IMAGES
of America

LAMPASAS COUNTY

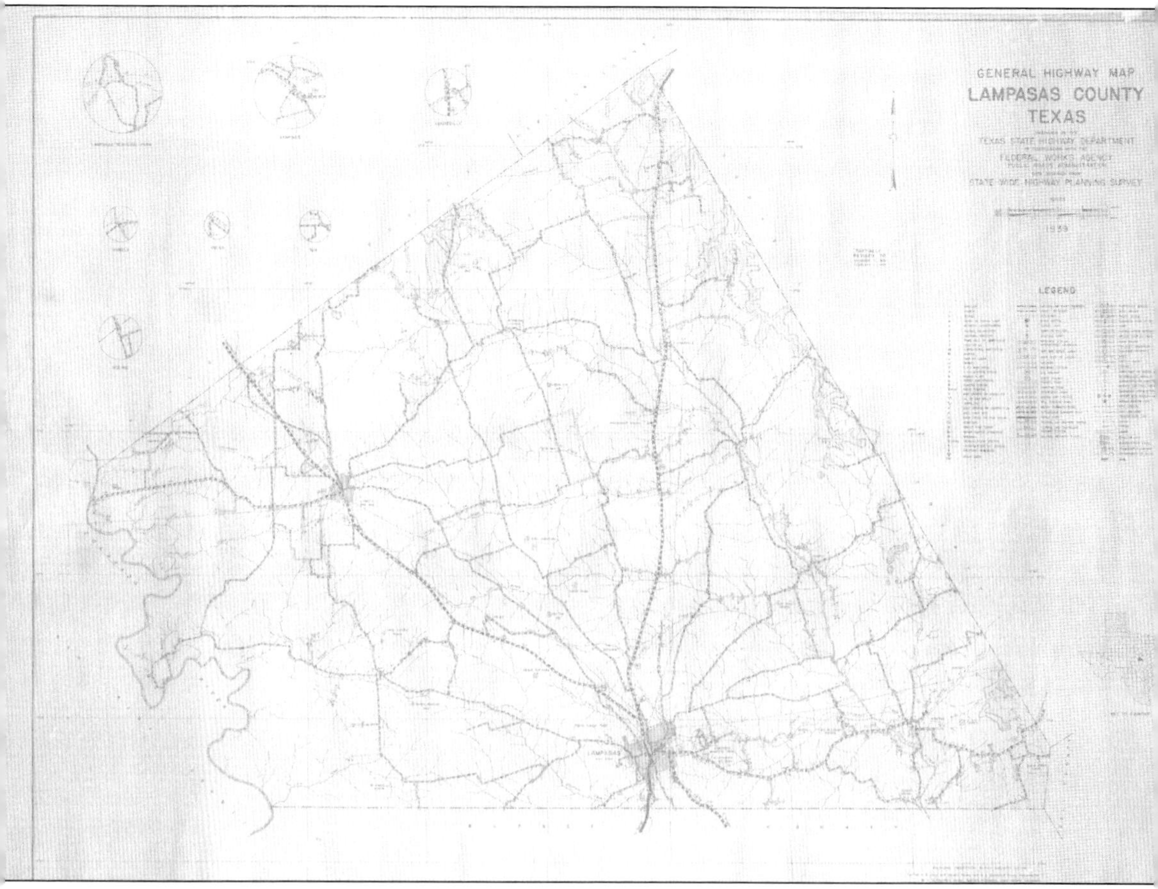

MAP OF LAMPASAS COUNTY, 1939. This map of Lampasas County shows some of the smaller communities in the area. (Courtesy of Jerry Goodson.)

ON THE COVER: Around 1902, picnickers spent leisurely Sunday afternoons at Pillar Bluff, just west of the city of Lampasas. Note the women's hats and fan. (Courtesy of Charlene Nash.)

IMAGES
of America

LAMPASAS COUNTY

Lampasas County Museum Foundation, Inc.

ARCADIA
PUBLISHING

ISBN 978-0-7385-5881-3

Published by Arcadia Publishing
Charleston SC, Chicago IL, Portsmouth NH, San Francisco CA

Printed in the United States of America

Library of Congress Catalog Card Number: 2008925030

For all general information contact Arcadia Publishing at:
Telephone 843-853-2070
Fax 843-853-0044
E-mail sales@arcadiapublishing.com
For customer service and orders:
Toll-Free 1-888-313-2665

Visit us on the Internet at www.arcadiapublishing.com

Contents

ACKNOWLEDGMENTS

The Lampasas County Museum Foundation, Inc., thanks the citizens of Lampasas County and the Lampasas County Historical Commission for their generous help with finding the photographs, fact-checking, and with writing this book.

All photographs, unless otherwise indicated, are from the collection of the Lampasas County Museum Foundation, Inc., and are housed at the Keystone Square Museum in Lampasas.

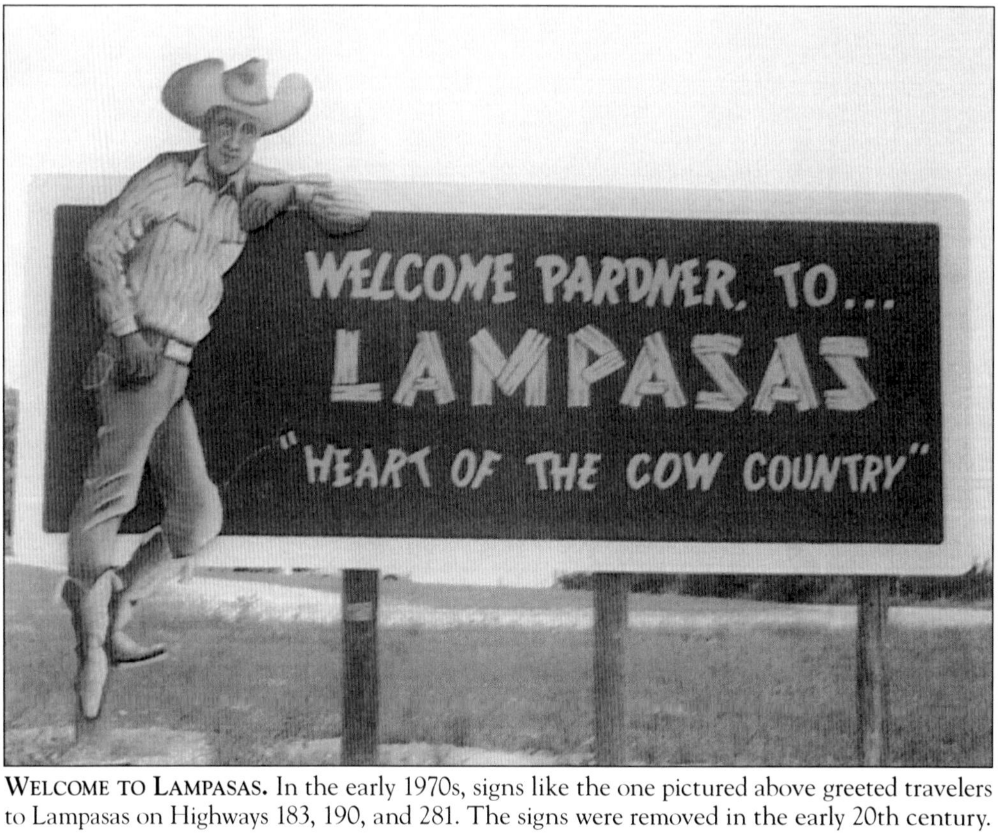

WELCOME TO LAMPASAS. In the early 1970s, signs like the one pictured above greeted travelers to Lampasas on Highways 183, 190, and 281. The signs were removed in the early 20th century.

INTRODUCTION

Lampasas County is now considered part of central Texas, but it was virtually on the edge of the state's vast western frontier when it was created in 1856. Bison still roamed the area, and prairie grasses stood stirrup high. First to be settled were the fertile river bottoms and lands along the many creeks and streams that flowed into the region's two main waterways, the Colorado and Lampasas Rivers.

Mineral springs in the area also produced an abundance of water and were legendary for possessing curative powers. It is said that when early Texas pioneer Moses Hughes first heard about the springs from Native Americans, he began to wonder if the mineral waters could heal his ailing wife. In 1853, Moses and his brother Nimrod moved their mother, their wives, and their children to the sulfur springs that the city of Lampasas would be near one day.

The Hughes are considered Lampasas's first permanent settlers; however, others soon followed and established farms and settlements elsewhere in the region. Within a few years, enough people had moved to the area to warrant petitioning the Texas Legislature to form a new county, and on February 1, 1856, Lampasas County was born.

The Civil War began only five years after Lampasas County was created. With man power diverted to the military effort, crime and Native American depredations increased on the home front. Despite the hardships of war and frontier existence, people continued to come.

After the war, there was an even larger influx of pioneers into the area, most from the war-torn states of the Deep South. Yet life throughout the former Confederacy was plagued by additional difficulties brought on by martial law and Reconstruction. Crime and violence such as the Horrell-Higgins feud remained a threat to civil order, and in the 1870s, Lampasas is said to have gained the reputation of being one of the roughest places in Texas.

Just how much violence actually touched the lives of ordinary citizens remains to be investigated, for the infamous decade also saw the rise of such civilizing forces as churches and schools. These institutions became central to scores of rural communities that once dotted county maps. As the 1870s drew to a close, the Farmers' Alliance was founded in Lampasas County as an organized political response to the plight of the small farmer.

The postwar era was also the heroic age of cowboys and cattle ranches. Lampasas County contributed its part to the making of the legendary epoch, as many a local cattle baron prospered and ranch hands "rode up the trail," driving vast herds to railheads and other points farther north.

With the 1882 arrival of the Gulf, Colorado, and Santa Fe Railway, Lampasas County's frontier period came to an end. The railroad created two new towns, Kempner and Lometa, and ushered in a new era of prosperity and unparalleled social change in Lampasas. People from all walks of life flocked to Lampasas hoping to profit from a greatly expanded trade territory and a thriving tourist industry based on the area's mineral springs.

A group of Houston and Galveston investors, which included Santa Fe executives, formed the Lampasas Springs Company and built the luxurious 200-room Park Hotel in 1883, the same year construction began on the Lampasas County Courthouse. The richly furnished hotel featured state-of-the-art amenities and a bathhouse built directly over one of the Hancock Springs where guests could "take the waters" in high style.

Across town at Hanna Springs a group of local businessmen united to build the grand Hanna Springs Pavilion, with hot and cold bathing facilities, elegant parlors, concession areas, and an orchestra on the first floor. A large hall, 60-by-120 feet, occupied the entire second story.

Other hotels were built, including the three-story Globe Hotel, which boasted the only elevator in town. Tracks were laid for a mule-drawn streetcar system to connect the Santa Fe depot north of town with the Park Hotel several miles to the west and to points in between. For a short while, Lampasas, advertised as "the Saratoga of the South," was the leading tourist destination in Texas.

When the railroad moved farther west in 1885, Lampasas's economy declined, and tourists eventually quit coming. Fires in Lampasas's central business district and drought further exacerbated the economic downturn. In time, agriculture returned to the county's economic forefront.

After the beginning of the 20th century, the wool and mohair industry in Lampasas County rose to preeminence with the arrival of the Houston and Texas Central Railway and the construction of a branch of the Gulf, Colorado, and Santa Fe Railway from Lometa to Eden. With the ready means of shipping in great quantity, wool and mohair buyers in Lampasas and Lometa became principals in the industry, establishing warehouses throughout central and west Texas and selling directly to textile mills in New England and Great Britain.

With several developments during the 1930s that helped boost the local economy, Lampasas County may have been spared the worst ravages of the Great Depression. Providing jobs were federally funded projects such as the construction of a new post office in Lampasas and the creation of Lampasas State Park. Among those who worked on federally financed dams along the Colorado River were a number of Lampasas County men. The routing of U.S. Highway 281 through the county likewise had a significant and positive long-term impact.

Life for Lampasas Countians during the years of World War II was likely similar to that of their compatriots throughout the country. Following the Japanese attack on Pearl Harbor, the county's young men volunteered in droves for service in the armed forces. Civilians bought war bonds, collected items for scrap metal drives, and remained watchful for any Lampasas County boys on casualty lists.

In September 1942, the U.S. Army opened Camp Hood about 20 miles from Lampasas. Established as a training facility for thousands of soldiers being shipped overseas, the military base provided Central Texans a rare glimpse into the development of America's preparations for war.

Camp Hood remained in operation after the war and was made a permanent installation that was renamed Fort Hood. The army base transformed the economies of communities in its neighboring counties by providing civilians with employment and contracts.

With rural electrification accomplished and its municipal infrastructures modernized, Lampasas County enjoyed postwar housing and baby booms, as did the rest of the country. However, marring the prosperity was a catastrophic drought that ravaged the state for almost seven years during the 1950s. Yet Lampasas, Lometa, and the county's rural communities, which at the time included Kempner, Adamsville, Bend, Izoro, Long Cove, Nix, Rumley, and Unity, all survived.

Ironically, what brought an end to the worst drought on record in Lampasas was its worst flood on record. The Mother's Day Flood of 1957 killed five people and destroyed the central business district around the courthouse square. However, with the resiliency of the people—displaying the same pioneer spirit as that of their predecessors a century earlier—Lampasas was soon rebuilt, and the community was restored.

One

OLD TOWN LAMPASAS

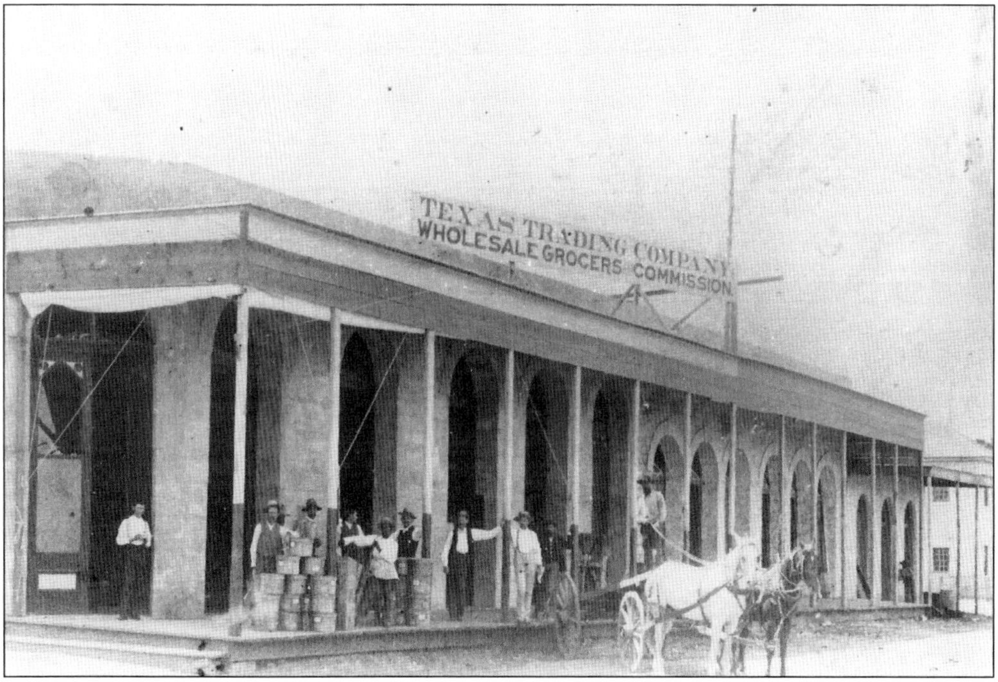

TEXAS TRADING COMPANY, 1880S. Wagon trains from the Texas Trading Company delivered goods to farmers and ranchers as far as 150 miles out of town. The business of Lampasas took place in "Old Town," an area that included the county courthouse and the courthouse square.

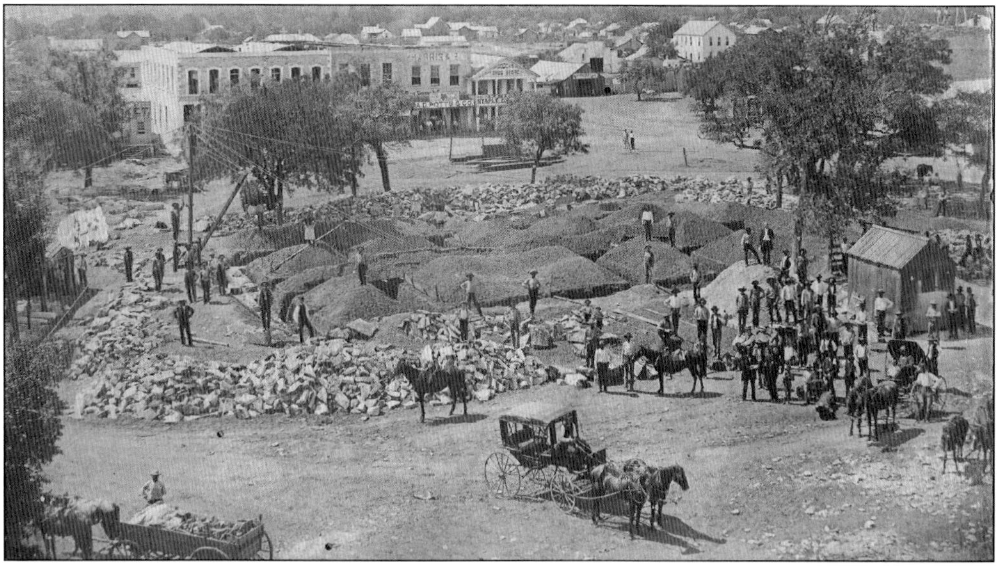

Groundbreaking for the Lampasas County Courthouse, 1882. In 1882, Waco architect W. C. Dodson designed a courthouse and jail for Lampasas. Dodson designed courthouses for at least five Texas counties. The native limestone structure would house all county offices in one building for the first time and was finished in 1883. This photograph shows workers excavating for the foundation in 1882.

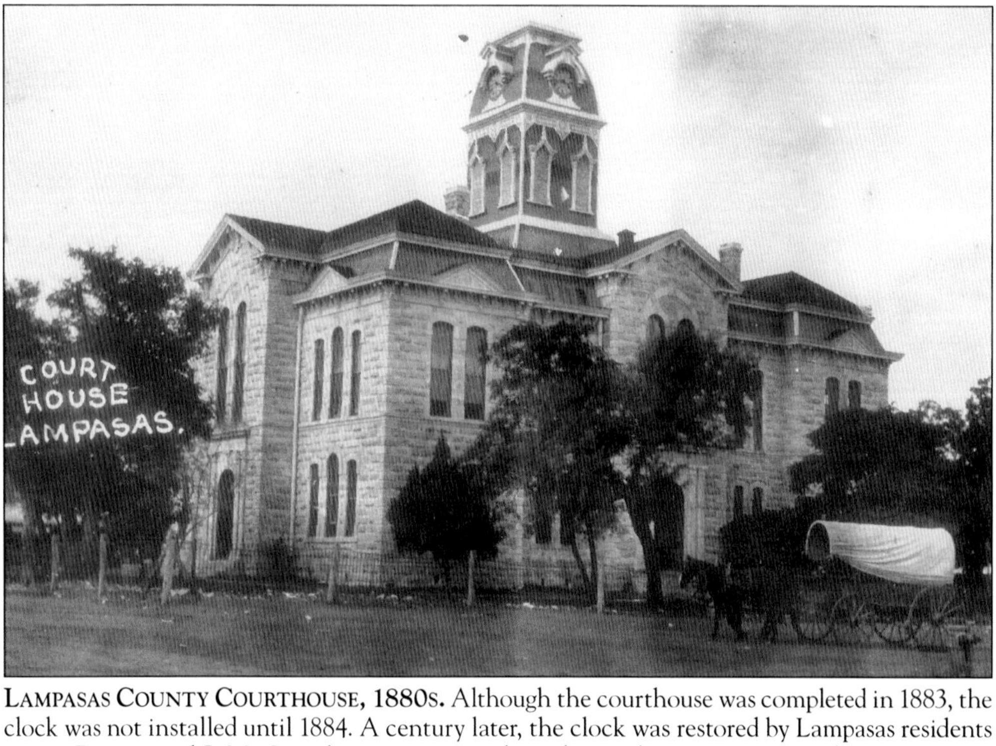

Lampasas County Courthouse, 1880s. Although the courthouse was completed in 1883, the clock was not installed until 1884. A century later, the clock was restored by Lampasas residents Major Dumas and J. M. Crumley to its original mechanical operation. Crumley and Dumas designed and custom-crafted parts they were unable to locate. At the project's end, the clock kept perfect time, and the 1,300-pound bell tolled the hours once again.

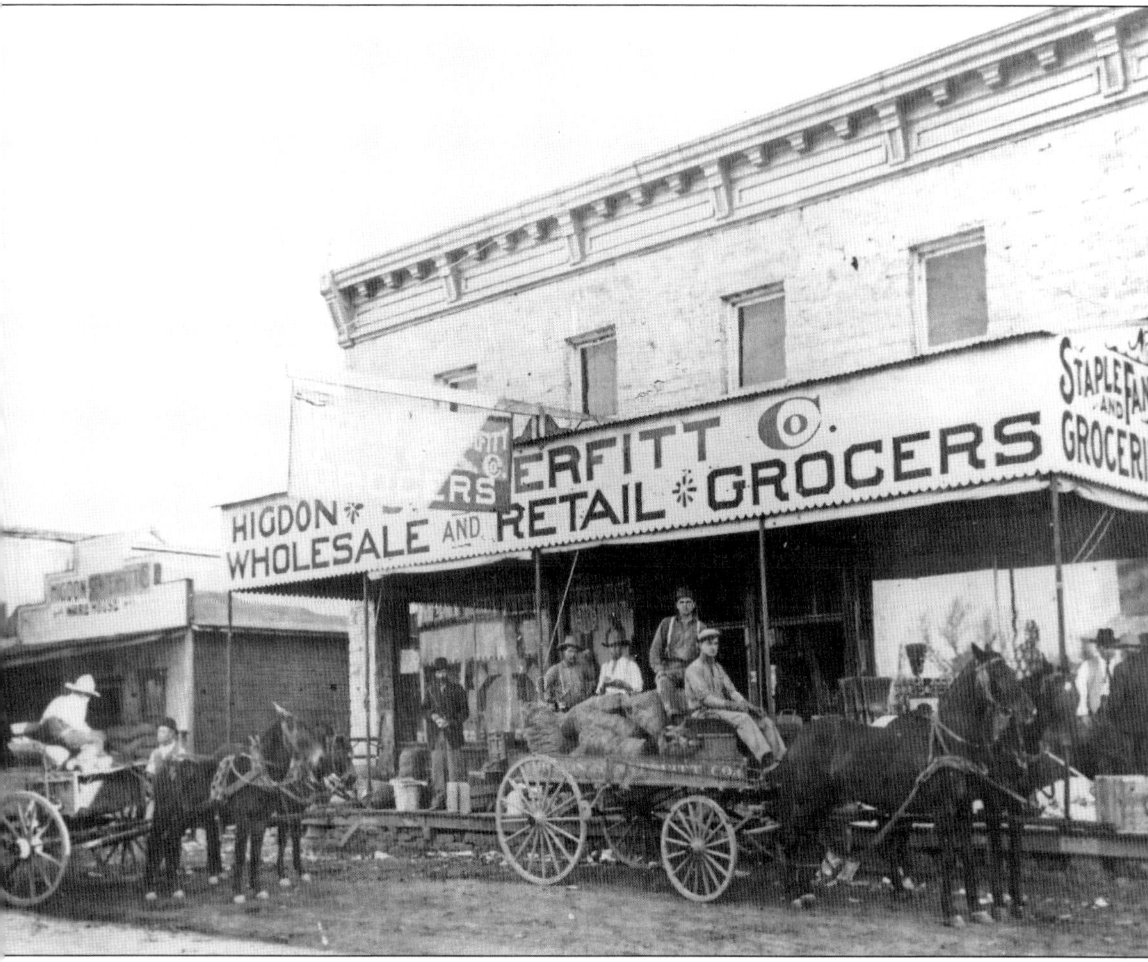

HIGDON-SENTERFITT COMPANY, WHOLESALE-RETAIL GROCERS, 1880S. In the late 1880s, A. L. Higdon and R. F. Senterfitt ran a successful wholesale and retail grocery business located on the corner of Third and Pecan Streets across from the county courthouse in Lampasas. Pictured here are the mule- and horse-drawn delivery wagons, which were loaded in front of the store and warehouse.

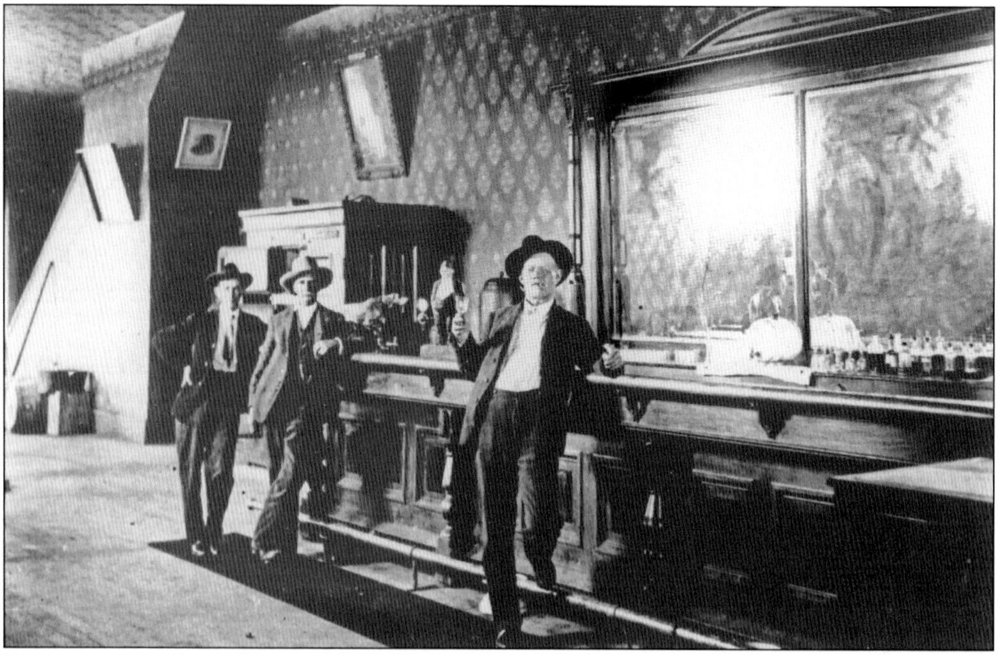

HOOVER AND NOYES, LATE 1870S. Hoover and Noyes Wines and Liquors, a saloon, was one of many on Third Street in the city of Lampasas. Saloons were a big part of city life in the late 1870s, when this photograph was probably taken. In the foreground, the saloon owner, A. W. Hoover, toasts the photographer.

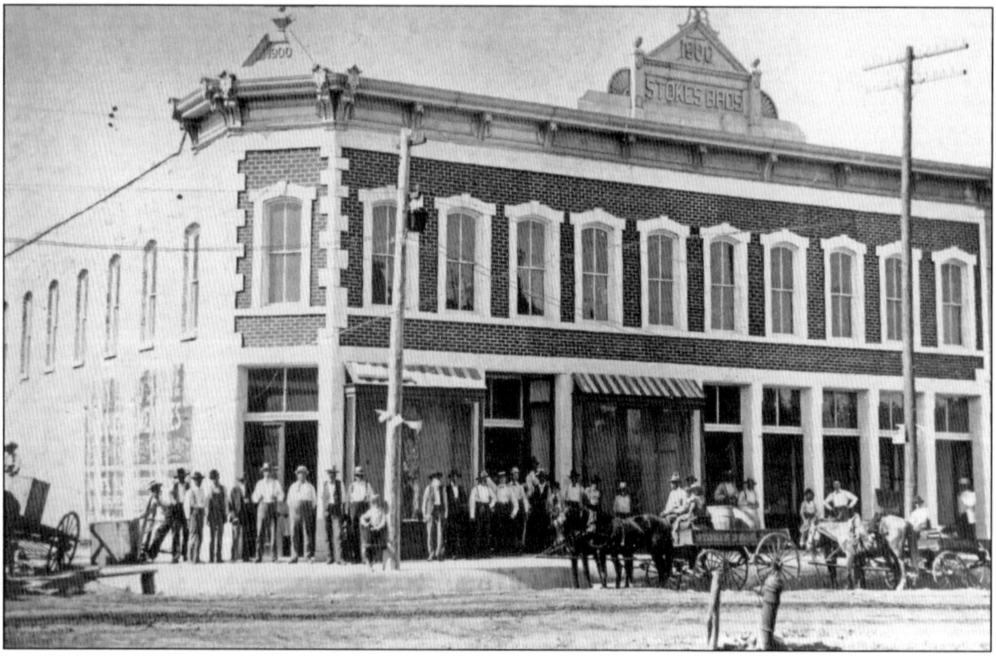

STOKES BROTHERS BUILDING. This view of the Stokes Brothers Building, erected in 1900, shows street life on the courthouse square. The Stokes Brothers delivery wagon is parked in front. The building later housed the First National Bank and was torn down in 1966 to make way for a more modern facility.

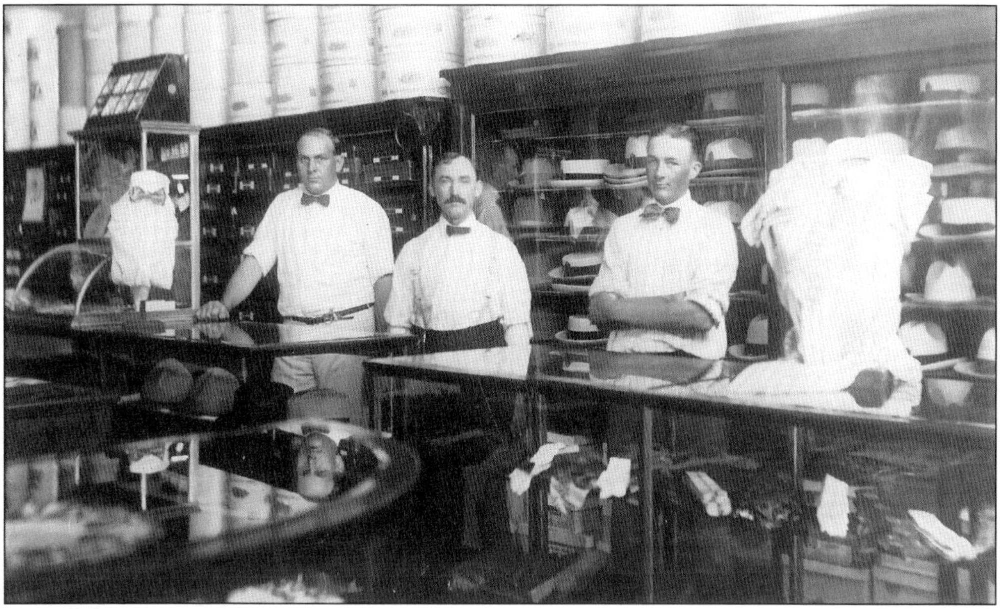

BRIGGS CARLILE COMPANY, C. 1918. David Todd Briggs III started his own mercantile on the north side of the courthouse square during World War I. He often told the story of the time he purchased too many $40 silk shirts. When they did not sell, he ended up giving them away. Pictured from left to right are Walter Mashbach, Briggs, and Clyde Mace. (Courtesy of Kay Briggs.)

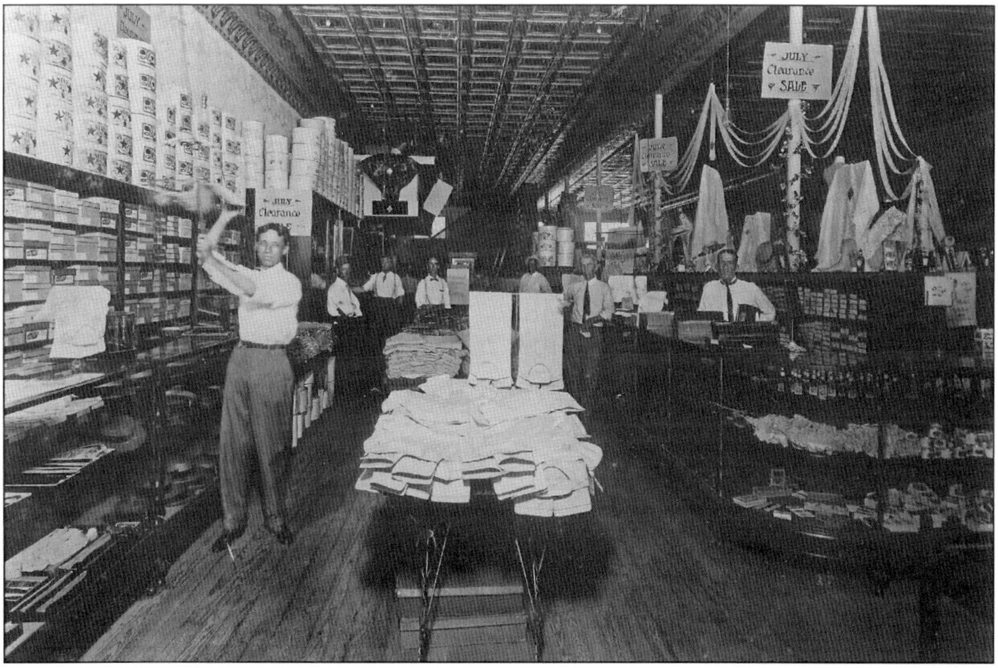

INTERIOR OF STOKES BROTHERS, C. 1916. The Stokes brothers ran a general mercantile in Lampasas as only one of their many enterprises. In this photograph, Stokes Brothers is holding a July clearance sale, and Jim Howard, at the left, is pulling stock from the shelves. Others in the photograph are, from left to right, Clyde Northington Sr., a Mr. Day, J. H. Andrew, A. Northington, P. C. Abney, and Martin Moses.

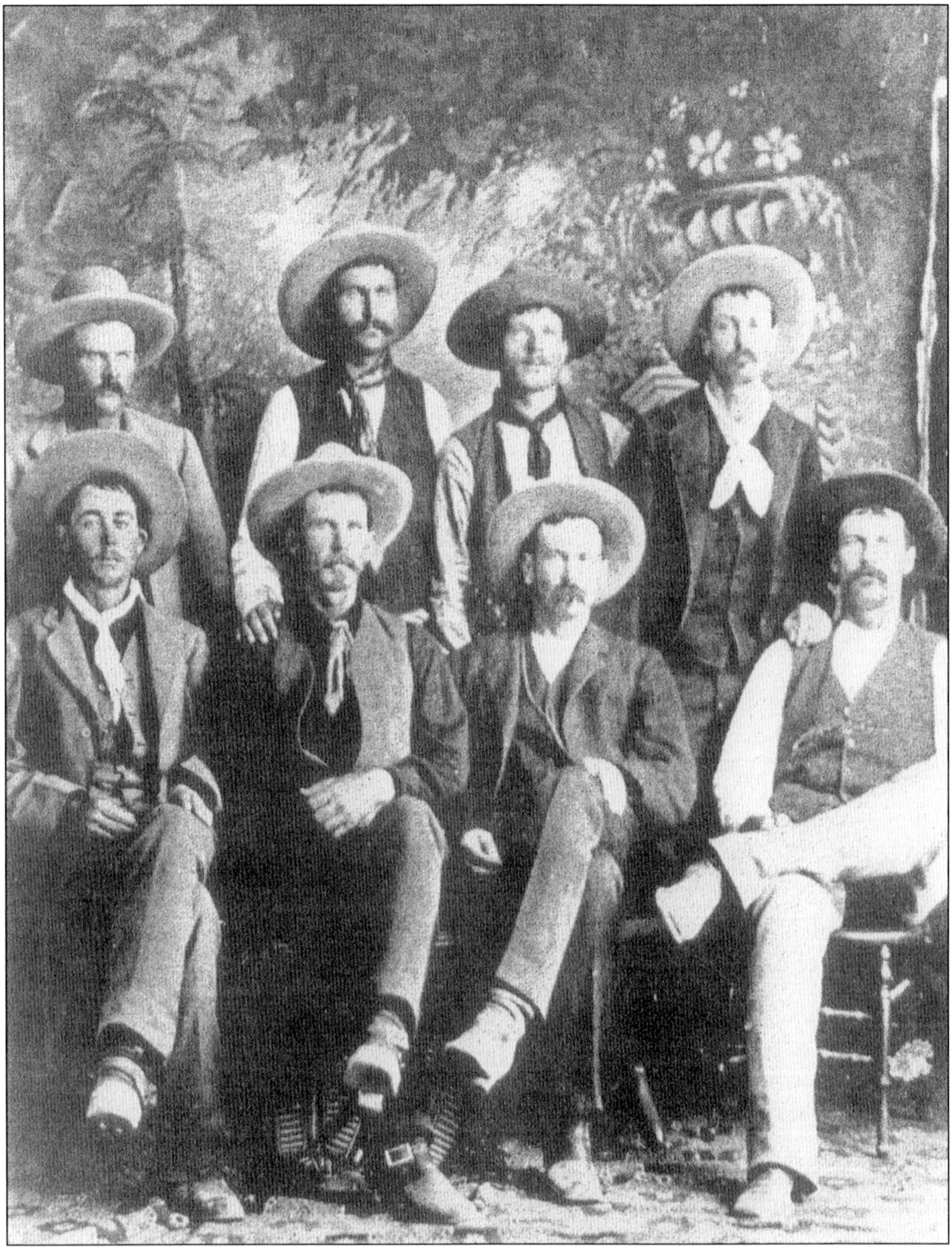

PINK HIGGINS AND HIS CREW. John Pinckney "Pink" Higgins (1851–1913), seated far right, is shown here with his crew after a cattle drive from Lampasas County to Kansas. Pink, a cowboy and gunfighter, is particularly famous for his part in the feud between the Horrell and the Higgins families, which took place in the 1870s over cattle rustling. Pink's killing of Merritt Horrell in 1877 on courthouse square in Lampasas earned him a reputation as a lethal marksman. (Courtesy of the Standard Studio, Lampasas.)

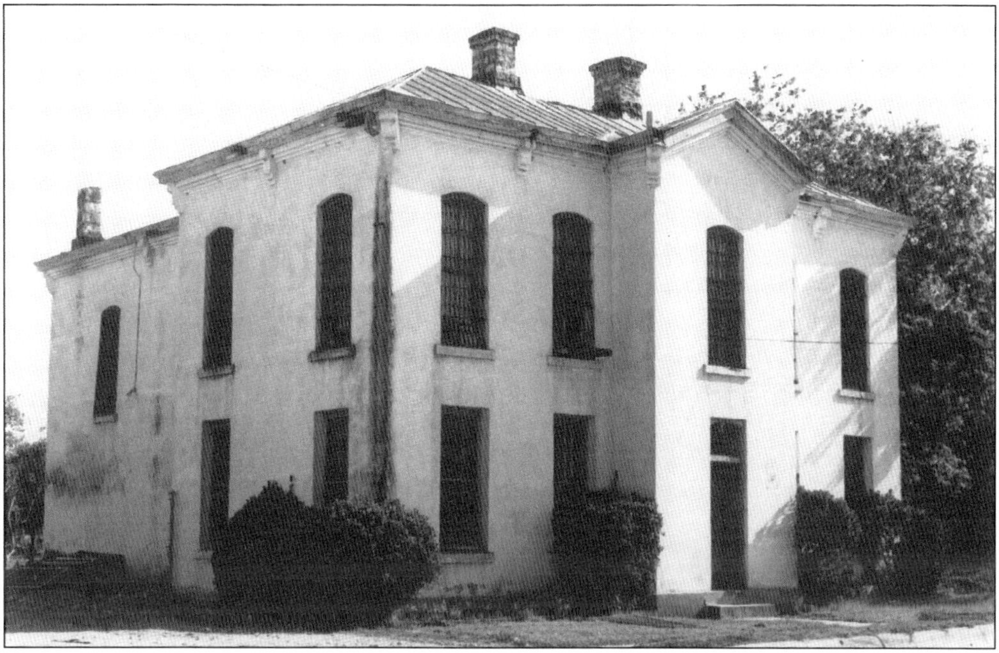

LAMPASAS COUNTY JAIL. The county jail was built of plaster over native limestone in 1883, the same year as the county courthouse. It was located on Fourth Street and was torn down in the early 1970s to make way for the present jail. (Photograph by Virgil Wooten.)

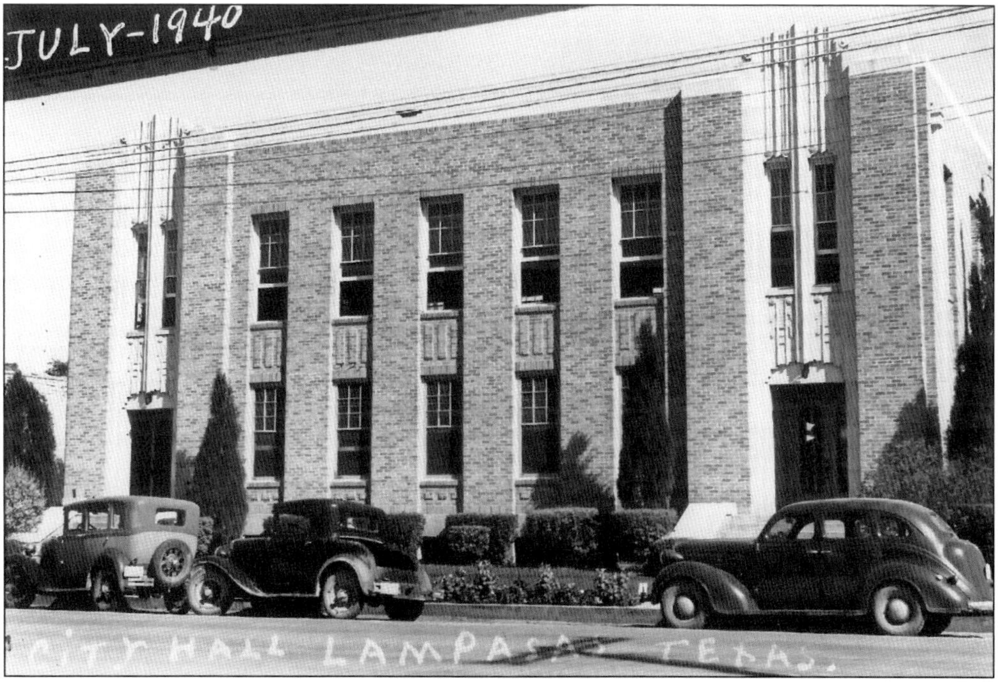

OLD CITY HALL, LAMPASAS, JULY 1940. The city hall was built in 1932 and was in use until the 1990s. It was originally built as a multipurpose building. The public library was on the second floor; city offices were at street level; and the basement was used for other functions. The building still stands on the corner of Third and Main Streets. (Photograph by Lucile Standard.)

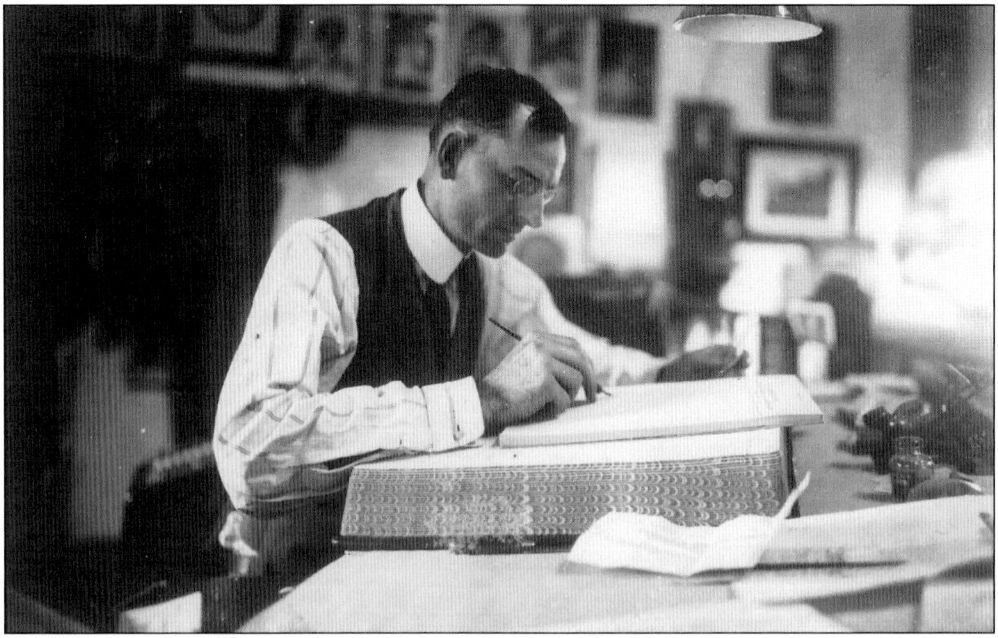

R. J. PAINE, EARLY 1900S. In the early 1900s, R. J. Paine was a bookkeeper for Key Brothers Grocery, which was then located at Third and Western Streets and was owned by James Richard "J. R." Key. Paine worked as an accountant at the Peoples National Bank before he started the Paine Agency, an insurance agency. In 1934, he and Charles Wachendorfer founded the Lampasas Federal Savings and Loan.

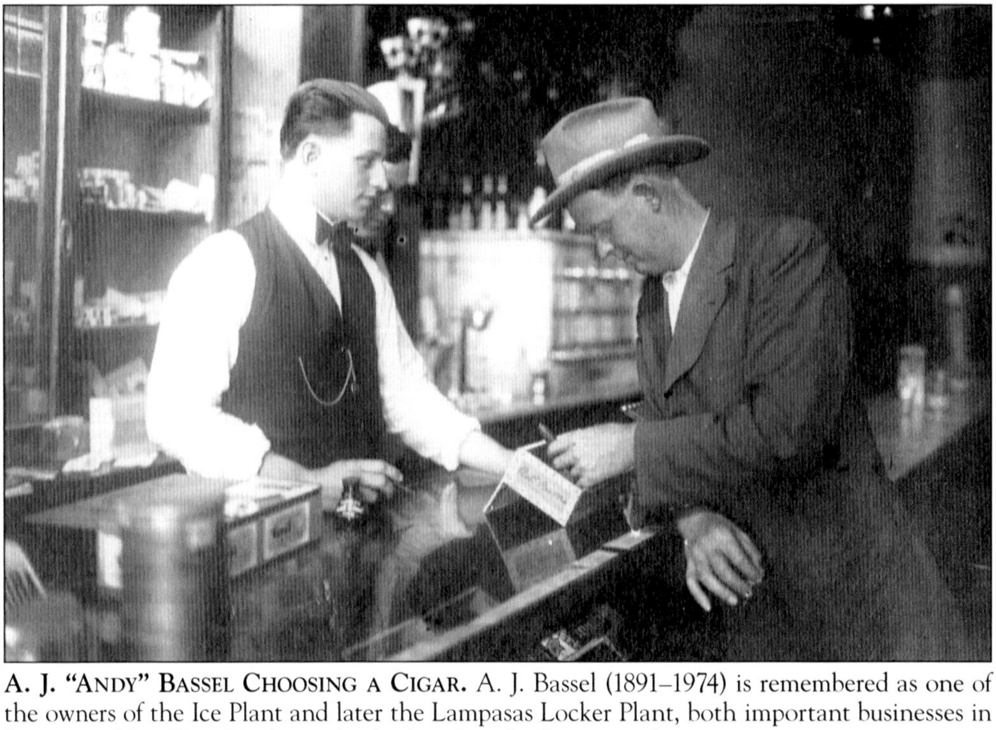

A. J. "ANDY" BASSEL CHOOSING A CIGAR. A. J. Bassel (1891–1974) is remembered as one of the owners of the Ice Plant and later the Lampasas Locker Plant, both important businesses in Lampasas. Here Bassel is shown in the interior of a downtown Lampasas concern.

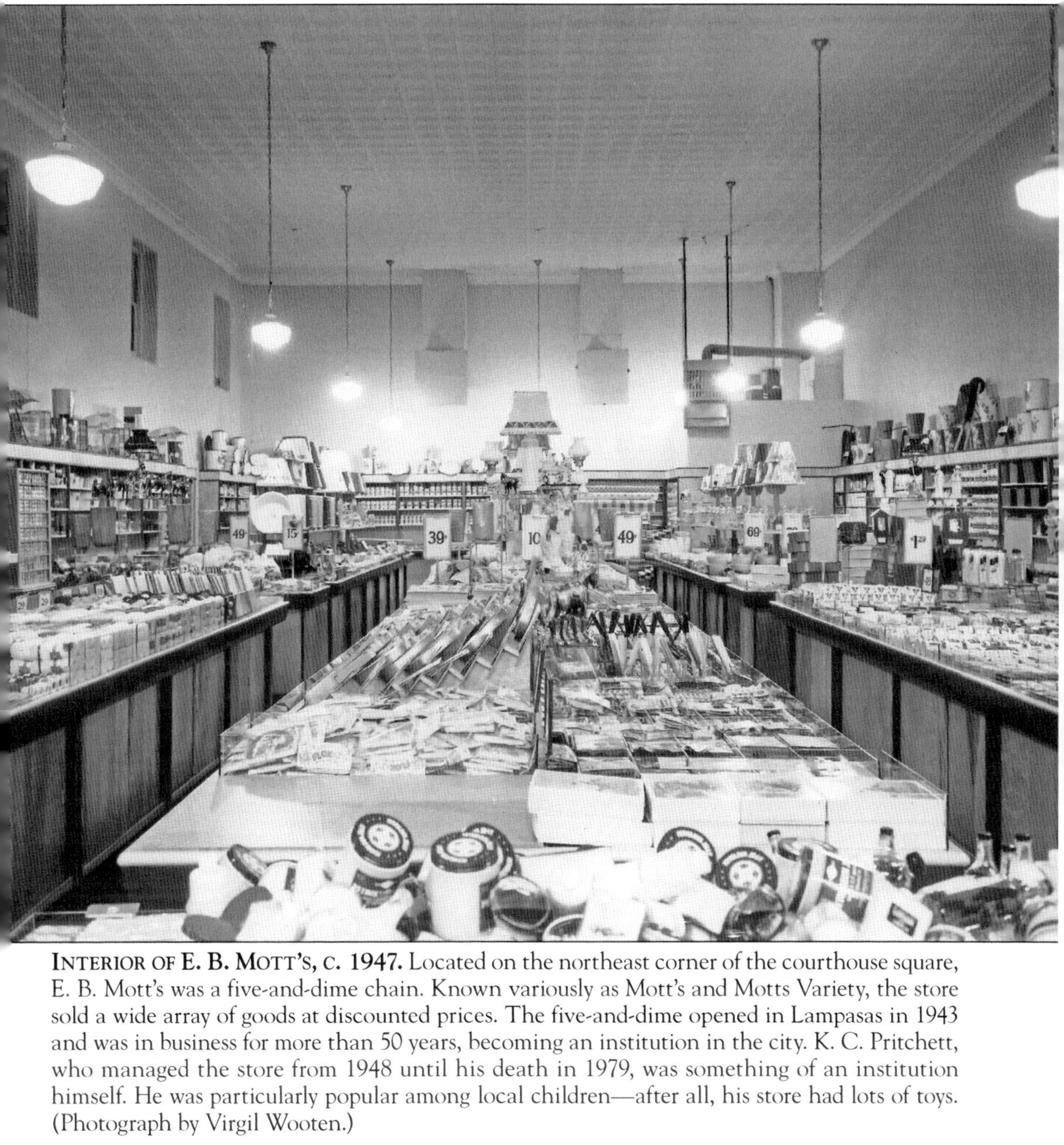

INTERIOR OF E. B. MOTT'S, C. 1947. Located on the northeast corner of the courthouse square, E. B. Mott's was a five-and-dime chain. Known variously as Mott's and Motts Variety, the store sold a wide array of goods at discounted prices. The five-and-dime opened in Lampasas in 1943 and was in business for more than 50 years, becoming an institution in the city. K. C. Pritchett, who managed the store from 1948 until his death in 1979, was something of an institution himself. He was particularly popular among local children—after all, his store had lots of toys. (Photograph by Virgil Wooten.)

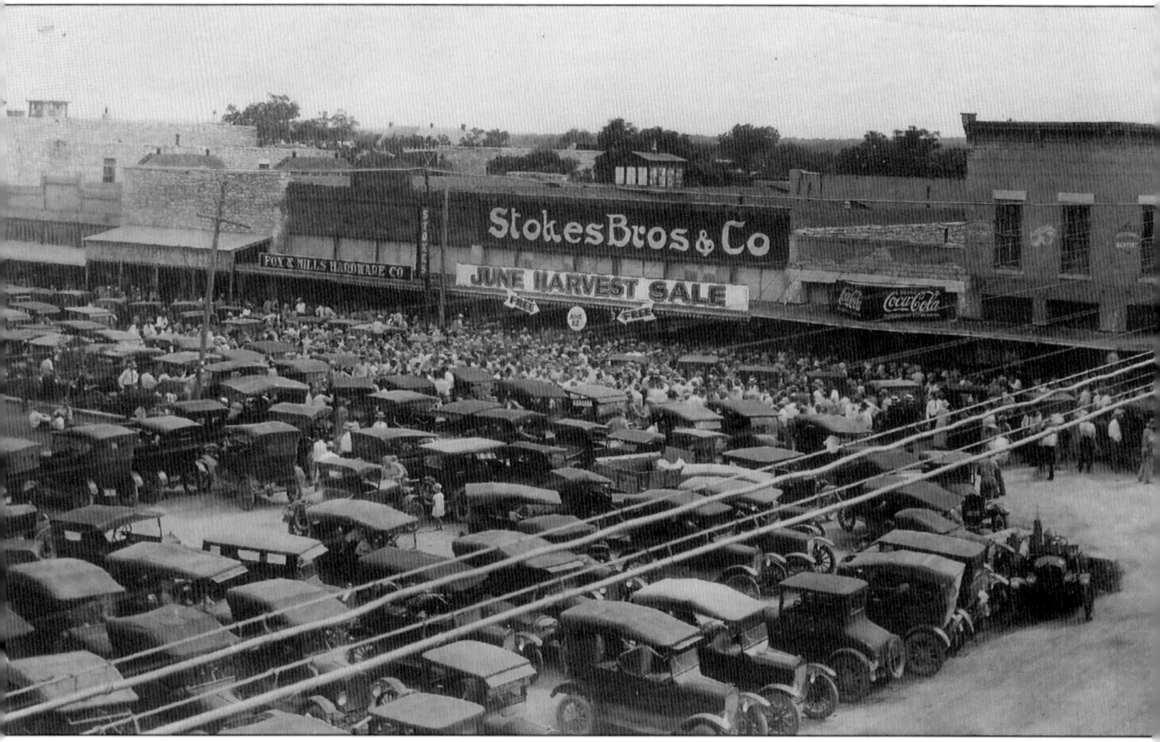

TRADES DAY, 1927. Trades Days were days that everyone, particularly those from rural areas, would come into town to shop. Parking spaces were not defined, and it was first come, first served. Here the west side of courthouse square is shown. Stokes Brothers and Company general mercantile figures prominently on Live Oak Street with its "June Harvest Sale" banner displayed across the entrance, enticing shoppers. The Stokes brothers later sold this store, and in time, it became Chastain-Miller Department Store.

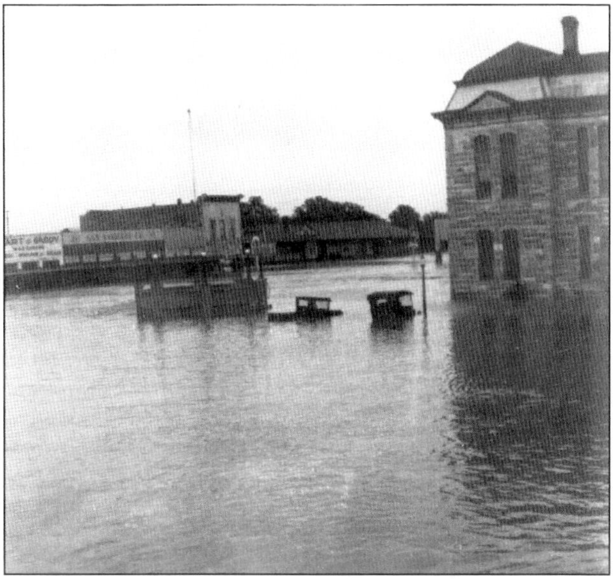

LAMPASAS COUNTY COURTHOUSE DURING THE 1936 FLOOD. Floodwaters rose high enough during the 1936 disaster to cause the wooden bandstand (center) to float, and the water nearly reached the first floor sills of the courthouse. The 1936 flood was the worst flood to date: floodwaters reached 5 feet in some areas of town, and property loss was estimated as high as $100,000.

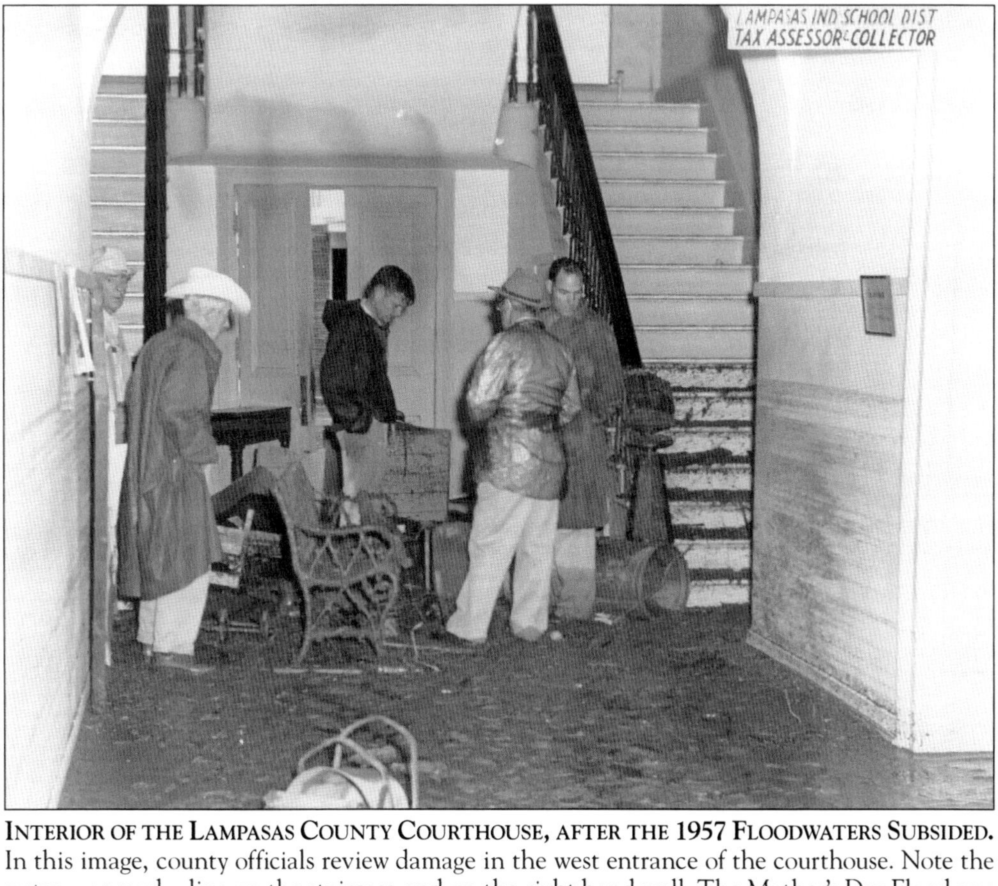

INTERIOR OF THE LAMPASAS COUNTY COURTHOUSE, AFTER THE 1957 FLOODWATERS SUBSIDED. In this image, county officials review damage in the west entrance of the courthouse. Note the water—or mud—line on the staircase and on the right-hand wall. The Mother's Day Flood was one of the most serious in the history of the city, and most of downtown was destroyed. (Courtesy of Gladden Corbin.)

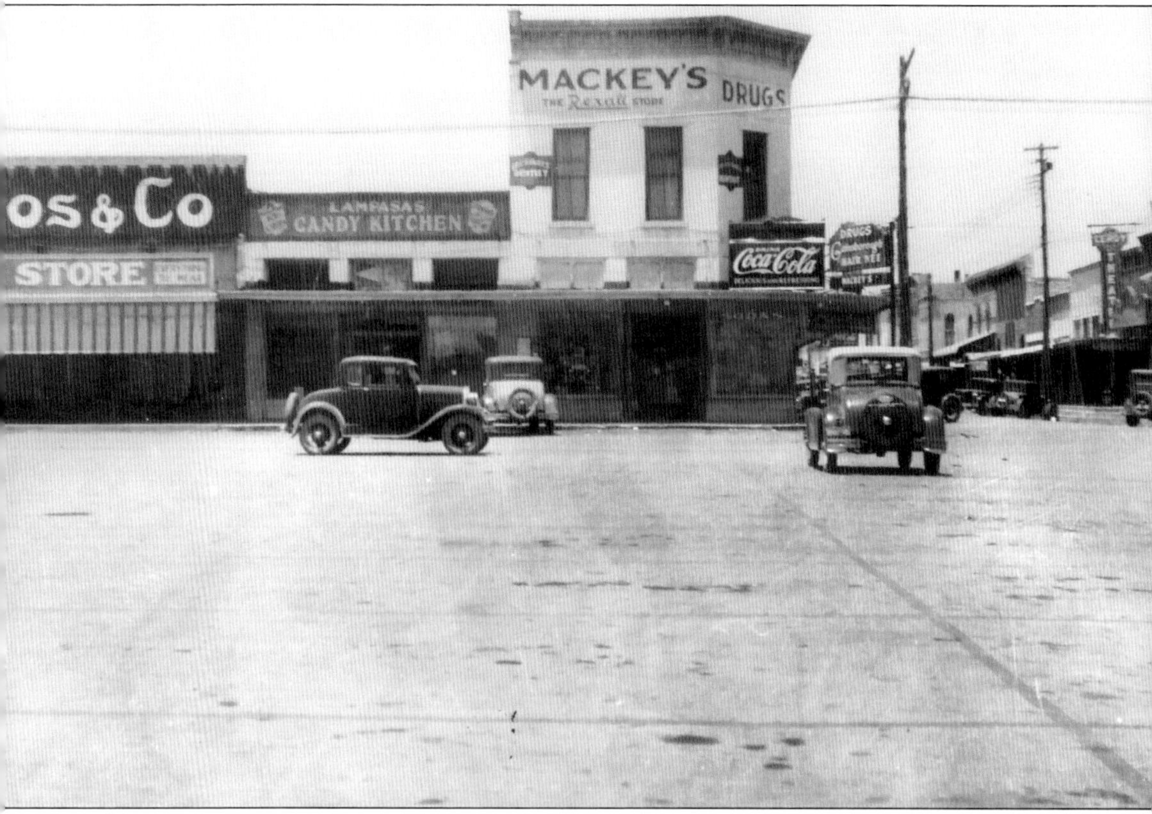

MACKEY'S AND THE CANDY KITCHEN, CORNER OF THIRD AND LIVE OAK STREETS, 1929. This photograph of the west side of the courthouse square prominently features the corner store, Mackey Drug, and the Candy Kitchen. Mackey Drug is on a site that has had several drugstores and was a gathering place for local men to discuss the news of the day. The Candy Kitchen, fragrant with the aroma of its namesake, was a favorite spot to enjoy ice cream after a movie, a day of shopping, or a special trip to partake of the confections dispensed from an elaborately carved bar. Dainty wire chairs and tables, typical of ice cream parlors, seated the dine-in patrons. Glass-enclosed display cases contained a selection of irresistible candies.

Two

COUNTY LIFE

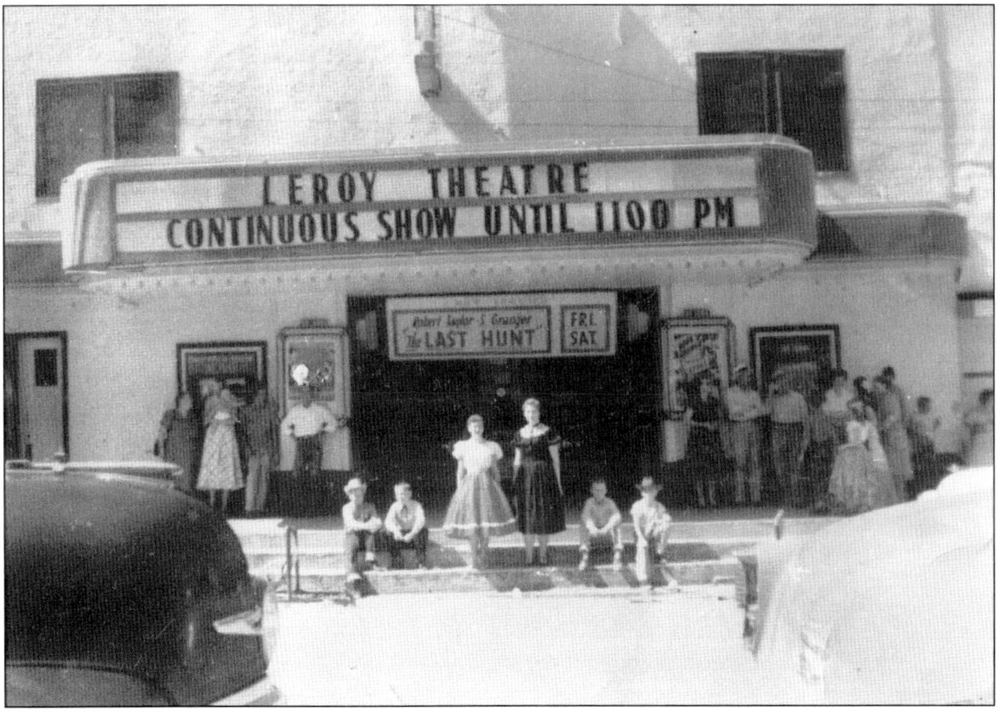

LEROY THEATER, 1950S. The last indoor picture show in Lampasas, the LeRoy Theatre was opened by brothers Lee and Roy Walker some time after 1917. In the 1950s, Saturday afternoon double features were standard fare, and the LeRoy was filled with kids of all ages. Fire destroyed the theater in 1970. Lometa also had movie houses from 1912 until 1963. "Going to the show" was a popular ritual of county life. (Courtesy of Mary Jane Bowman.)

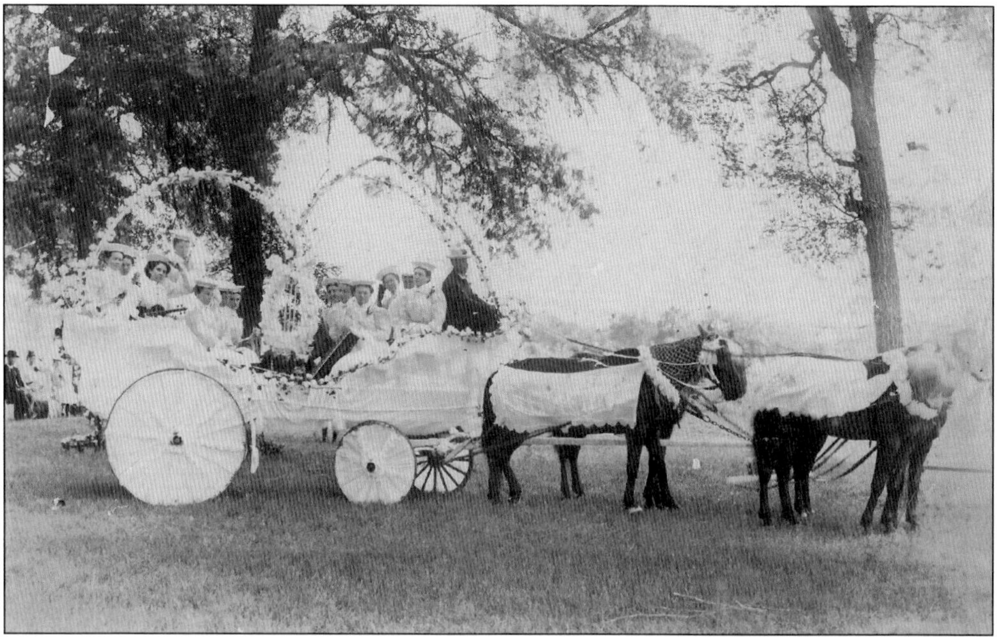

Yvonette Orchestra, c. 1898. Also known as the "Ladies Orchestra," this group is shown here on its float for the firemen's parade around 1898. The group played at a variety of events, including the firemen's picnic, openings of local shops, and at a Lampasas celebration of San Jacinto Day. The orchestra was made up of young women led by their director, Mrs. Cal Montgomery. Dude Brown is their driver.

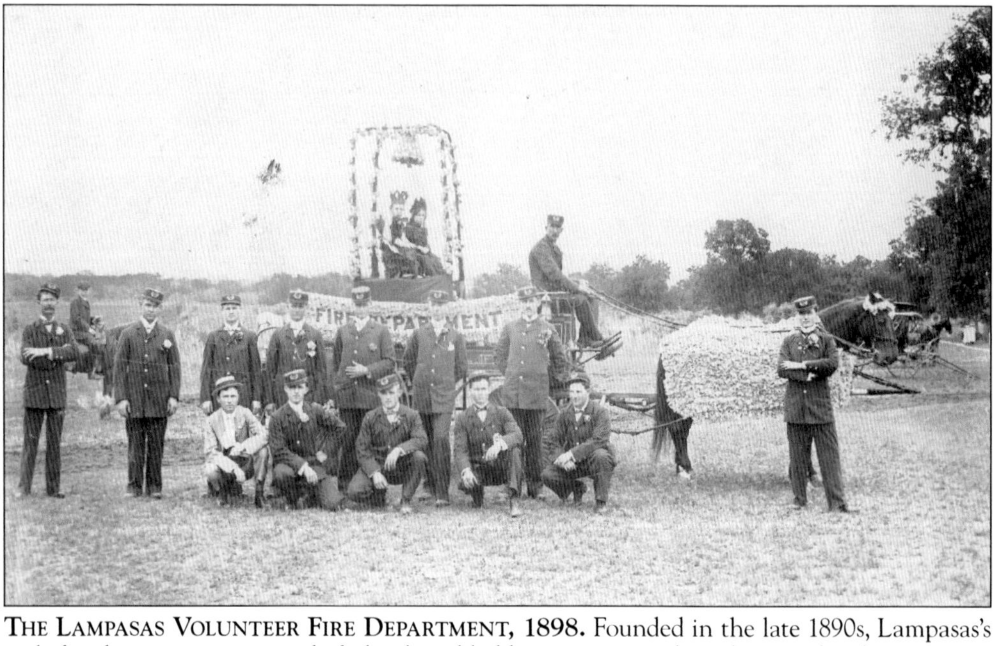

The Lampasas Volunteer Fire Department, 1898. Founded in the late 1890s, Lampasas's early fire department consisted of a hook-and-ladder company and two hose-and-reel companies. Pictured here are the firemen with their float on San Jacinto Day at the firemen's picnic. On the float are the San Jacinto Day King and Queen, Powell Harris and Ruth Cauthen Spann. The horses, Jack and John, were the most famous fire team in Lampasas.

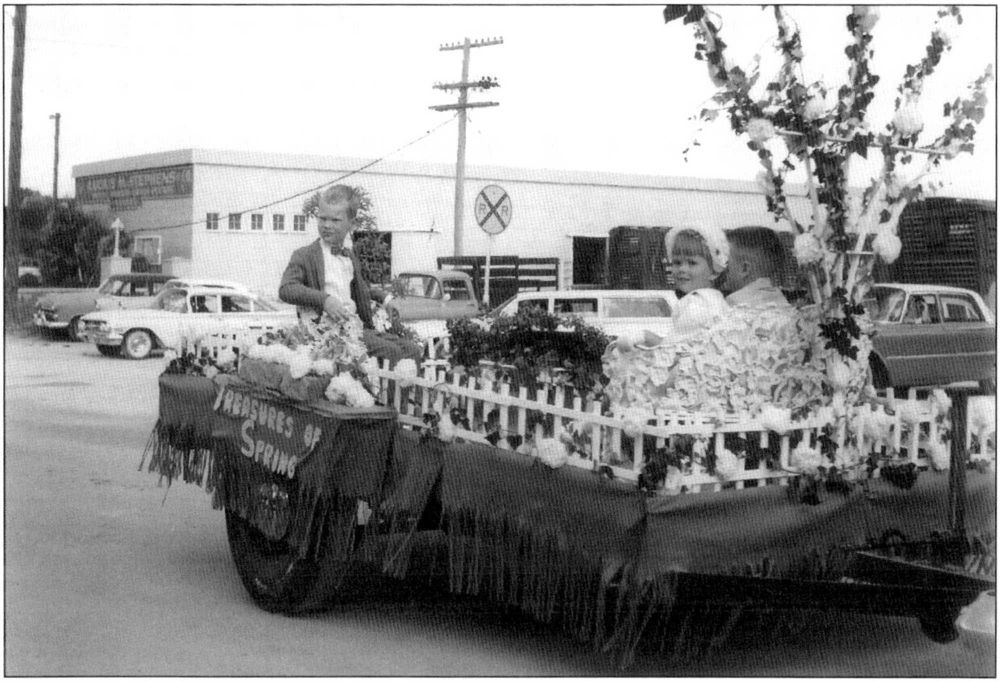

"Treasures of Spring" Float in a Parade in Lometa, 1961. Parades were and are an important part of Lampasas County life. This float most likely was decorated by the active L-M Garden and Civic Club of Lometa. In the background, the Lucius M. Stephens Company is visible. Stephens was prominent in the wool and mohair business but also traded pecans, another regional crop.

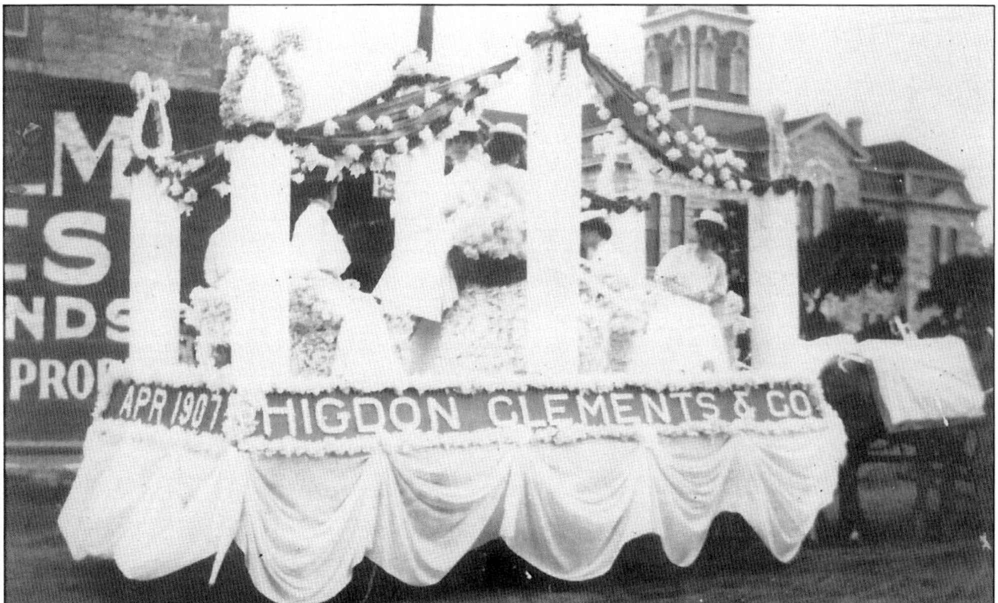

Higdon Clements and Company Float in a Lampasas Parade, 1907. Local companies created floats for Lampasas city and county parades to advertise their business and to show goodwill and community spirit.

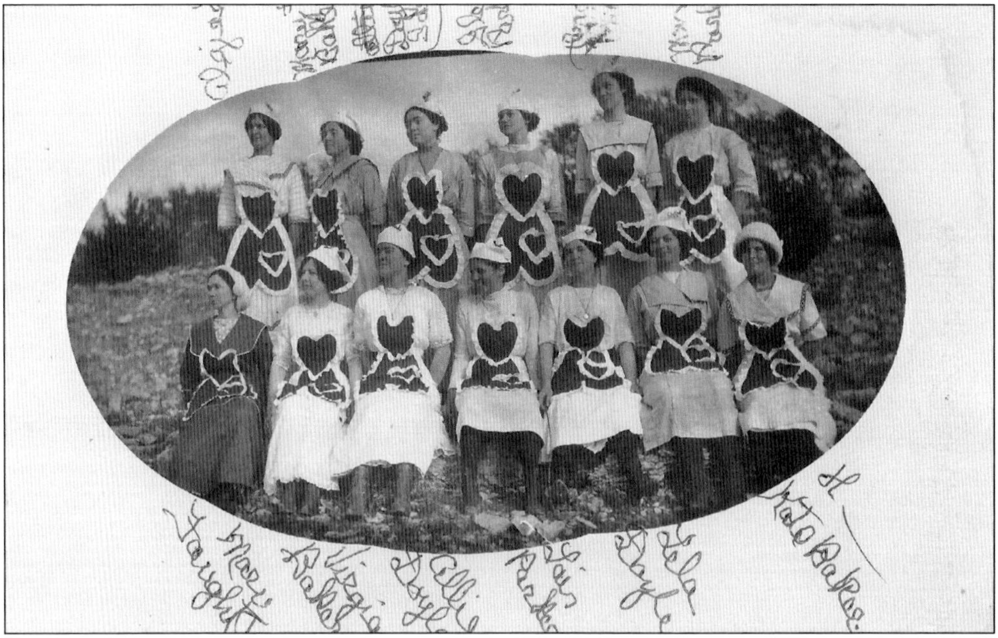

THE NIX VALENTINES, 1908. The small community of Nix is located west of the county seat and was settled in the late 1860s. In 1908, Mary S. Baker of Nix invited her friends and neighbors to a Valentine's Day luncheon and asked them to wear white. When the day arrived, Mrs. Baker provided each of the guests with a red valentine apron she had made. (Courtesy of Christine Wright.)

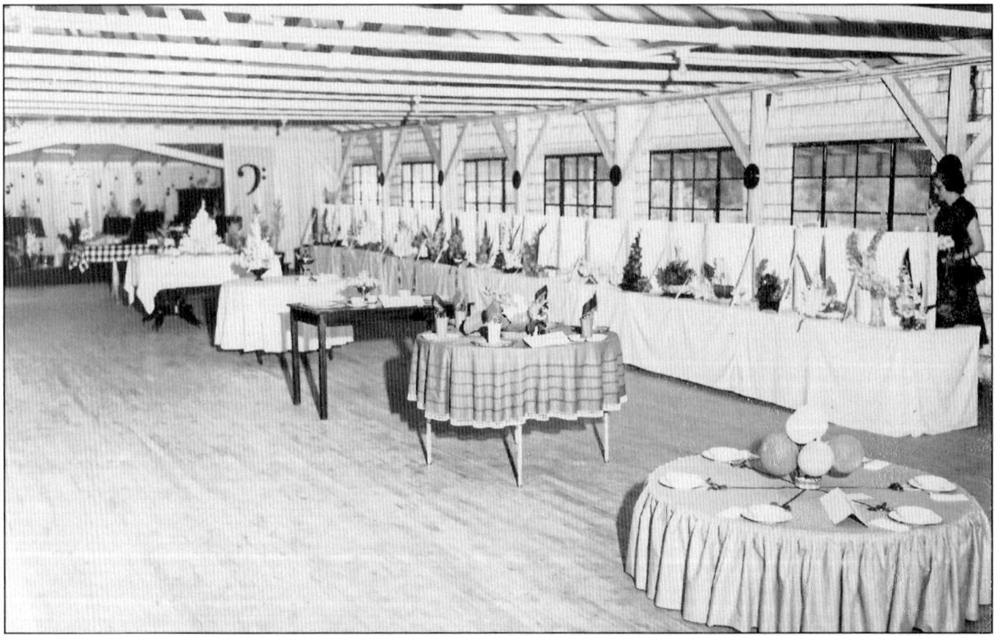

FLOWER SHOW AT THE HOSTESS HOUSE, EARLY 1960S. The Lampasas Council of Garden Clubs held flower shows all over town, including at the armory, the Hostess House, and the school gymnasiums. The flower shows often had themes. Each year, the group sponsored the Annual Chrysanthemum Show Festival, complete with a Chrysanthemum Queen and her court. This flower show was held at the Hostess House in Hancock Park.

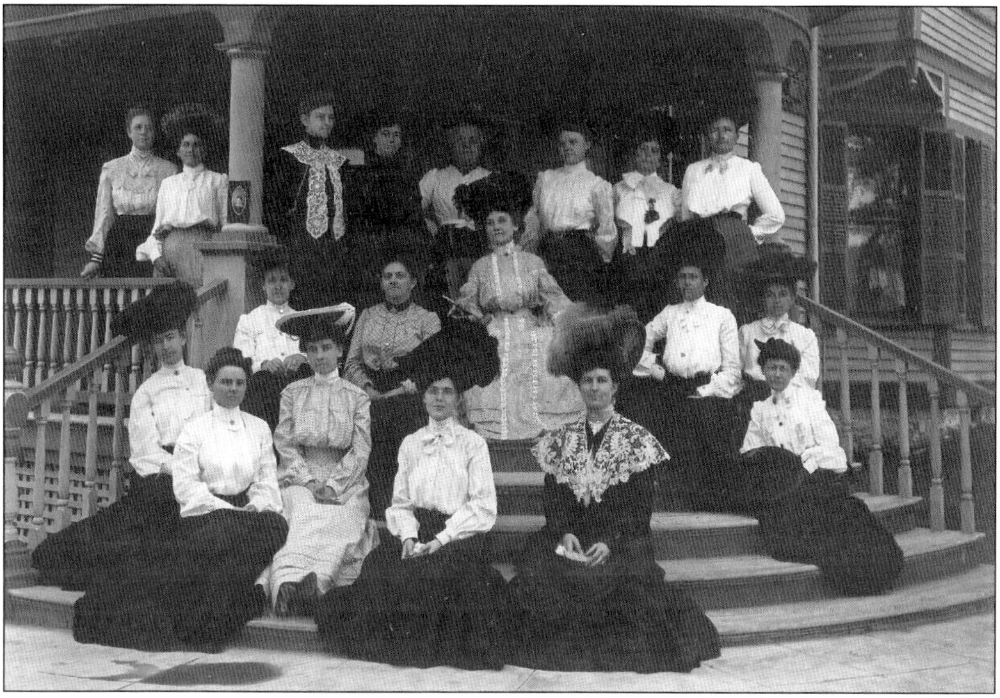

THE PIERIAN CLUB IN FRONT OF THE JOHN HALL HOUSE. In 1904, the charter members of the Pierian Club gathered at the home of Virginia Hall, which stands at the corner of Fourth and Broad Streets in Lampasas. Organized and federated in 1902 and still active today, the club was instrumental in founding the Lampasas County Library.

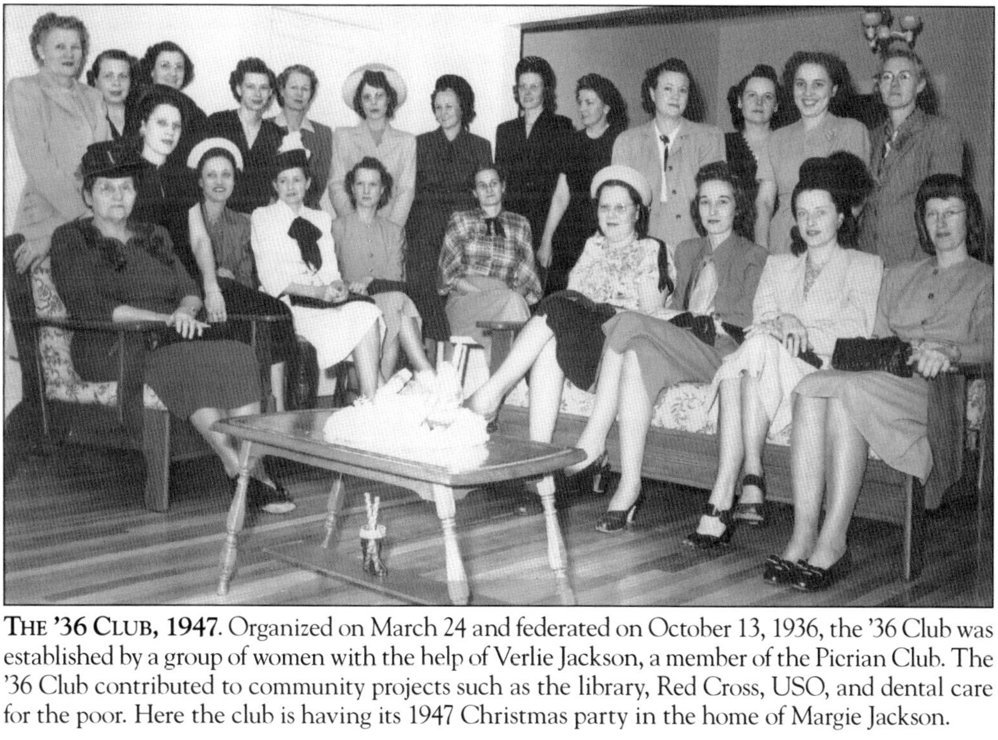

THE '36 CLUB, 1947. Organized on March 24 and federated on October 13, 1936, the '36 Club was established by a group of women with the help of Verlie Jackson, a member of the Picrian Club. The '36 Club contributed to community projects such as the library, Red Cross, USO, and dental care for the poor. Here the club is having its 1947 Christmas party in the home of Margie Jackson.

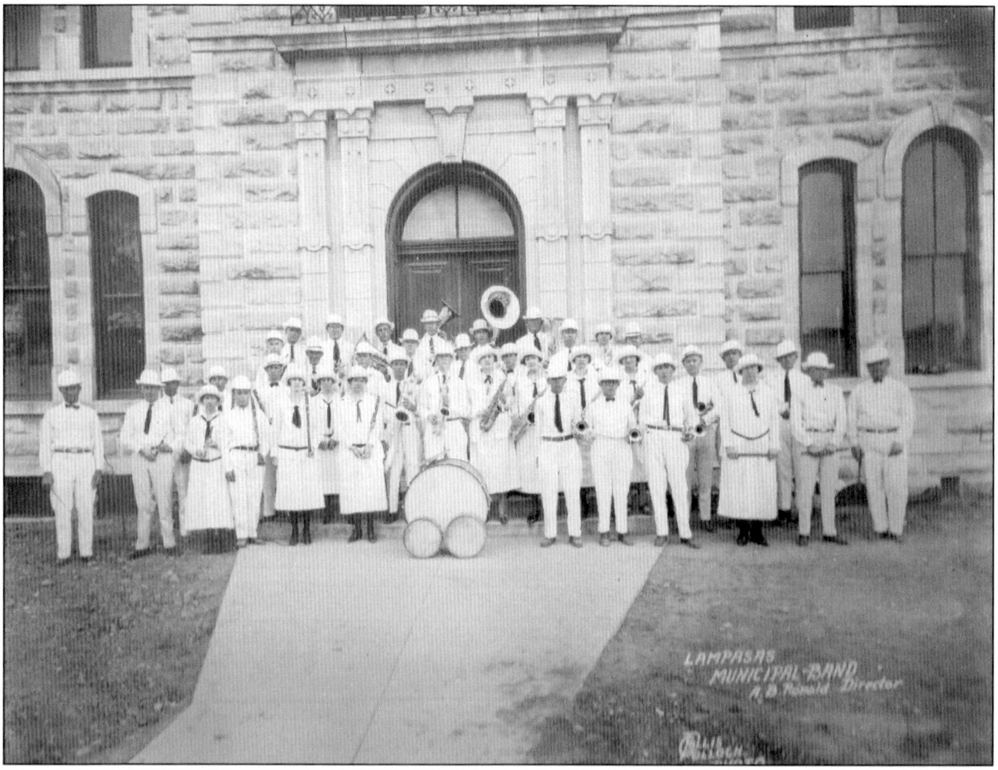

LAMPASAS MUNICIPAL BAND. Pictured in front of the south entrance of the Lampasas County Courthouse is the Lampasas Municipal Band with director A. B. Ronald. Established around 1922, the band played Friday evenings on the courthouse lawn in spring and summer, drawing large audiences. Ronald's original composition, "The Lampasas March," closed every concert.

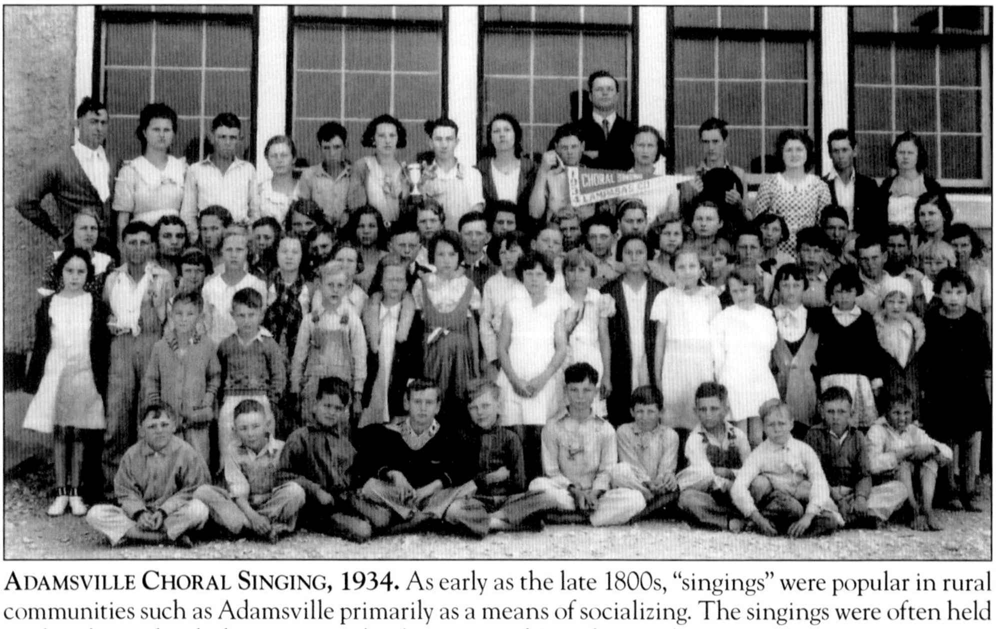

ADAMSVILLE CHORAL SINGING, 1934. As early as the late 1800s, "singings" were popular in rural communities such as Adamsville primarily as a means of socializing. The singings were often held in churches, schools, homes, or parks. (Courtesy of Wanda Lang.)

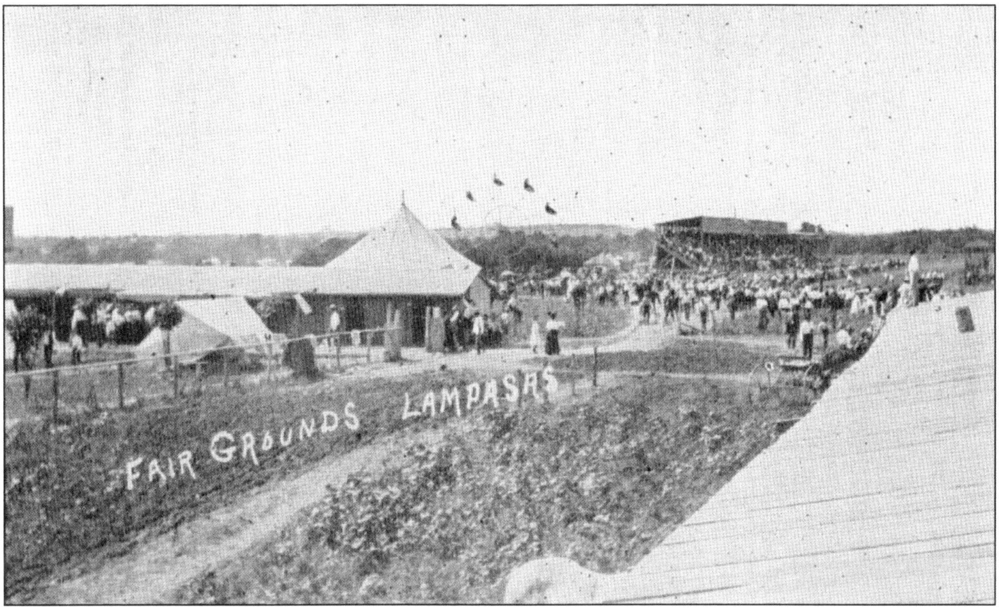

FAIRGROUNDS, LAMPASAS. The Lampasas Fairgrounds were located in the southwest section of the city near Sulphur Creek after 1900. The county agricultural fair and races were held there. There was a horse track that was one-mile around. This picture postcard shows the fair in full swing.

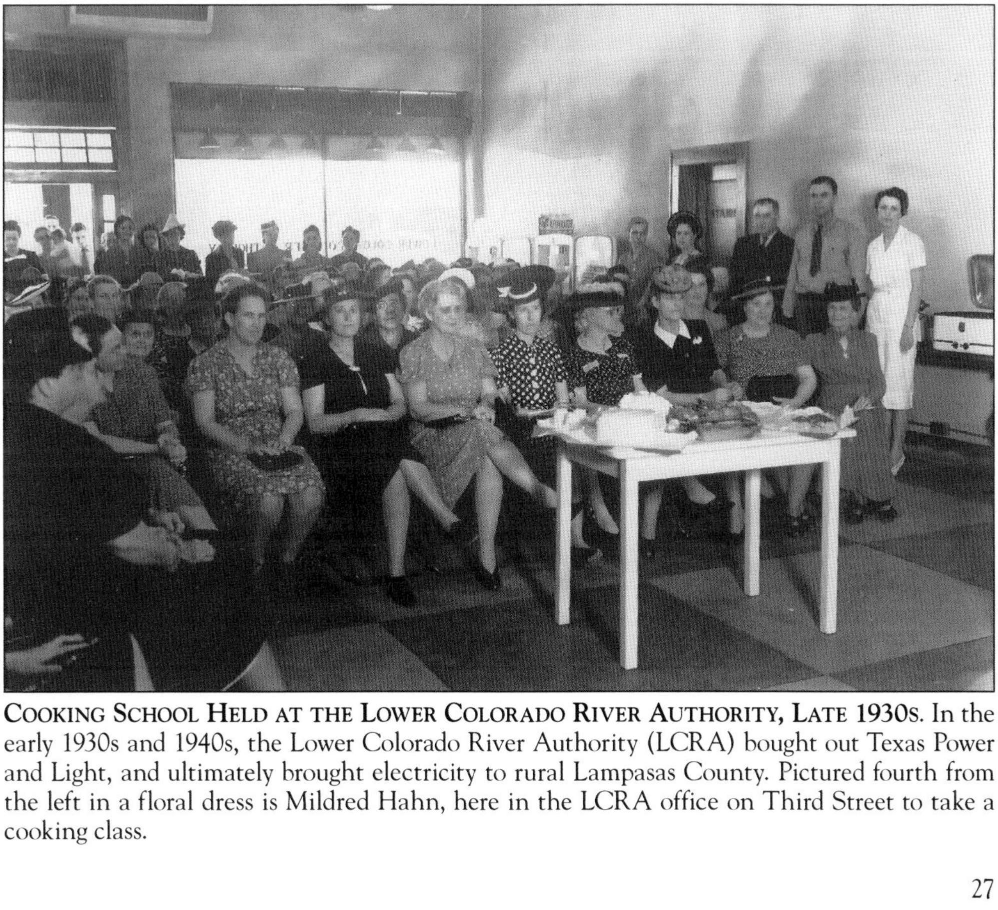

COOKING SCHOOL HELD AT THE LOWER COLORADO RIVER AUTHORITY, LATE 1930S. In the early 1930s and 1940s, the Lower Colorado River Authority (LCRA) bought out Texas Power and Light, and ultimately brought electricity to rural Lampasas County. Pictured fourth from the left in a floral dress is Mildred Hahn, here in the LCRA office on Third Street to take a cooking class.

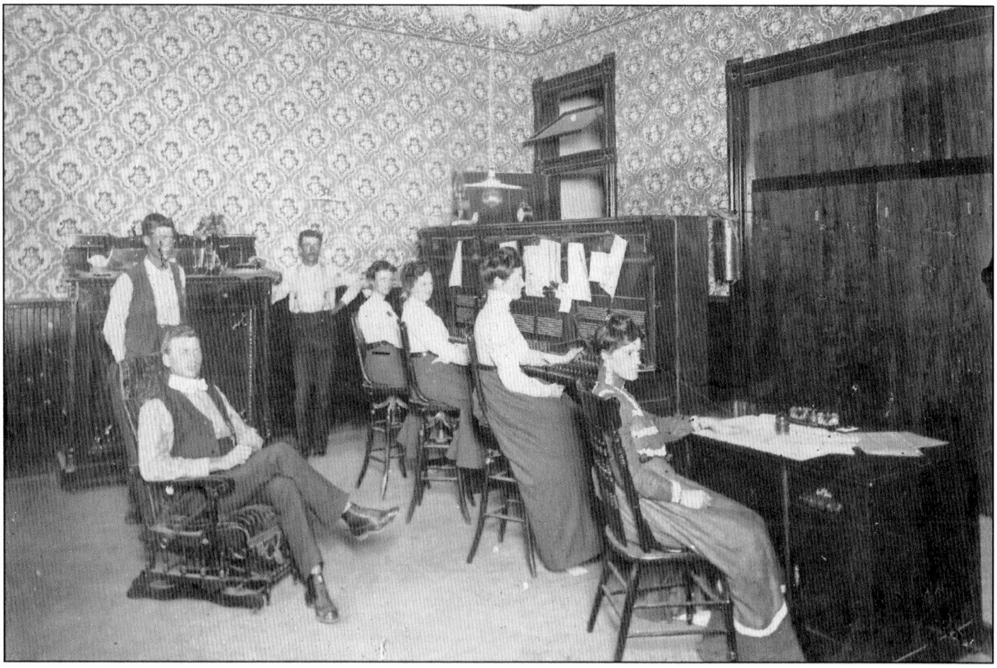

TELEPHONE COMPANY, LAMPASAS, EARLY 1900S. The Rural Telephone Company was an early company in Lampasas County. It was founded in Center in 1914 and at one point had offices on Live Oak Street in Lampasas. Another early phone company was Southwestern Bell. Here three women sit poised at the switchboard, ready to put calls through.

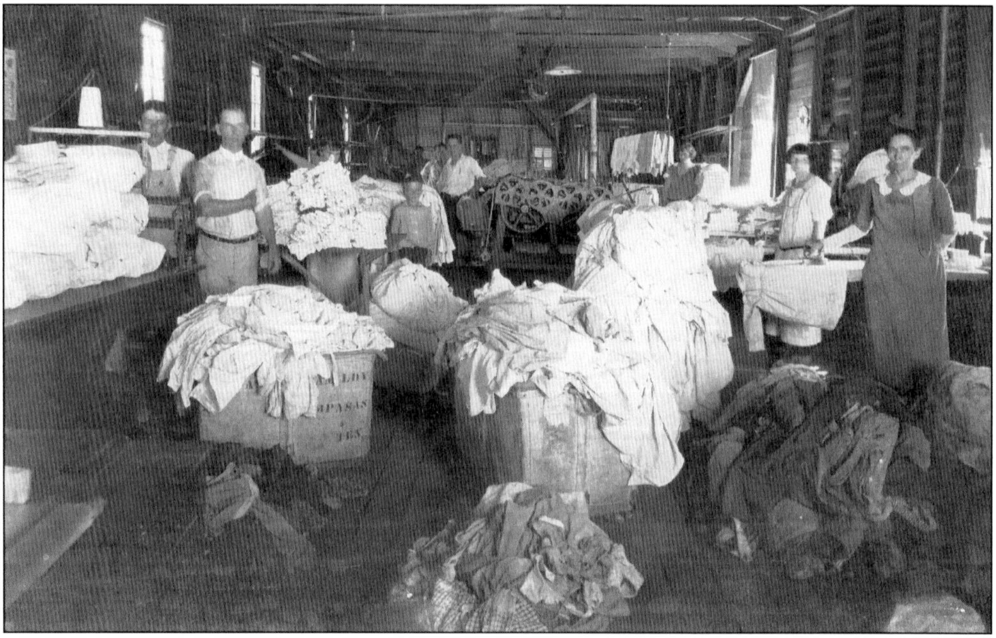

LAMPASAS STEAM LAUNDRY, 1920S. The Lampasas Steam Laundry was located on Elm Street, off of Fourth Street, across from W. C. Gillen's cotton gin. In the 1950s, every day at noon and at 5:00 p.m., the laundry sounded a whistle that could be heard across town. Here men and women work side by side in what must have been a hot and exhausting job.

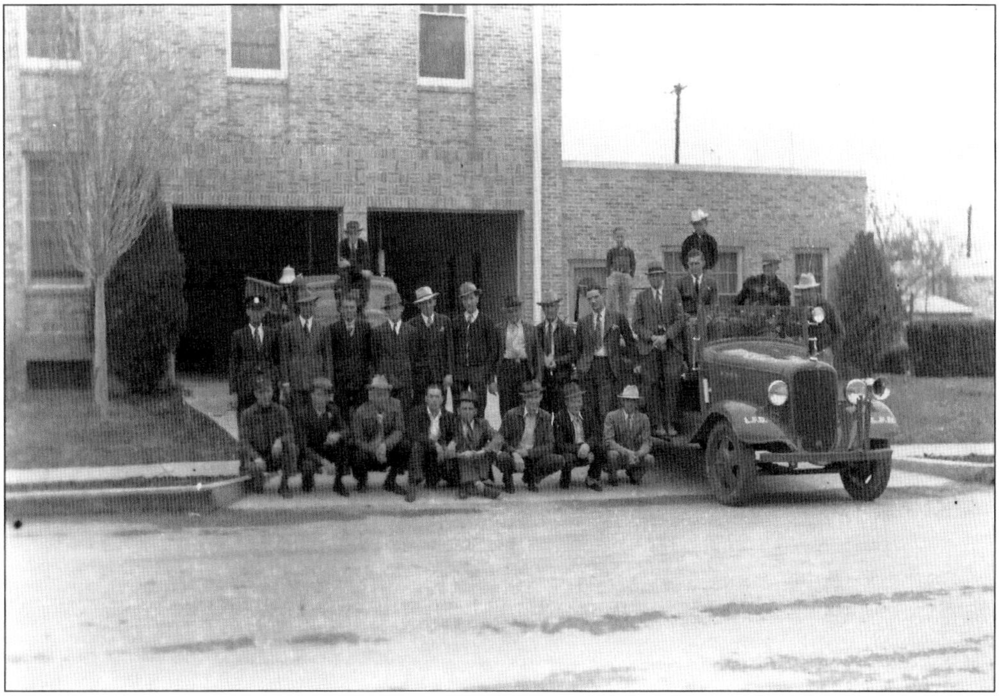

Lampasas Firehouse. The first building the Lampasas Volunteer Fire Department occupied was rented from R. E. Noble. As the department grew, it required more space. It was moved to the Higdon Gin Stable in June 1896. From the early 1930s to 1989, the fire station, pictured here, was located in part of city hall on Third and Main Streets. (Photograph by Lucile Standard.)

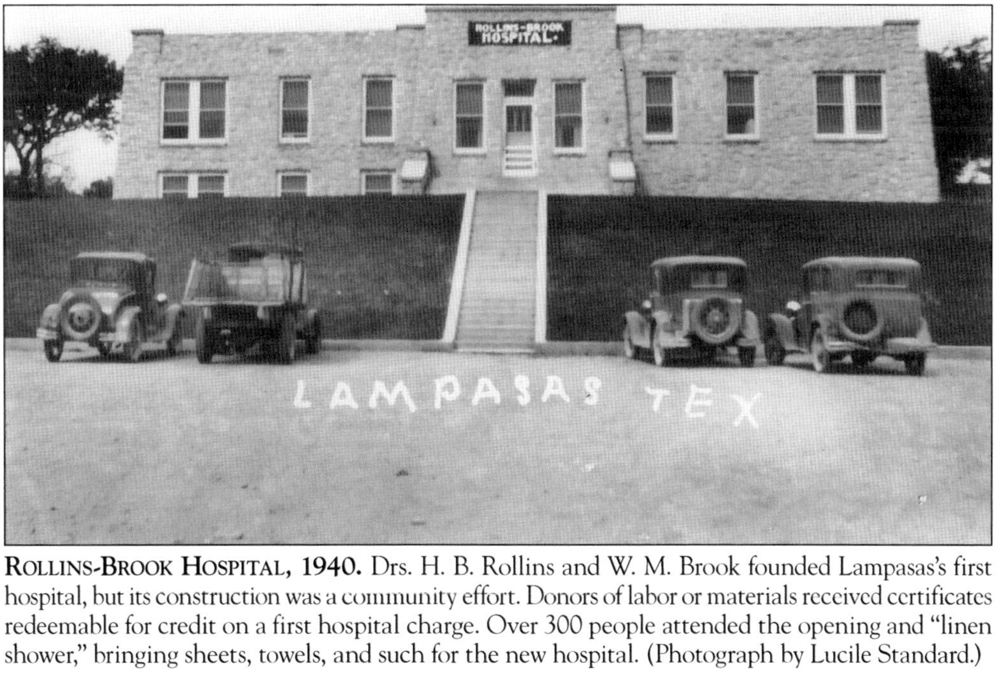

Rollins-Brook Hospital, 1940. Drs. H. B. Rollins and W. M. Brook founded Lampasas's first hospital, but its construction was a community effort. Donors of labor or materials received certificates redeemable for credit on a first hospital charge. Over 300 people attended the opening and "linen shower," bringing sheets, towels, and such for the new hospital. (Photograph by Lucile Standard.)

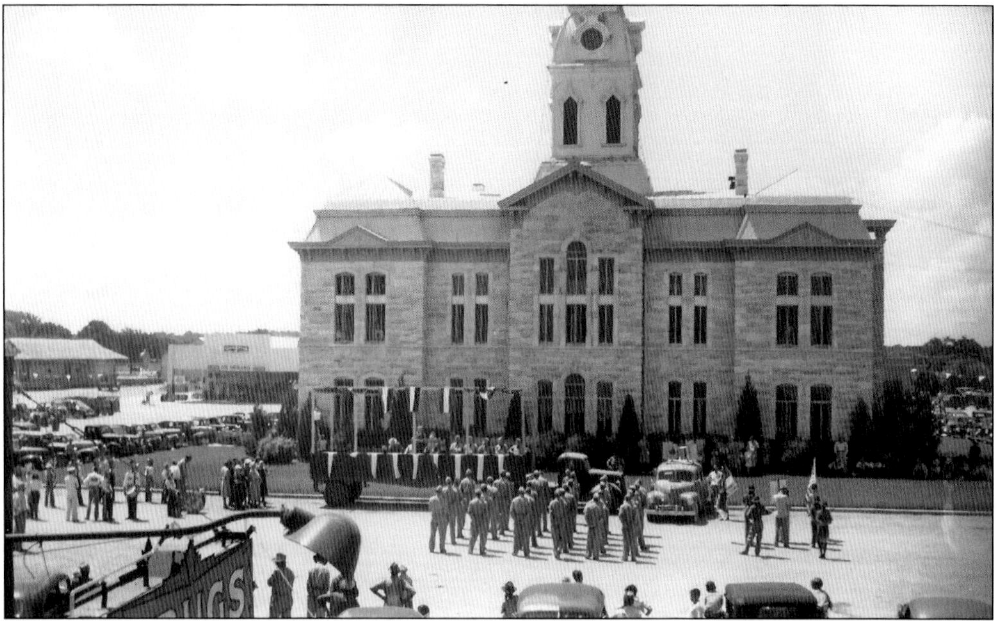

Operation Long Horn, Lampasas, 1952. In March and April 1952, the U.S. Army set up maneuvers in Lampasas County to update the skills of soldiers who had been trained in World War II. More than 115,000 servicemen participated, staging a mock occupation and liberation of the city by enemy forces. These maneuvers were known as Operation Long Horn.

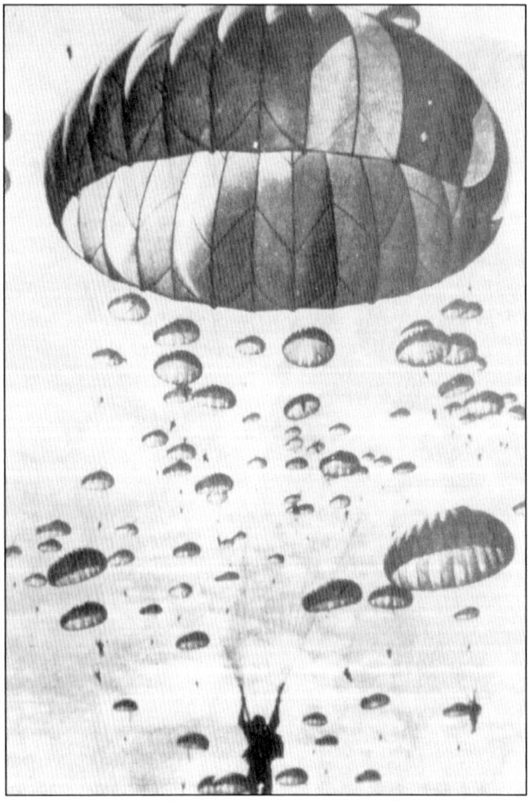

Operation Long Horn, Lometa, 1952. More than 2,500 paratroopers were dropped near Lometa during Operation Long Horn, military exercises staged by the U.S. Army in Lampasas County. More than 25,000 people watched the operation, which reportedly cost $3.3 million and 10 human lives. (Courtesy of Ruth Gadbury.)

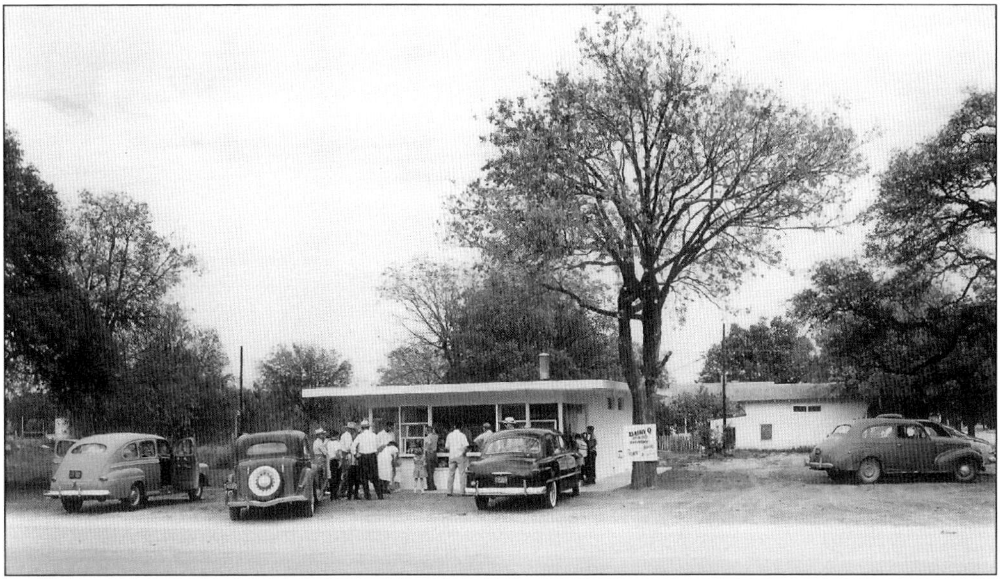

DAIRY CUE. The Dairy Cue opened in 1950, serving ice cream and milk shakes and, later, hamburgers and Cokes. Opened by James Buchanan Storm (1901–1985) and his wife, Robbie IraDell Upton Storm (b. 1911), the restaurant was renamed Storm's Drive-In and was expanded into a small chain. In the 1950s, Elvis Presley was stationed at Fort Hood in nearby Killeen, and it is said that he came to the restaurant often.

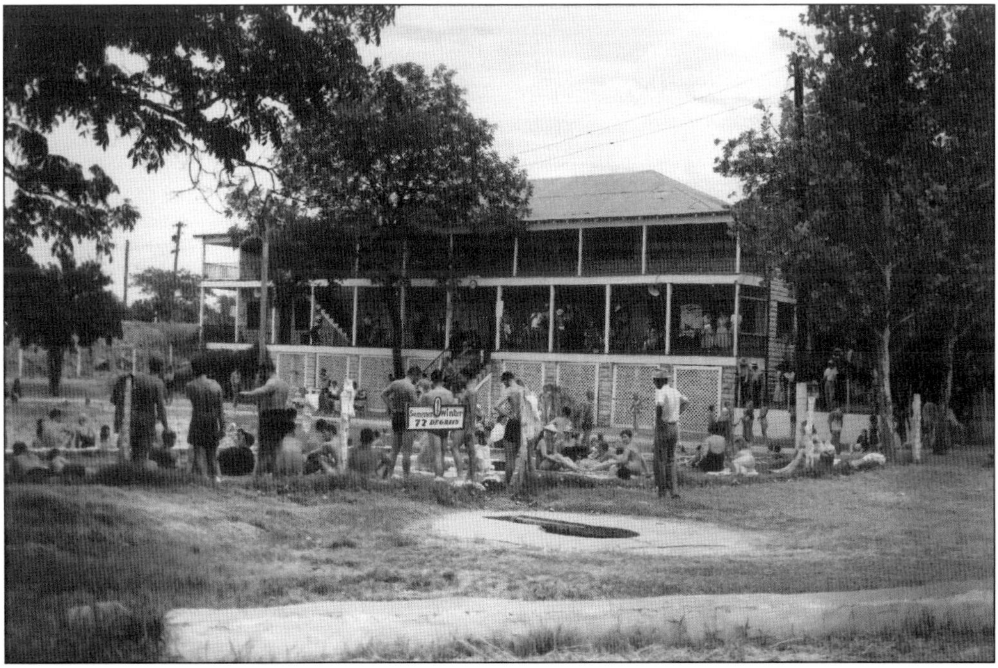

SUMMER AND WINTER, 72 DEGREES ALL YEAR-ROUND. Hancock Park swimming pool, shown here in 1947, boasts a year-round constant temperature of 72 degrees Fahrenheit. The Hostess House, visible just behind the spring-fed pool, was built in 1929 with an office, a sandwich bar, and dressing room. Later an apartment was added for the Hancock Park manager. In 1949, the Hostess House was remodeled and was sided in limestone.

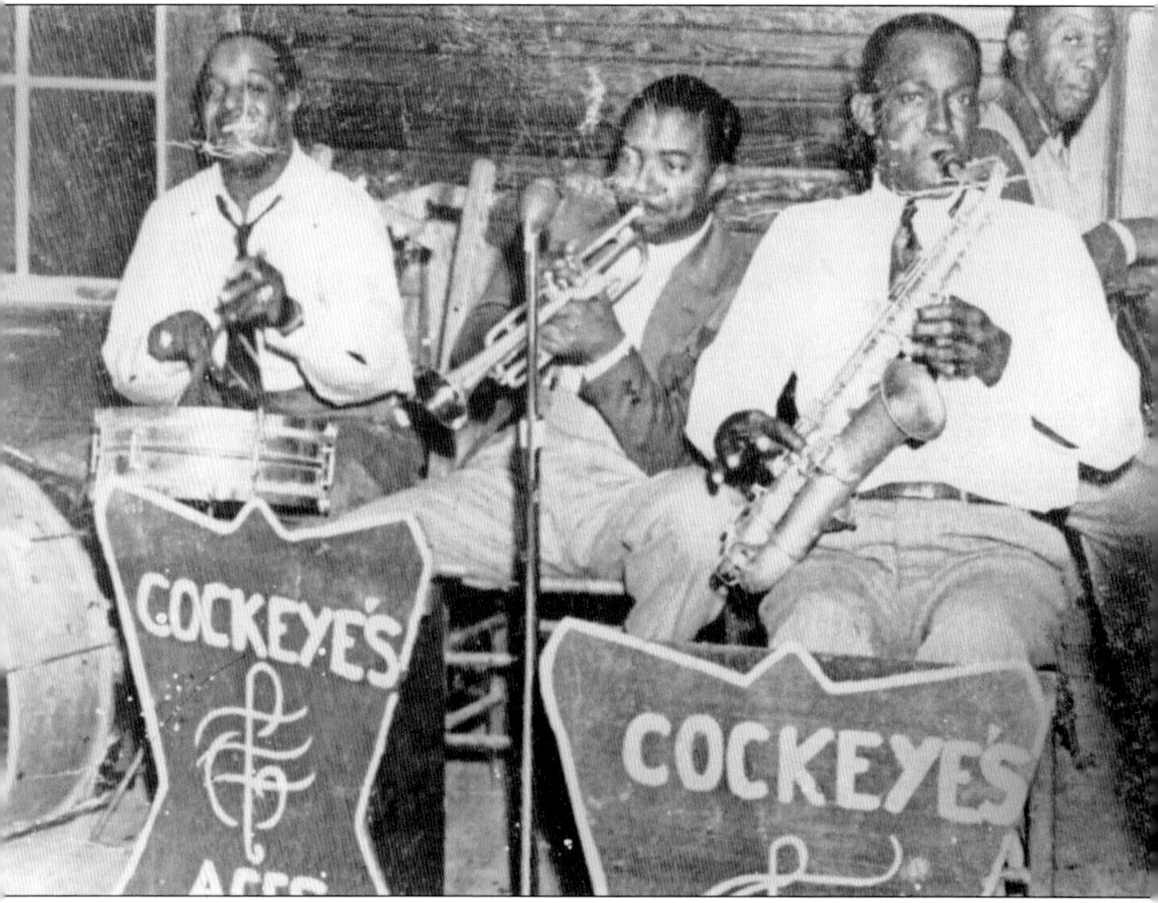

COCKEYE'S ACES, 1949. Many a night was danced away to the music of Fay "Cockeye" Brown and his band. Pictured from left to right are Brown on drums, Hubert Pickett on trumpet, Woodrow "Woody" Tipton on saxophone, and Fred Phillips at the piano. From time to time, Brown also played string bass. The well-known group (with varying members) performed at dances in the surrounding area for several decades beginning in the 1920s. Their repertoire included jazz, blues, and country and western, as well as popular tunes of the day. County life, at least for dancers, had to include a turn to the music of Cockeye's Aces.

Three

THE SARATOGA OF THE SOUTH

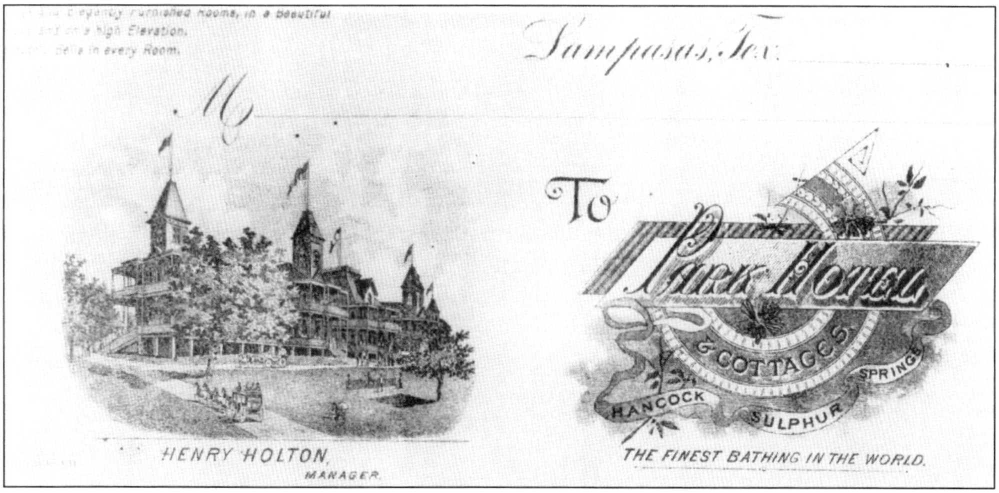

PARK HOTEL LETTERHEAD. This photograph shows an artist's rendering of Lampasas's legendary Park Hotel, which was built in 1883 by a group of Houston and Galveston investors who aimed to develop a spa that catered to the affluent. "Here one met the right people and enjoyed all the amenities of a cultured life—at the *Saratoga of the South*," read one advertisement of the day, enticing people to come to Lampasas that they, too, might luxuriate in the healing spring waters at the elegant, 200-room Park Hotel.

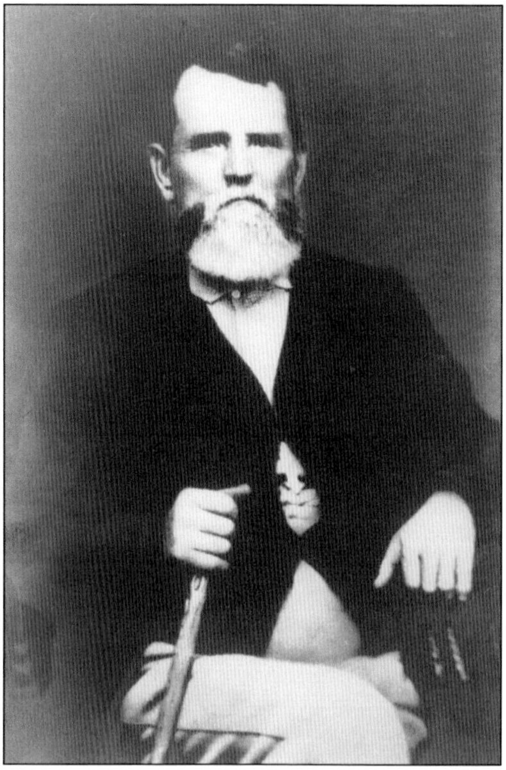

MOSES AND HANNAH HUGHES. Among the first permanent settlers in the future city of Lampasas, Moses Hughes and his brother, Nimrod, brought their families, including their mother, Rebecca Hughes, from Williamson County to the mineral springs in and around Sulphur Creek in 1853. The Hughes had heard about the healing properties of the springs from Native Americans and hoped to improve the ill health of Moses wife, Hannah. Moses and Hannah, with her health restored, lived near their mill on Sulphur Creek. Later they bought land west of Lampasas and built a two-story native-limestone house. Constructed during 1855–1856, the home still stands. The brothers remained active in community affairs, signing the petition for the creation of Lampasas County and serving in defense militias. Moses built Lampasas's first mill, and Nimrod served on Lampasas County's first commissioner's court.

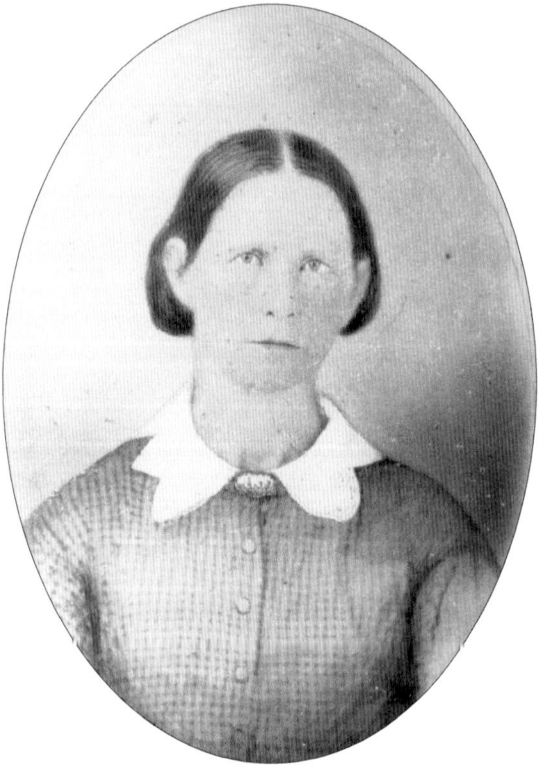

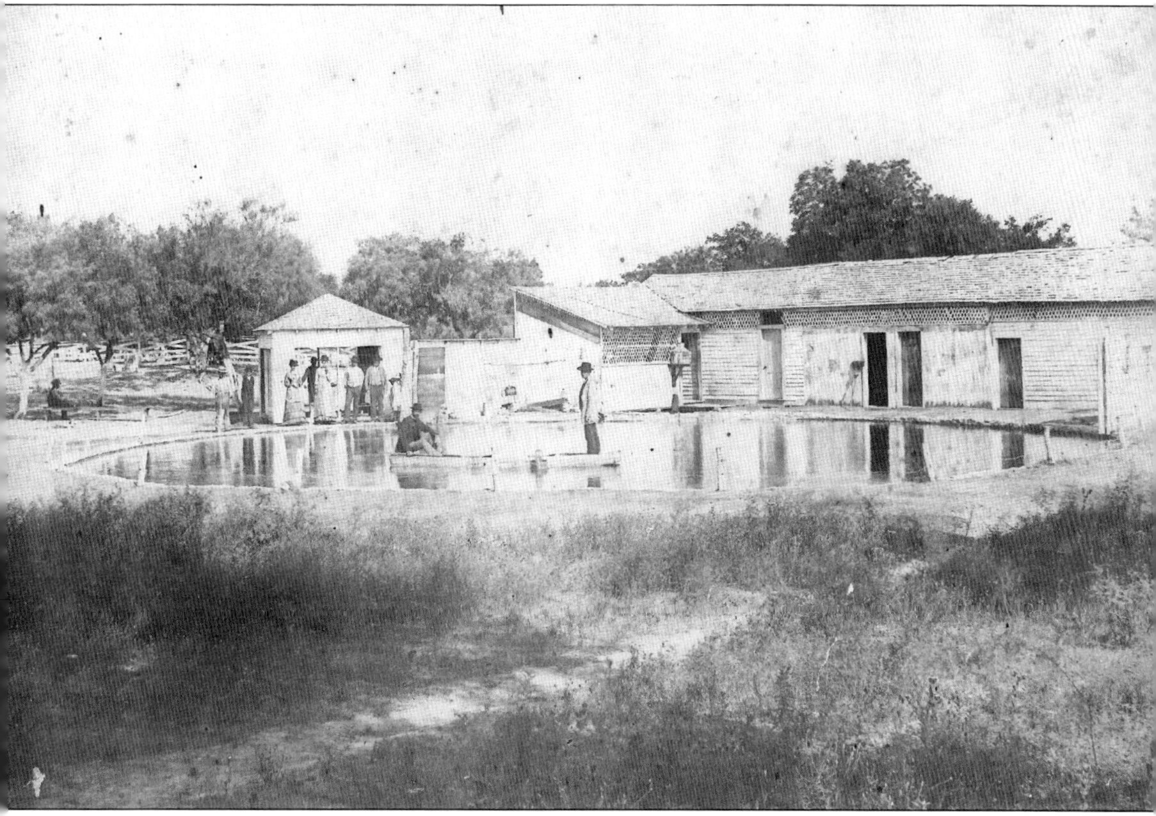

HANNA SPRINGS BATH HOUSE. Commercial development of Hanna Springs began soon after the town site of Burleson (later named Lampasas) was laid out and lots sold in 1855. It is said that during the preparation of the site for the first bathhouse, the spring had to be cleared of numerous bison bones. Pictured is one of the earliest photographs of Hanna Springs known to exist. John Hanna became owner of the facility in 1867, and the Hanna name has remained associated with the spring since then.

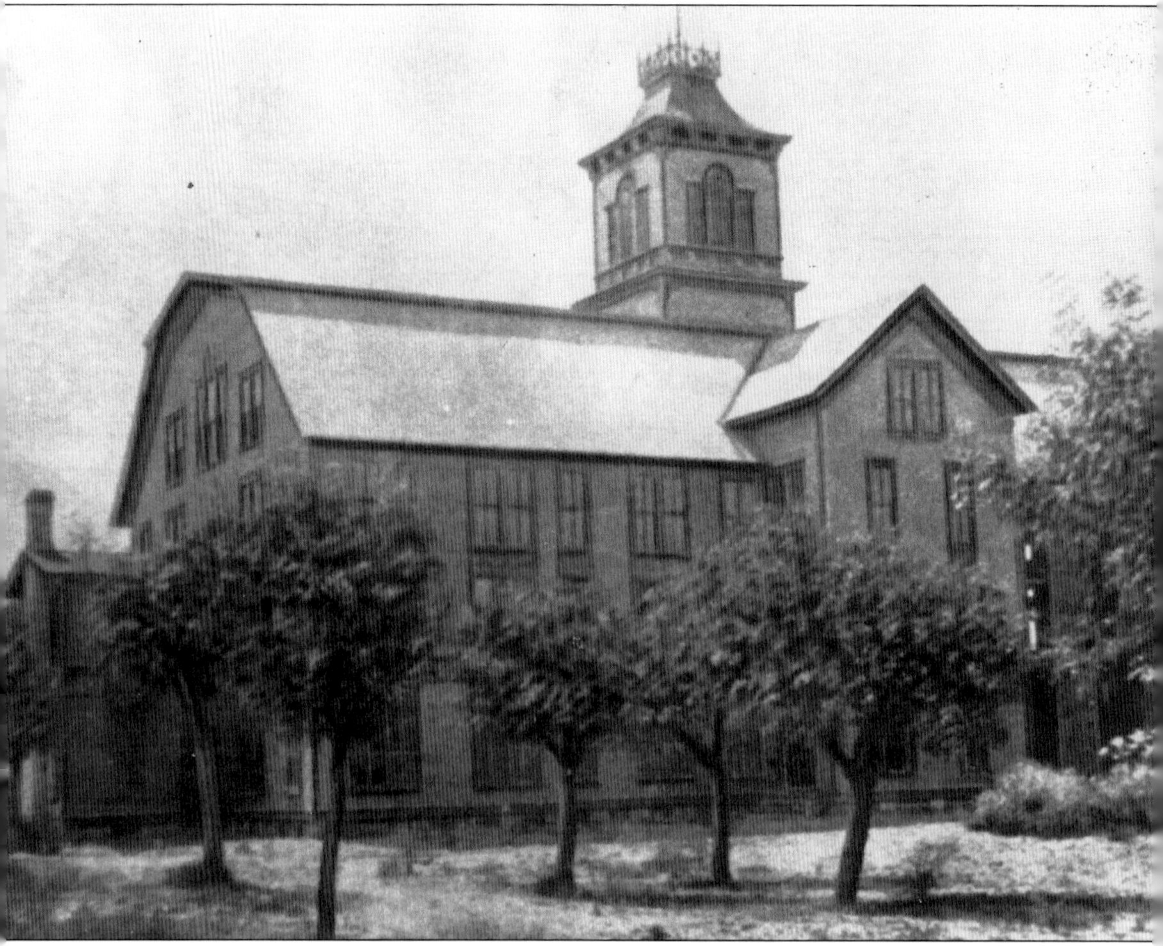

HANNA SPRINGS PAVILION. Following the 1882 arrival of the Gulf, Colorado, and Santa Fe Railway, Lampasas became a boomtown and fashionable health resort. The Hanna Springs Pavilion and Bath House offered hot and cold baths, swimming pools, dressing rooms, and elegantly furnished parlors on the first floor. The entire upper floor served as a great hall, measuring about 60 by 120 feet. Accessed by exterior staircases at either end of the building, the hall was the site for musical and theatrical events often attended by formally attired ladies and gentlemen. In 1892, Texas Democrats convened at the Hanna Springs Pavilion to elect delegates to the party's national convention some months later. Delegates convened in Houston in late summer to select Democratic nominees for statewide offices.

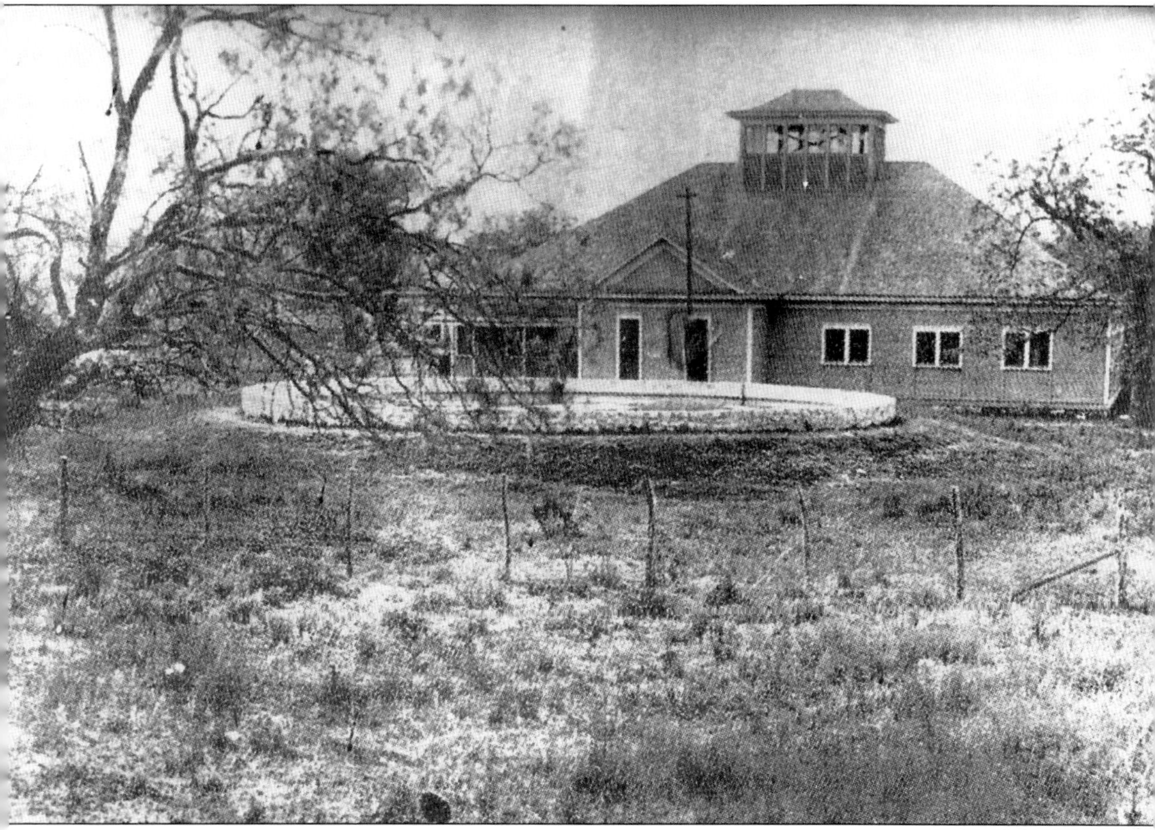

HANNA SPRINGS REVISITED. Pictured here is one of the bathhouses built at Hanna Springs during Lampasas's first several decades. Besides facilities in which their patrons could "take the waters," early proprietors built hotels, enabling guests to extend their visits. In 1855, George and Martha Scott acquired the springs and its environs, and became its first hoteliers.

PARK HOTEL

AND COTTAGES.

THE ONLY FIRST-CLASS HOTEL IN LAMPASAS.

200 Large, Airy and Elegantly Furnished Rooms in a Beautiful Grove. Electric Bells in Every Room.

ALTITUDE 1,500 FEET. ✣ RATES, $2.50 AND $3.00 PER DAY.

HANCOCK SULPHUR SPRINGS.

Hot, Cold and Vapor Baths; also, Large Swimming Pools. The Finest Bathing in the World. Can Bathe 500 Persons Daily.

FLOW FROM ONE SPRING 4,000 GALLONS PER MINUTE.

STREET CARS FROM HOTEL TO TOWN EVERY 15 MINUTES.

LAMPASAS HOTEL CO., Proprietors. HENRY HOLTON, Manager.

SAMPLE ROOMS IN CITY FOR COMMERCIAL TRAVELERS.

CERTIFICATE OF ANALYSIS

OF THE

HANCOCK SPRINGS,

By E. WALLER, Ph. D., of New York.

Per U. S. Gallon of 231 Cubic Inches.

INGREDIENTS.	GRAINS.
Chloride of Sodium,	49.835
Bromide of Sodium,	traces
Bi-carbonate of lithia,	0.186
Bi-carbonate of lime,	24.282
Bi-carbonate of iron,	0.052
Chloride of magnesium,	18.265
Chloride of Calcium,	8.040
Sulphate of Potassa,	2.024
Sulphate of lime,	3.462
Alumina,	0.059
Silica,	0.496
Organic matter,	trace
Total,	106.701

ELWYN WALLER, Ph. D.

New York, August 28, 1883.

PARK HOTEL ADVERTISING CARD. Listing the many amenities the Park Hotel offered its guests while in Lampasas, this bit of promotional material devoted half of its space to a listing of the mineral content of the water from the nearby Hancock Springs. "Taking the waters"—drinking it, bathing in it, and swimming in it—was a popular and fashionable pastime throughout the United States and Europe during the late 19th century. Other advertising of the day enticed tourists to "come to the Park Hotel and meet the socially correct." For a short time, Lampasas, with facilities at both the Hancock and Hanna Springs, became the leading tourist destination in Texas.

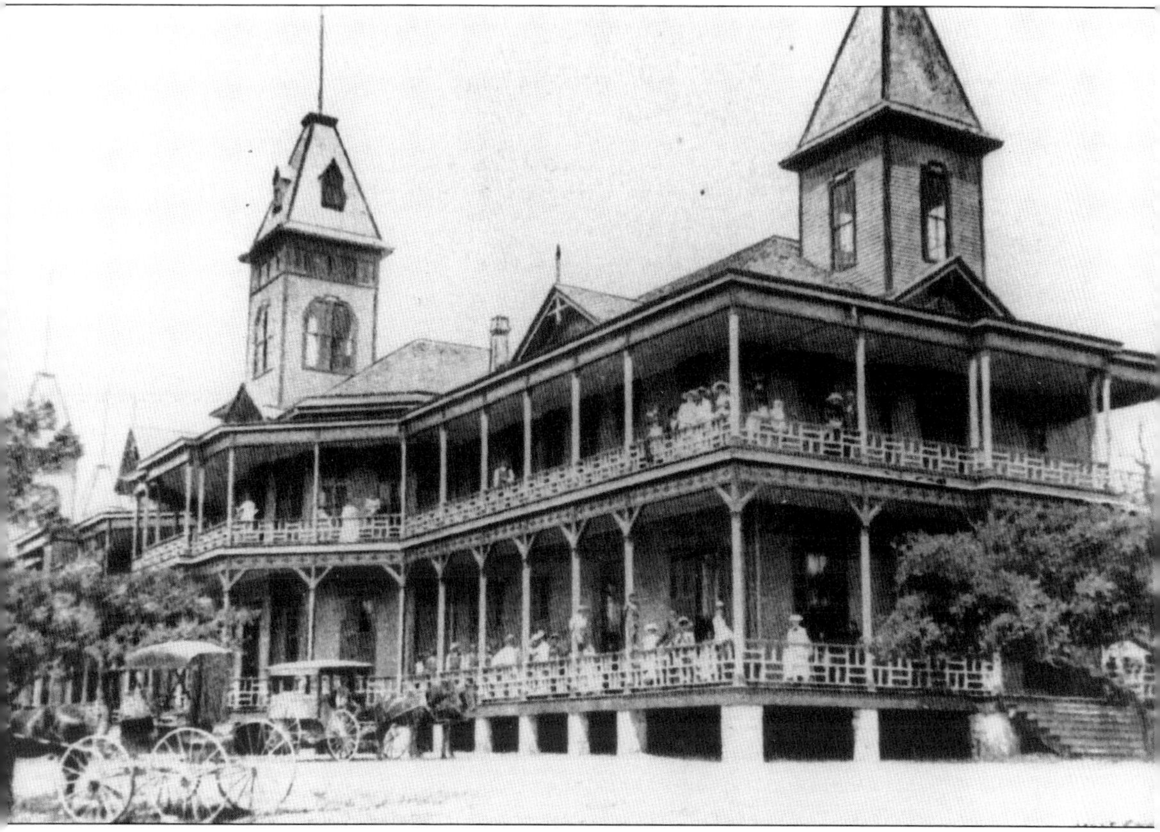

PARK HOTEL. Built in 1883 by a group of Houston and Galveston businessmen that included George and John Sealy, the elegant Park Hotel was situated on 200 acres of land that included the Hancock Springs. Sporting a footprint about the size of a football field, the Park Hotel was said to have been one of the largest wood-frame hotels in the country. Equipped with electric bells in each of its 200 guest rooms, the luxury hotel also featured richly furnished parlors; music, reading, and writing rooms; a billiard room with four tables; and a grand dining room. Its staff included an English manager, a liveried orchestra, and French chefs. The hotel burned to the ground one icy night in February 1895.

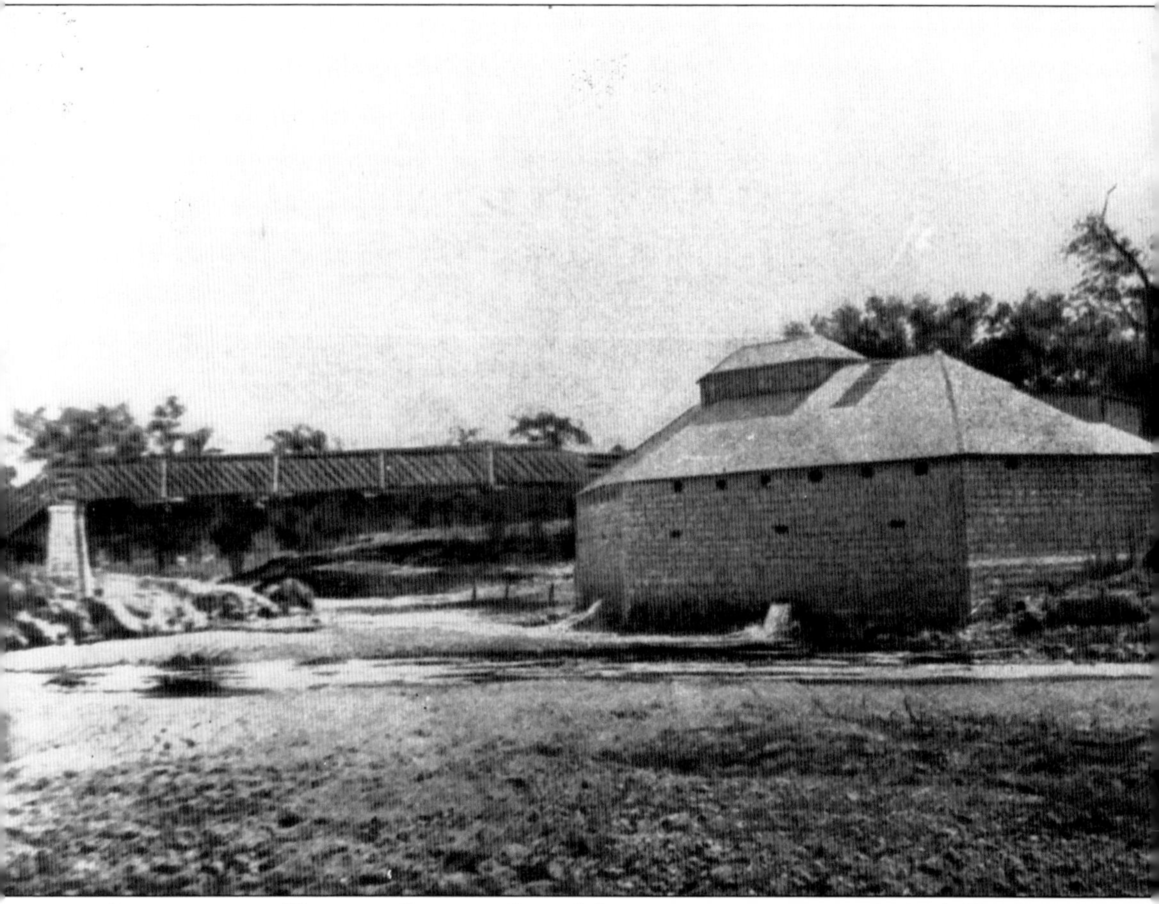

BATHHOUSE AT HANCOCK SPRINGS. One of the primary attractions at the Park Hotel was its large bathhouse on the south side of Sulphur Creek. Built directly over one of the Hancock Springs, the bathhouse enclosed two swimming pools, one for men and the other for women. Although the old bathhouse lost its roof long ago, remnants of its exterior stone walls—and the bubbling spring within—can still be seen today at Hancock Park. Built for the convenience of guests at the Park Hotel, a boardwalk and a small suspension bridge provided a way to get to the Hancock Springs bathhouses on the other side of Sulphur Creek. Another transportation amenity was a mule-drawn streetcar system that carried people between the train depot and the Park Hotel. The trolley also made stops as it wound its way through the courthouse square and past other hotels of the day.

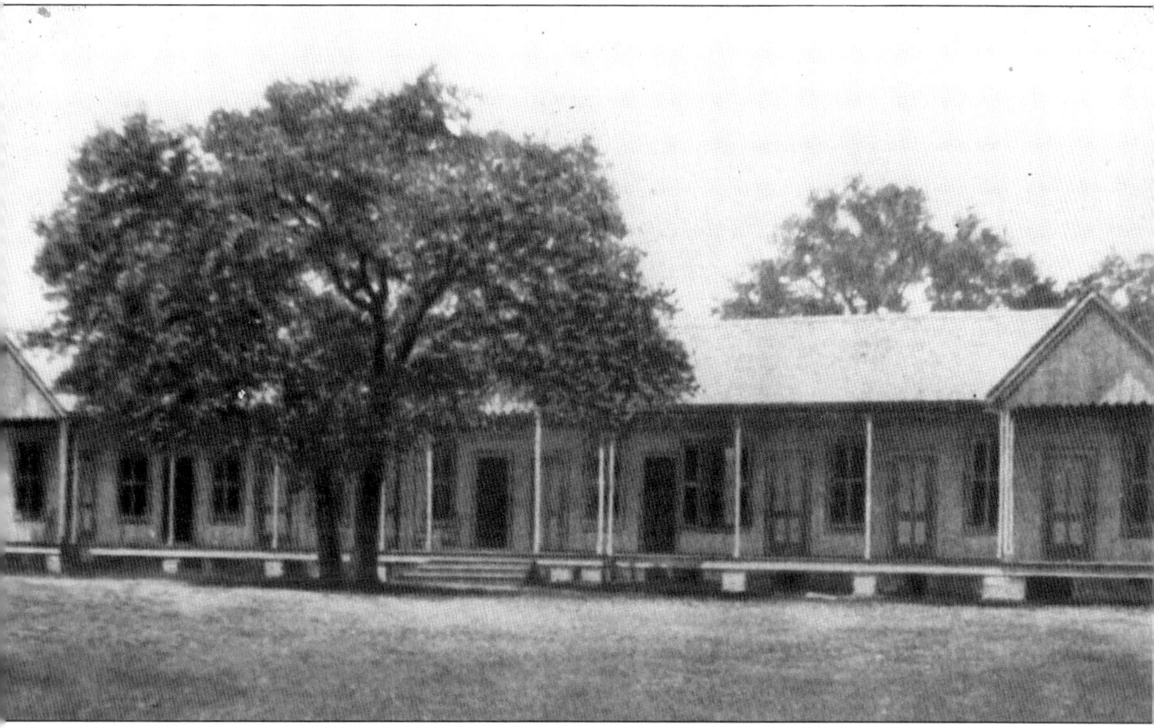

BACHELORS ROW. In addition to 200 rooms in the hotel proper, the Park Hotel also offered guests the privacy of cottages. Built in rows behind the hotel, one row of cottages was reserved for families, while cottages in the opposite row were rented to bachelors. In front of the hotel, which faced Sulphur Creek to the south, was a pavilion in which guests danced almost nightly. Beyond the pavilion was a boardwalk and a footbridge that led to the bathhouses across the creek.

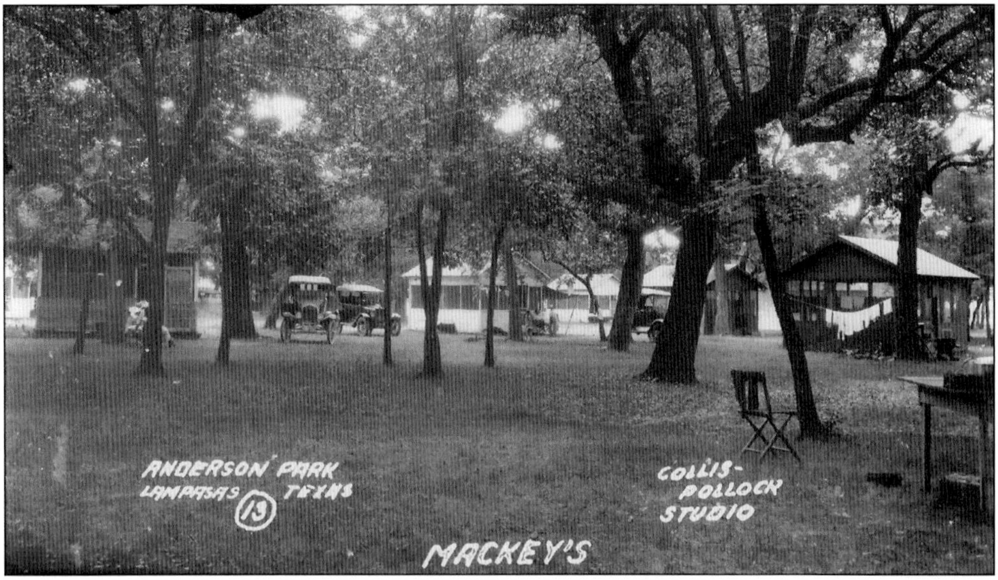

ANDERSON PARK. The Central Texas Baptist Encampment first convened at Hancock Park in the summer of 1905. With the success of the first year, the Encampment Association bought the park and operated it for almost 25 years. The park was renamed "Anderson Park" in honor of A. P. Anderson, a deacon in the First Baptist Church of Lampasas. The facility went by that name until 1929, when it was sold to L. N. Little and Frank Baker.

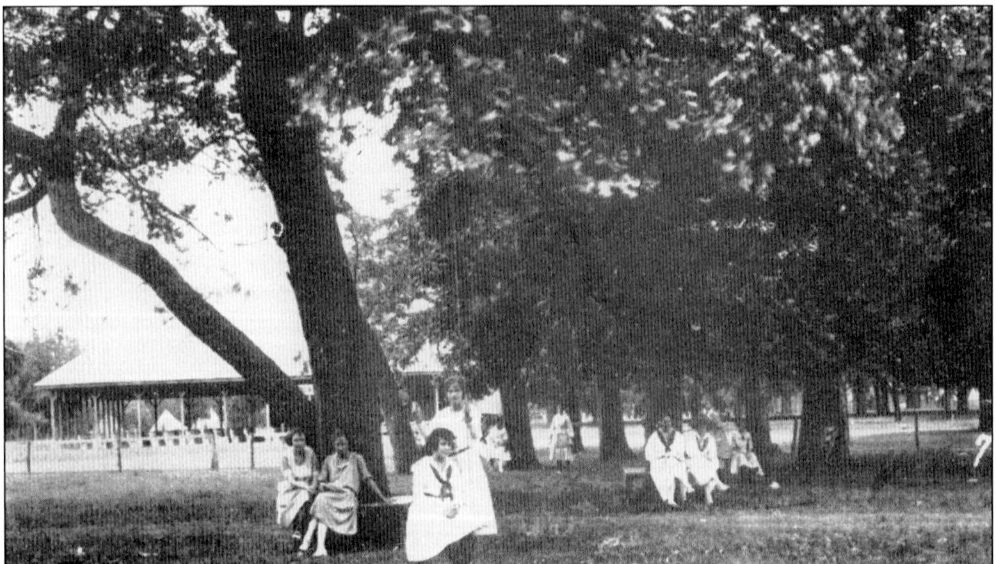

RELAXING AT ANDERSON PARK. Cabins were built for people attending the annual 10-week Baptist summer encampments. Time for rest and recreation were planned into each day. Visible in the background of this photograph is Dickson Auditorium, which could seat 2,500 to 3,000. It was named for J. H. Dickson of Lampasas, who first had the idea of using the old Park Hotel grounds as a Baptist encampment.

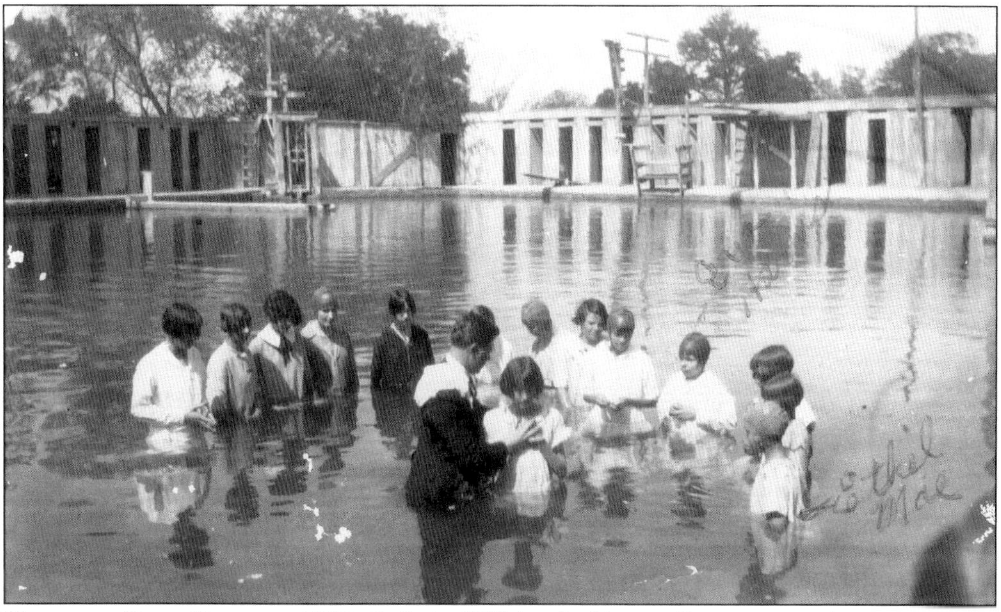

HANCOCK POOL BAPTISM, 1927. Built in 1911 by the Baptist Encampment Association, the spring-fed Hancock Pool was often used for baptisms, as well as for swimming. Pictured here is the baptism of a young girl in 1927. Other improvements made at Anderson Park included pavilions, the Hostess House, and a telephone facility.

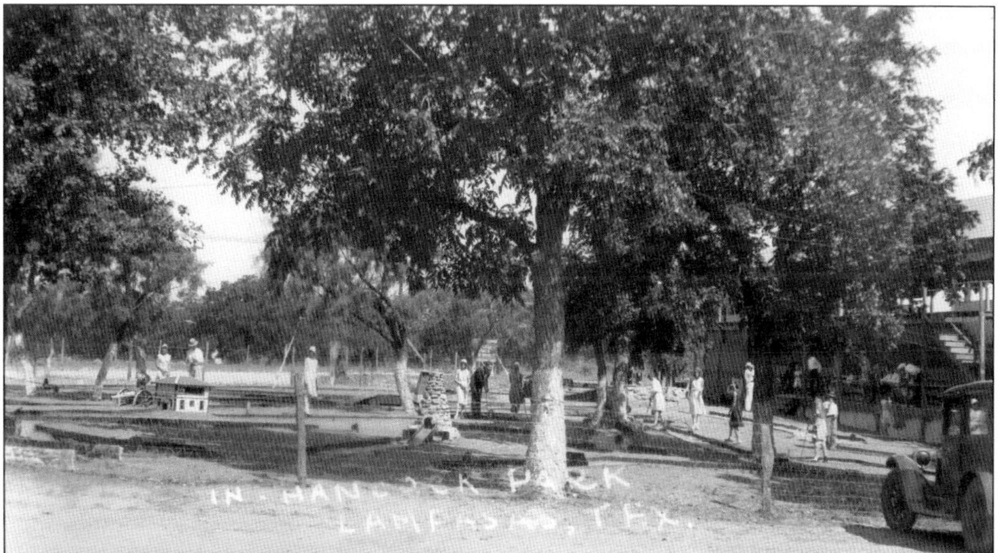

MINIATURE GOLF COURSE. One of the many improvements Charles Baker and L. N. Little made to Anderson Park after they bought it from the Central Texas Baptist Encampment was this miniature golf course. The two men operated the park as the Baker and Little Swimming and Boating Company from 1929 to 1936. The City of Lampasas bought the recreation facility in 1936 and changed its name to the original Hancock Park.

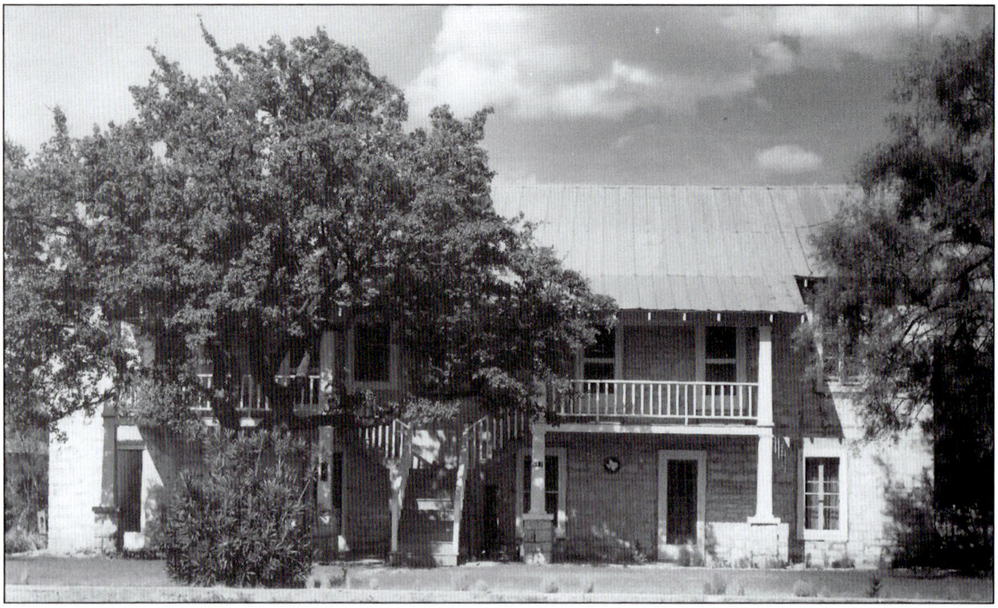

Hart Hotel Stage Stop. Built shortly after the Civil War, the Hart Hotel was originally a two-room, two-story stagecoach stop. It was enlarged twice, and later it was converted into apartments. The Hart Hotel was also known as the Hart House, and at one time, it was named the Commercial Hotel. Located at 511 South Western Avenue, the hotel is one of the oldest structures in Lampasas County.

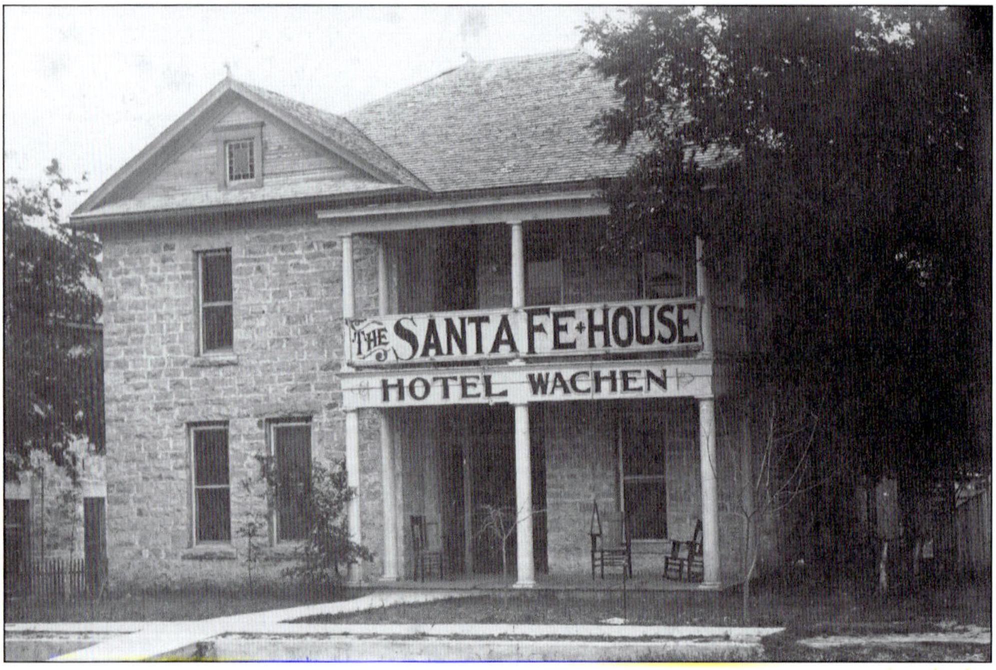

Santa Fe House—Hotel Wachen. Originally the home of Regimus and Maria Wachendorfer, this two-story native-stone property was later converted into a hotel by their son Charles and his wife, Verna. In operation as early as the 1920s, the Hotel Wachen stood at Second and Pecan Streets, a block north of the courthouse square. It was destroyed by fire in 1968.

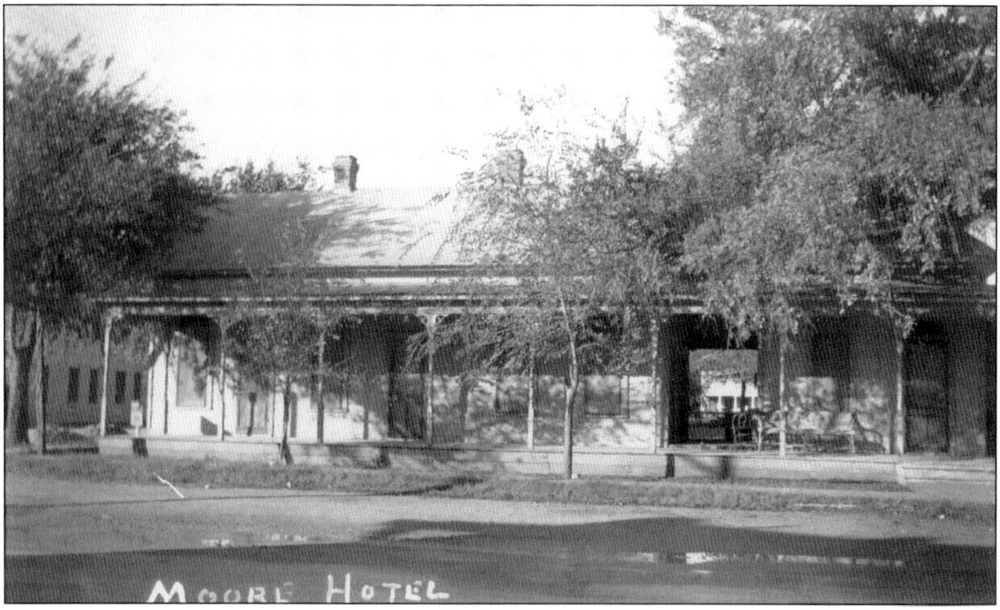

MOORE HOTEL. Located at Live Oak and Second Streets, the Moore Hotel once stood across the street from the Santa Fe depot. The business was owned and operated by W. R. and Maria Moore. It opened during the 1920s. It was closed after Moore ("Uncle Billy") died in 1936. Moore spent his early years in the printing business and was the father of Dudley Moore, a much-beloved Lampasas educator.

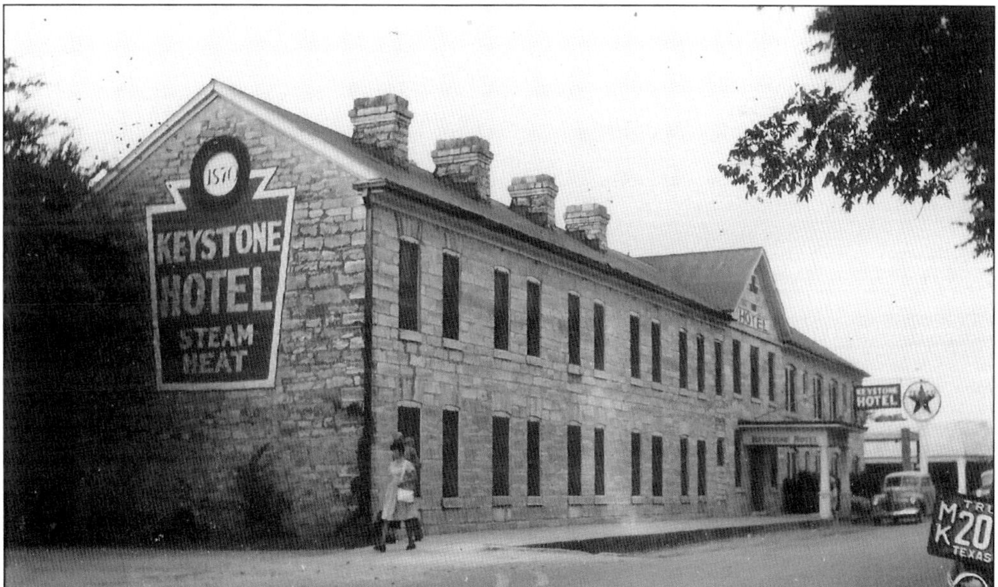

KEYSTONE HOTEL. Originally named the Star Hotel, this native-limestone structure was built about 1870 by J. N. and Harriet Gracy as a stagecoach stop. During the 1920s, J. R. Key bought the property and changed its name to the Keystone Hotel. Key added a new wing to the hotel and installed a steam heating system. The hotel still stands at 404 East Second Street.

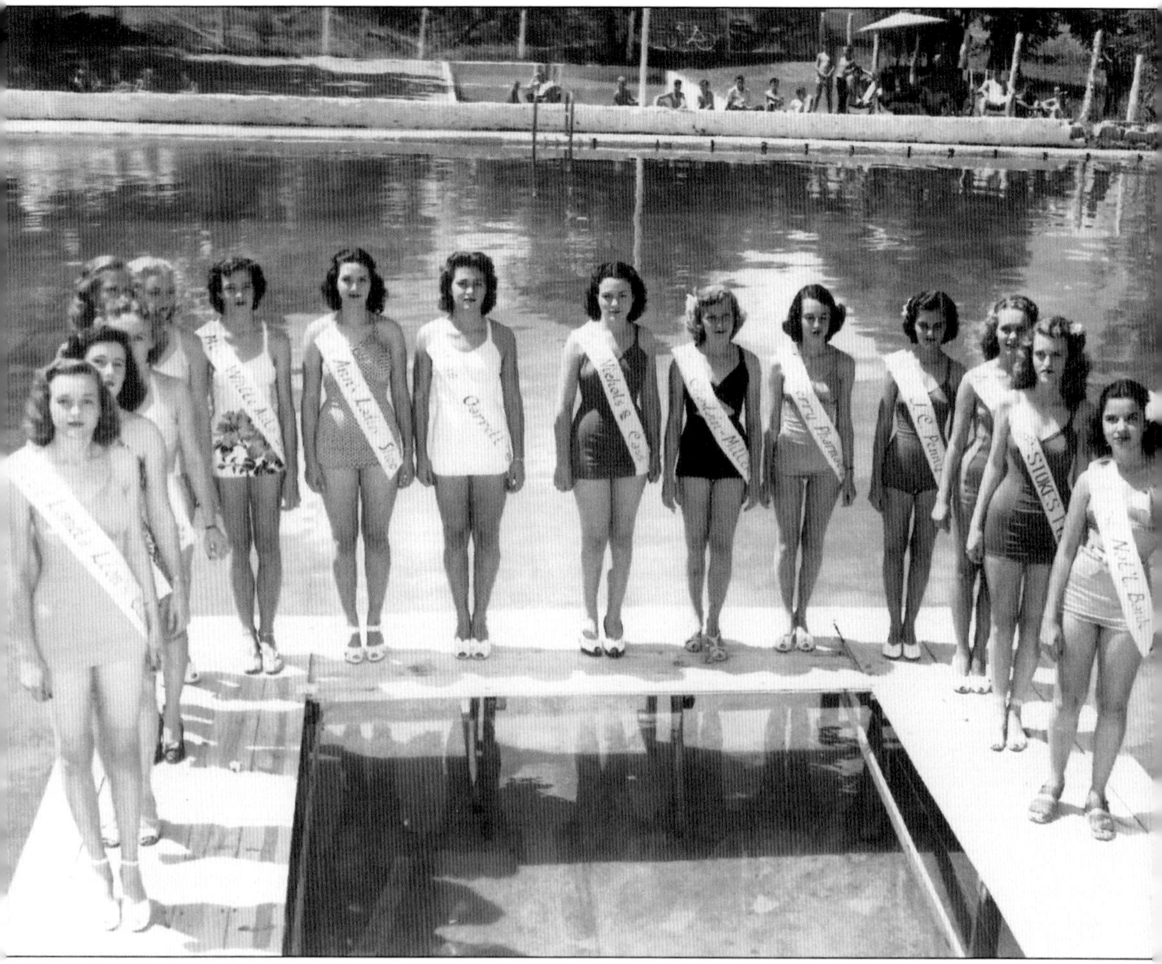

BATHING BEAUTIES AT HANCOCK POOL, C. 1948. A "Bathing Beauty Contest" was held during festivities surrounding the rededication of Hancock Park about 1948. During World War II, the City of Lampasas had leased the park to Camp Hood as a recreation spot for soldiers. At that time, the facility was called Panther Recreation Park. After the war, the city resumed management, changed the name back to Hancock Park, and made extensive improvements, including a nine-hole golf course. Each "beauty" wore a sash with her sponsor's name emblazoned across it. Sponsors included Stokes Brothers, J. C. Penney, Garrett's Dry Goods, and Cowan Pontiac. The Bathing Beauties are, from left to right, Frieda Jo Kirby, Delores Glover, Gloria Young, Evelyn Moore, Carolyn Harman, Cleo McGhee, Peggy Nell Hoover, Alice Langford, Charlene Wright, Nina Lee Jones, Vernell Gunter, Mary Jane Fretwell, Beverly Burns, Bobbie Nell Dellis, and Anna Wolfe. (Photograph by Virgil Wooten.)

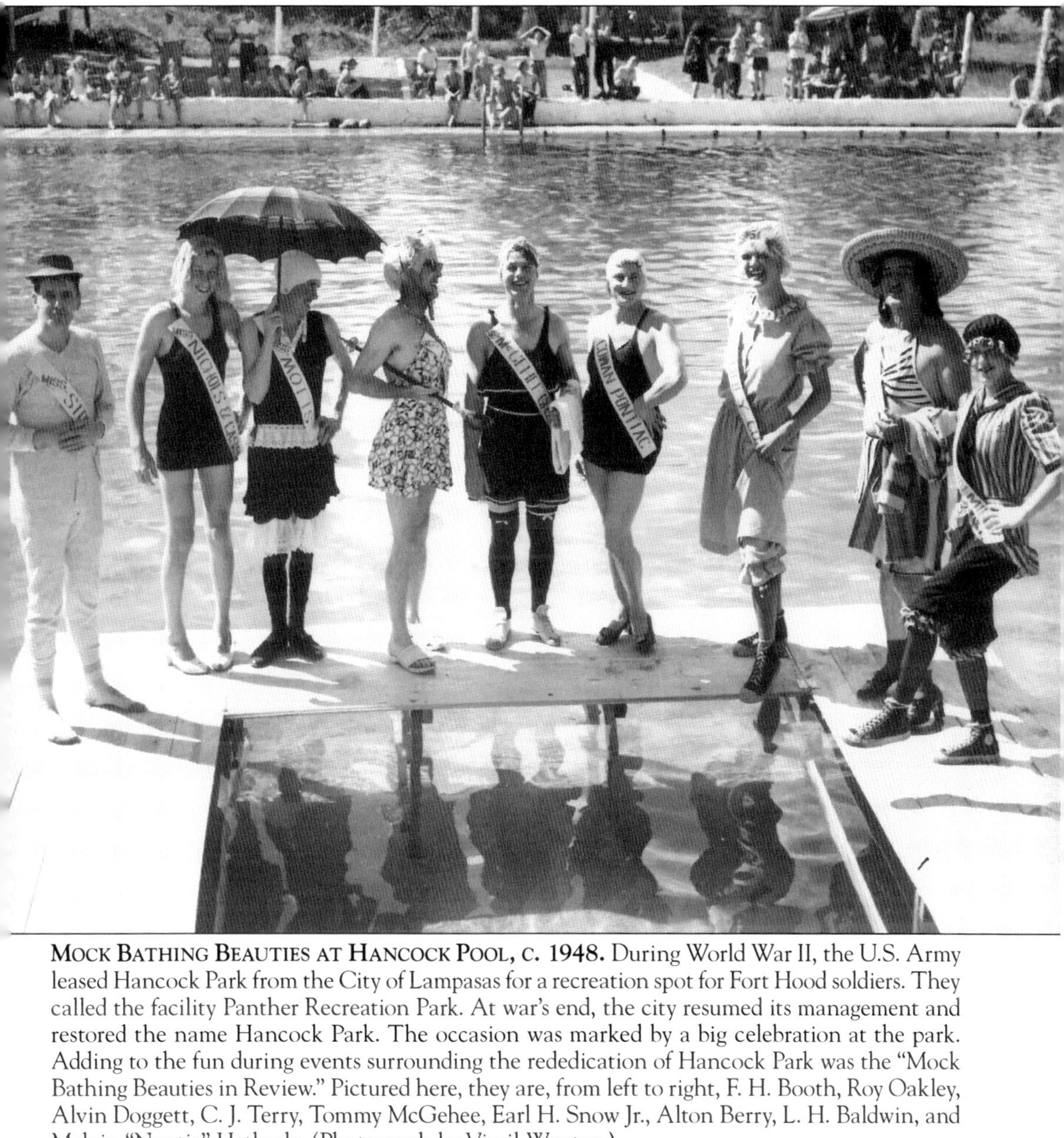

MOCK BATHING BEAUTIES AT HANCOCK POOL, C. 1948. During World War II, the U.S. Army leased Hancock Park from the City of Lampasas for a recreation spot for Fort Hood soldiers. They called the facility Panther Recreation Park. At war's end, the city resumed its management and restored the name Hancock Park. The occasion was marked by a big celebration at the park. Adding to the fun during events surrounding the rededication of Hancock Park was the "Mock Bathing Beauties in Review." Pictured here, they are, from left to right, F. H. Booth, Roy Oakley, Alvin Doggett, C. J. Terry, Tommy McGehee, Earl H. Snow Jr., Alton Berry, L. H. Baldwin, and Melvin "Nootie" Hetherly. (Photograph by Virgil Wooten.)

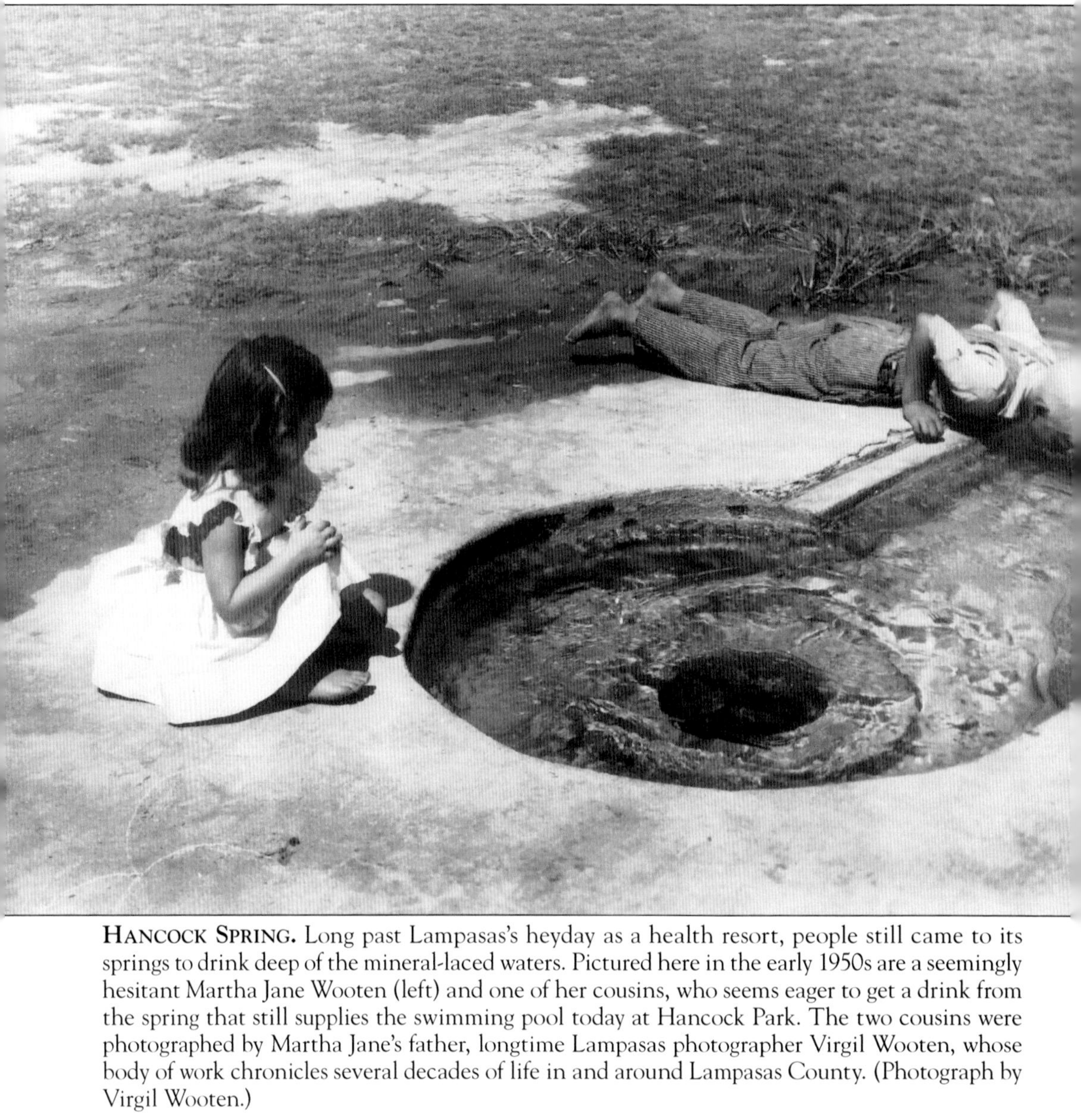

HANCOCK SPRING. Long past Lampasas's heyday as a health resort, people still came to its springs to drink deep of the mineral-laced waters. Pictured here in the early 1950s are a seemingly hesitant Martha Jane Wooten (left) and one of her cousins, who seems eager to get a drink from the spring that still supplies the swimming pool today at Hancock Park. The two cousins were photographed by Martha Jane's father, longtime Lampasas photographer Virgil Wooten, whose body of work chronicles several decades of life in and around Lampasas County. (Photograph by Virgil Wooten.)

Four

Travelin' around the County

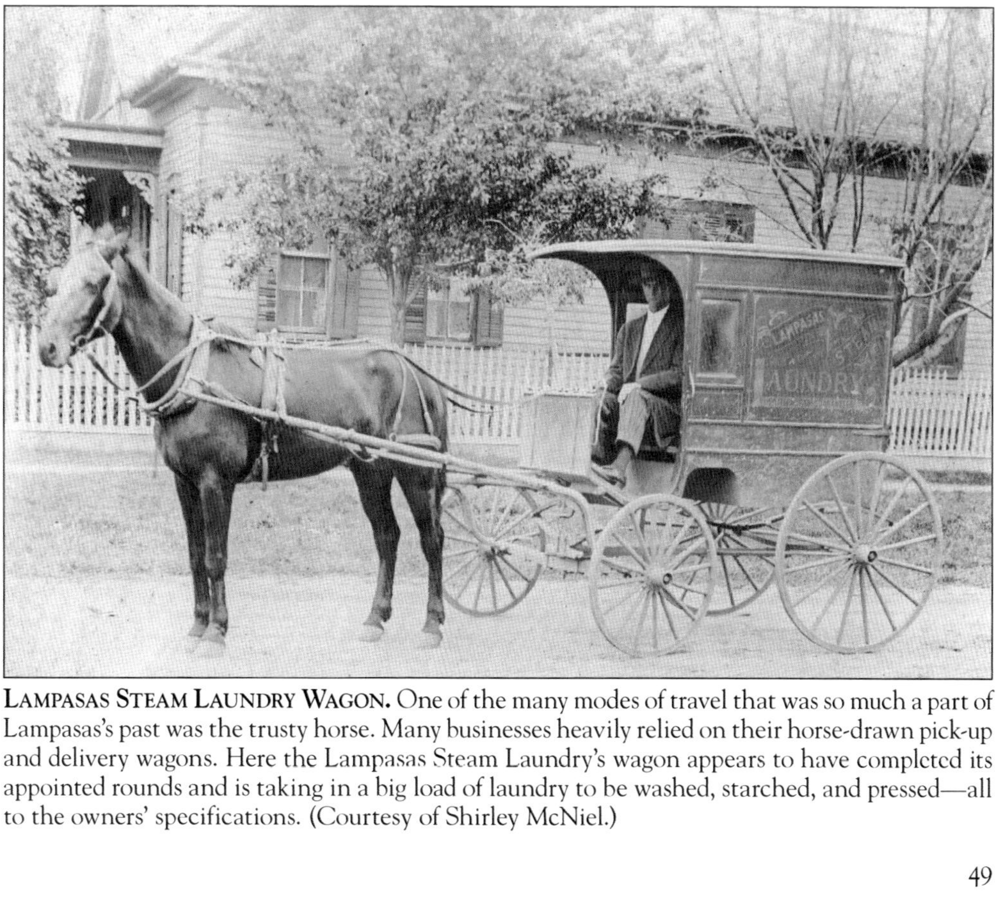

Lampasas Steam Laundry Wagon. One of the many modes of travel that was so much a part of Lampasas's past was the trusty horse. Many businesses heavily relied on their horse-drawn pick-up and delivery wagons. Here the Lampasas Steam Laundry's wagon appears to have completed its appointed rounds and is taking in a big load of laundry to be washed, starched, and pressed—all to the owners' specifications. (Courtesy of Shirley McNiel.)

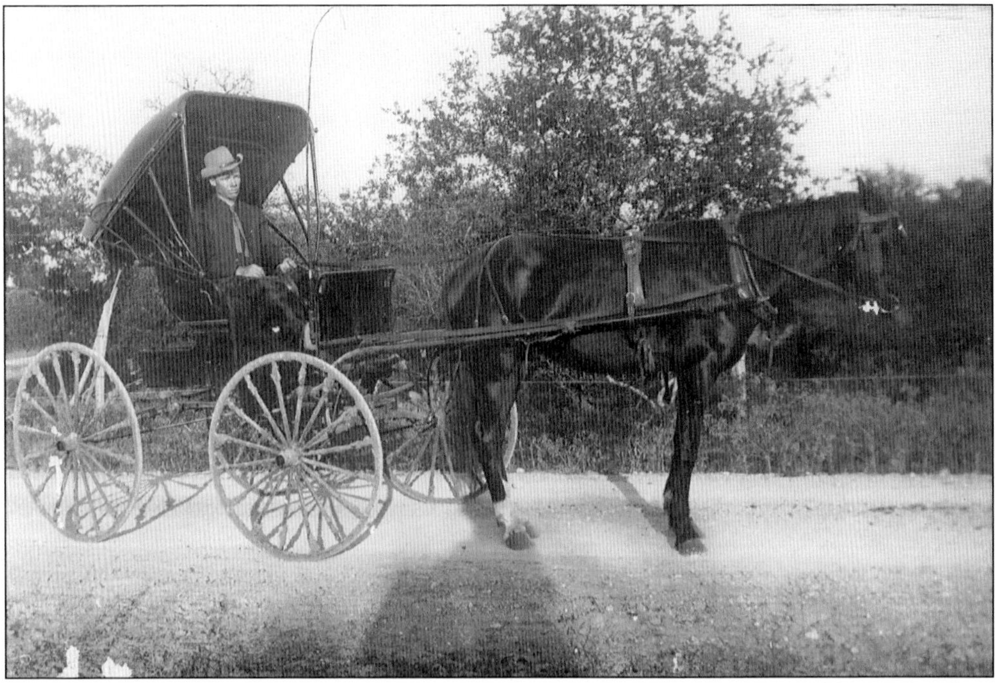

FRANKLIN RICHARDSON IN HIS ONE-HORSE BUGGY, 1910S. In 1913, Franklin Richardson (1888–1969) drove this buggy to a party where he met 15-year-old Lena Carter (1897–1983). They were married as they sat in this buggy later that year. (Courtesy of private collector.)

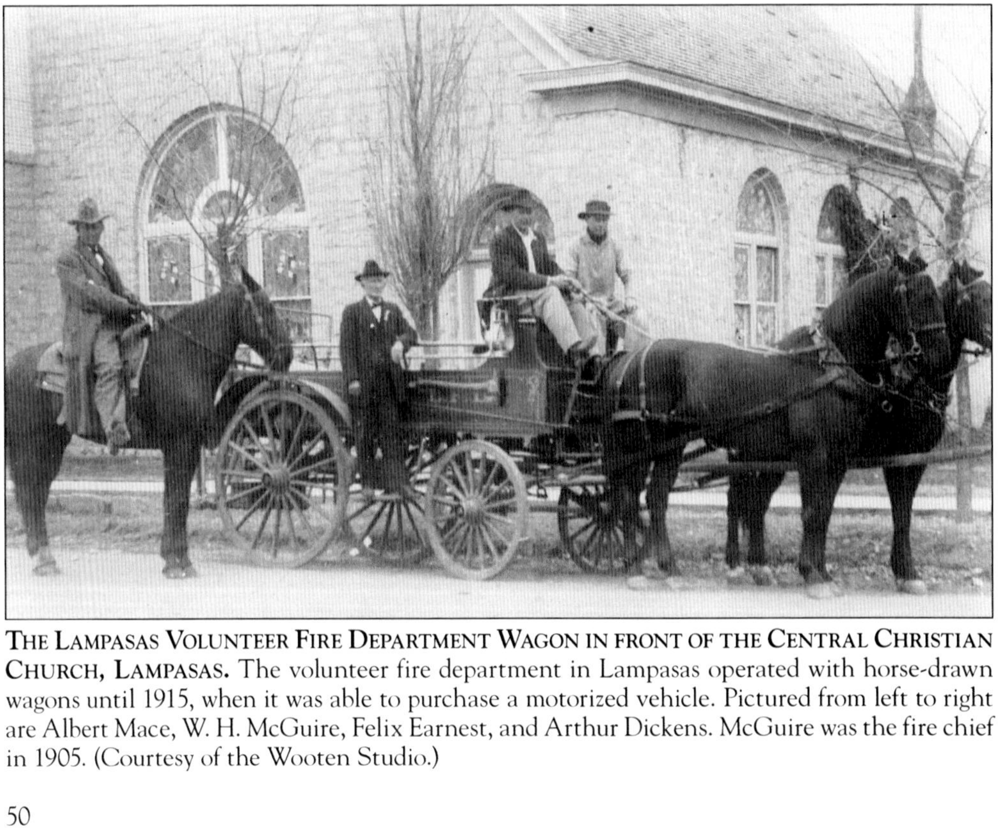

THE LAMPASAS VOLUNTEER FIRE DEPARTMENT WAGON IN FRONT OF THE CENTRAL CHRISTIAN CHURCH, LAMPASAS. The volunteer fire department in Lampasas operated with horse-drawn wagons until 1915, when it was able to purchase a motorized vehicle. Pictured from left to right are Albert Mace, W. H. McGuire, Felix Earnest, and Arthur Dickens. McGuire was the fire chief in 1905. (Courtesy of the Wooten Studio.)

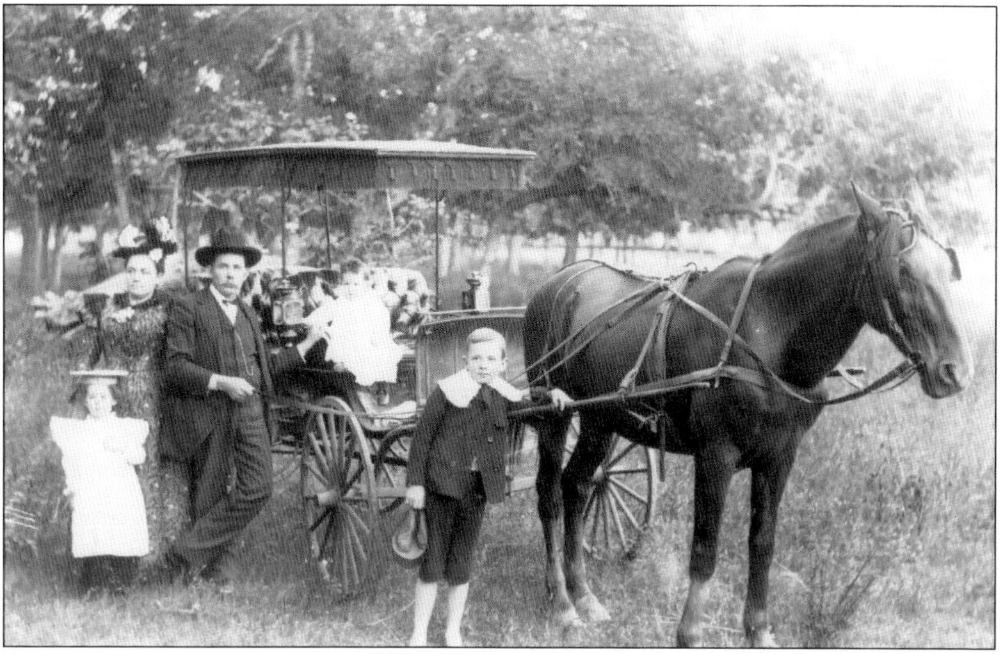

George W. and Annie Clements with Children Bernice, Annie Lois, and Elbert. G. W. Clements was influential in Lampasas as owner of a major wholesale and retail grocery and, later with his son, Elbert, in the land loan business. In 1925, it is said that he was the largest taxpayer in Lampasas. His prosperity is evident in the luxurious family carriage pictured here. Note its tasseled canopy and tufted leather seating.

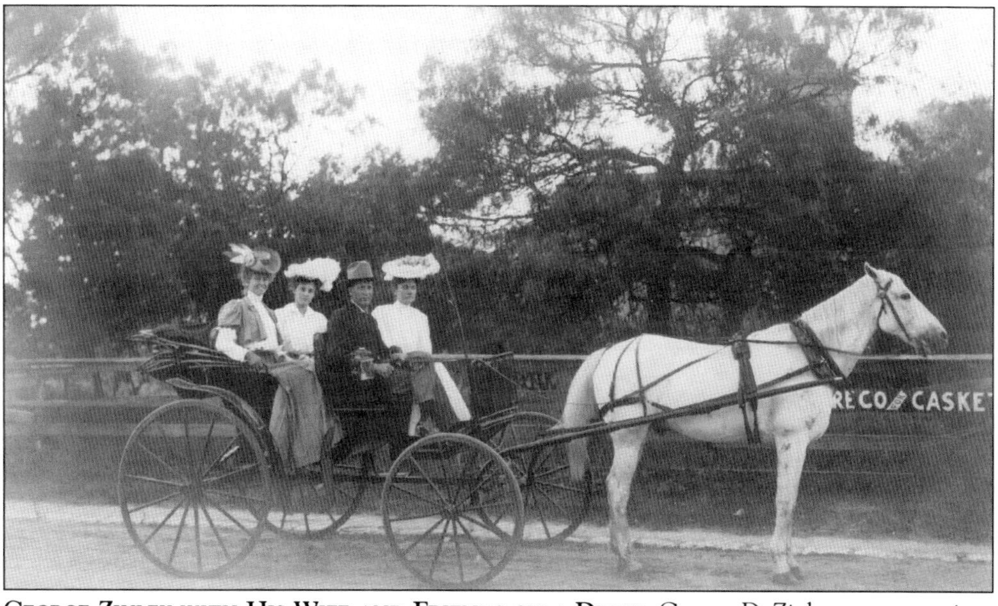

George Zivley with His Wife and Friends on a Drive. George D. Zivley was, at various times, city marshal of Lampasas, deputy sheriff of Lampasas County, and sheriff of Bell County. Here he takes his wife, Leta Witcher (to his left), and friends for a drive, a pleasant way to spend an afternoon.

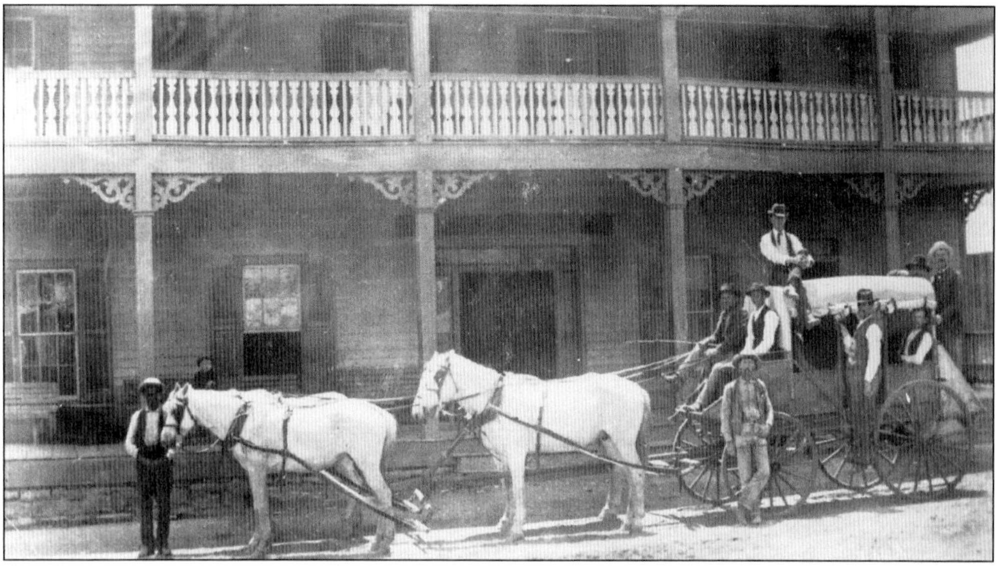

OLD STAGECOACH IN FRONT OF THE DOFFLEMYER BUILDING, C. 1890. The stagecoach picked up passengers and mail at the Dofflemyer Building in San Saba before traveling on to Lometa and Lampasas. Prior to the arrival of the railroad in Lampasas in 1882, the stagecoach prevented county citizens from becoming isolated from the outside world.

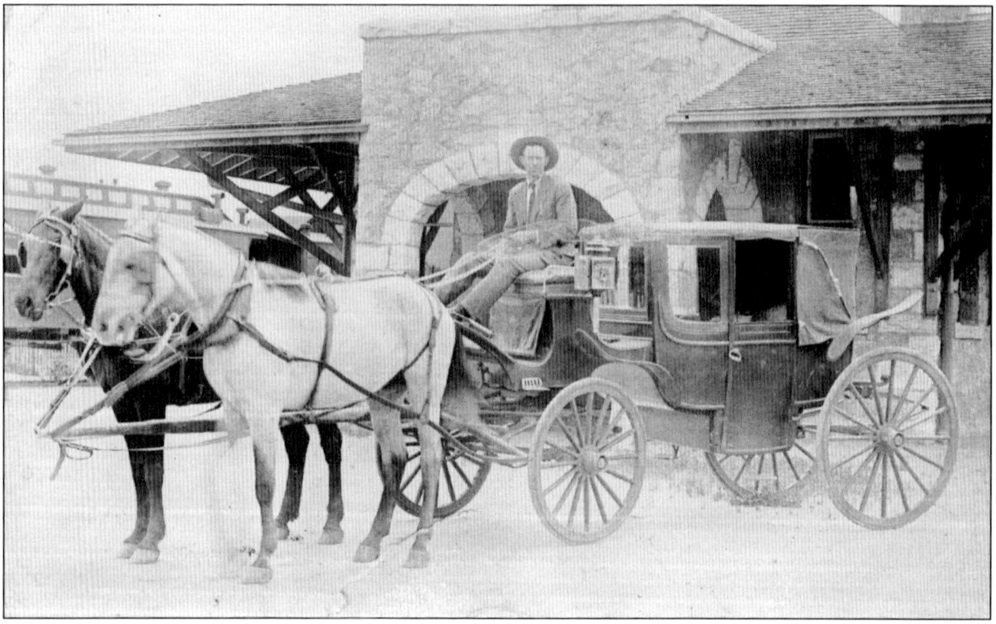

JOE B. MASSEY IN FRONT OF THE H&TC RAILROAD DEPOT, C. 1903. A horse and buggy, sometimes for hire, was a common means of traveling to and from the railroad station. Here Joe Massey sits with his reins in hand. The Houston and Texas Central (H&TC) depot was located on the southeast corner of the courthouse square.

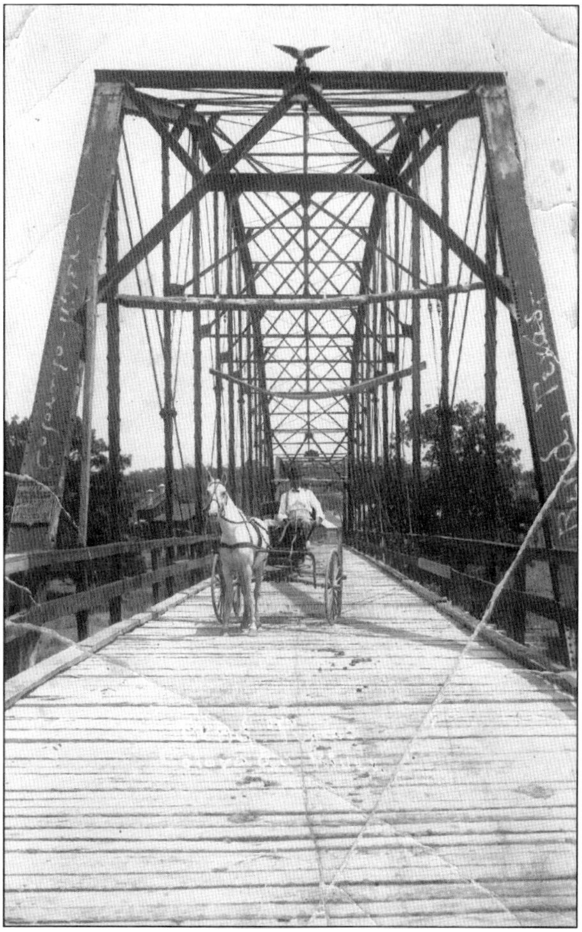

Bridge at Bend, over the Colorado River. This bridge crossed the Colorado River at Bend. It had large metal eagles at either end, honoring the spot's original name, Eagle Ford Crossing. (Courtesy of Merritt Romans.)

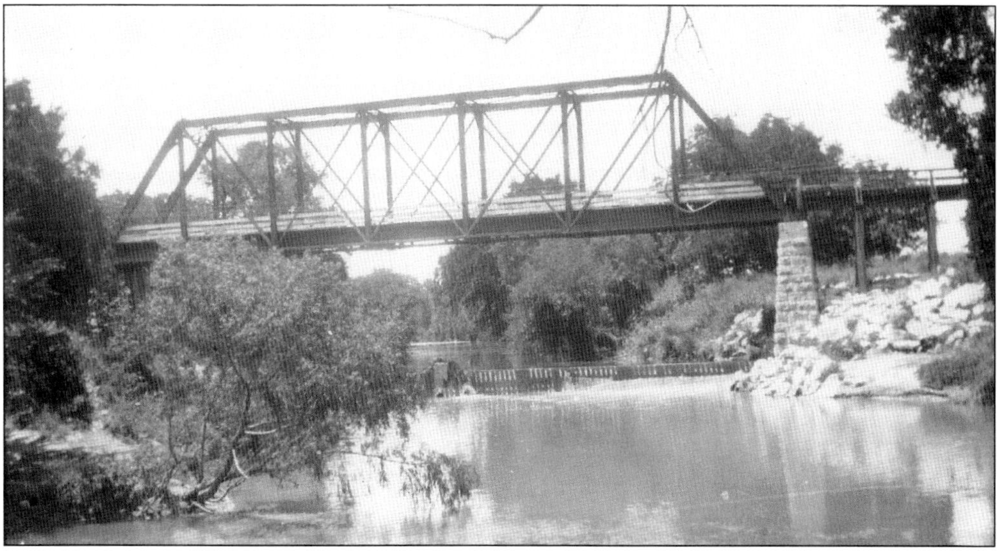

Bridge over the Lampasas River at Kempner. The railroad crossed the Lampasas River at Kempner over this iron bridge.

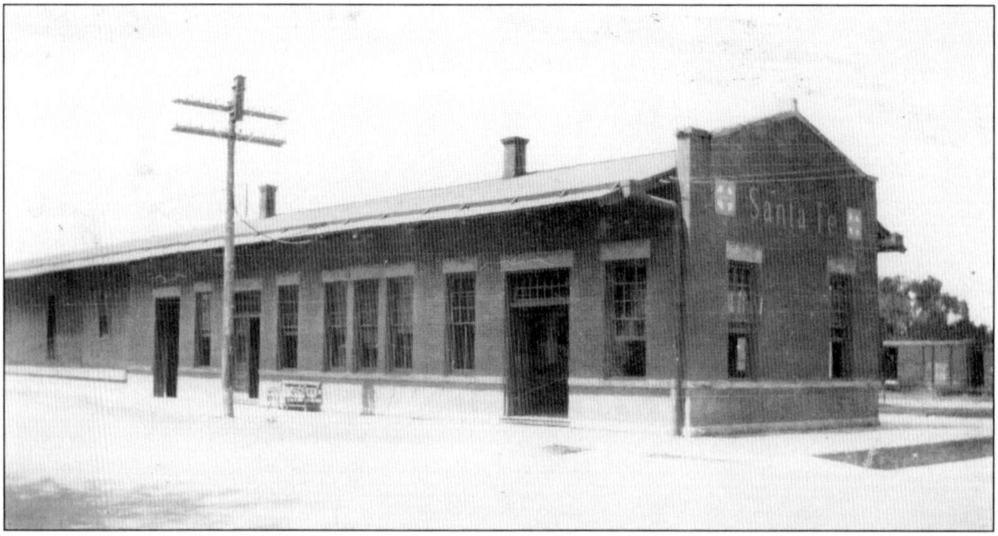

Santa Fe Depot, Lampasas. With the arrival of the railroad in Lampasas in May 1882, the city experienced a boom unlike any before or since. It was the western terminus of the Gulf, Colorado, and Santa Fe Railway for three years. This depot, located at Second and Live Oak Streets, was built in 1904.

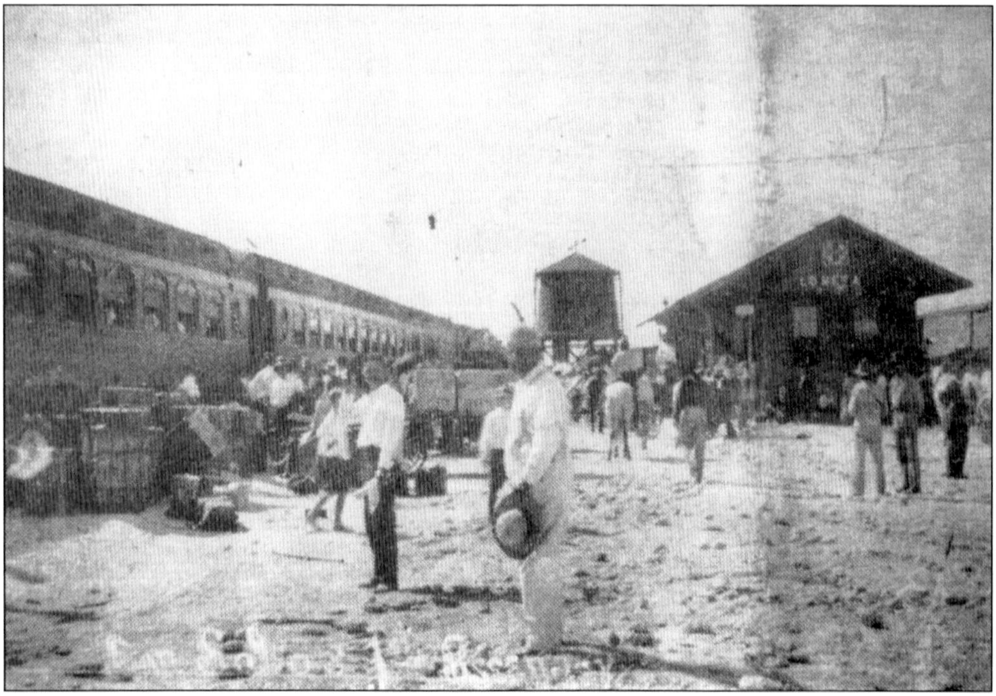

First Passenger Train from Lometa to San Saba, Texas, 1911. The Gulf, Colorado, and Santa Fe Railway completed tracks as far as San Saba in 1911. In this image, passengers board the train at the Lometa depot, while their baggage sits on the ground beside the train. (Courtesy of Ruth Gadbury and Joyce Hightower.)

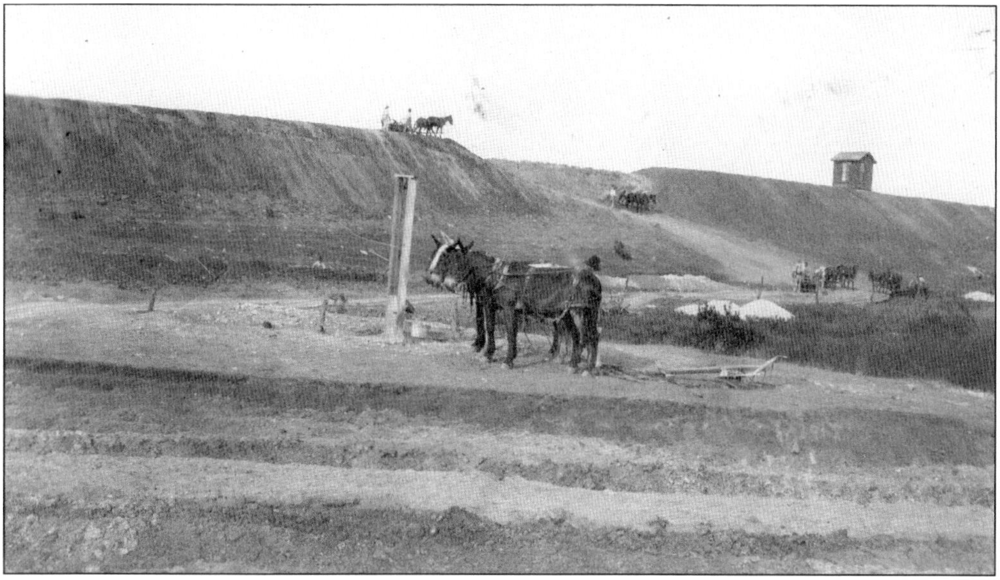

CONSTRUCTION OF THE SANTA FE RAILROAD LAKE AT LOMETA, C. 1902. Thomas Edward Romans and his team help others create a lake northwest of Lometa to provide water for the steam engines of the new trains. The reservoir covered approximately 25 acres. (Courtesy of Merritt Romans.)

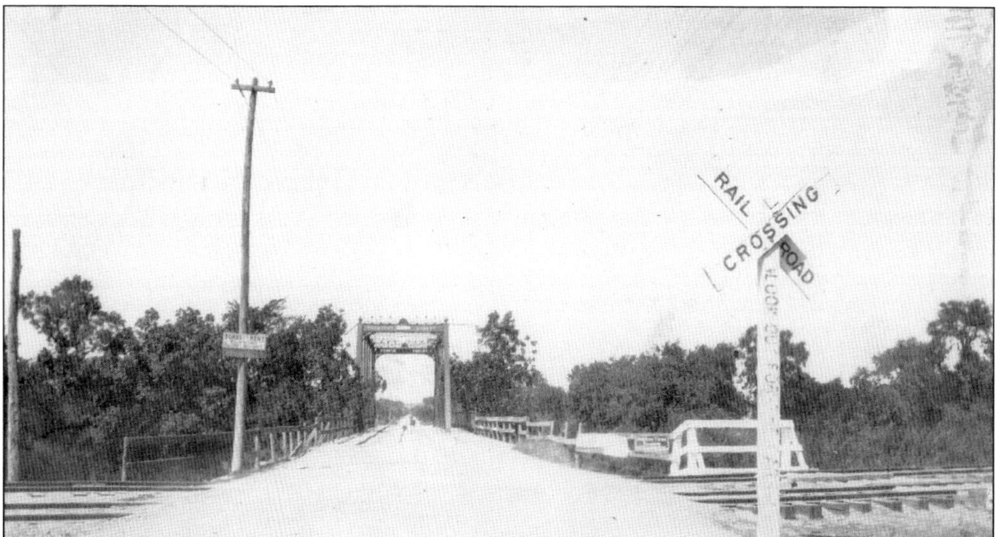

CHESTNUT STREET BRIDGE, LAMPASAS. This bridge was one of the few iron bridges in Lampasas. Note the railroad crossing sign warning drivers to "Look Out For Cars" and the advertisement at the left on the telephone pole, "Fords for Rent."

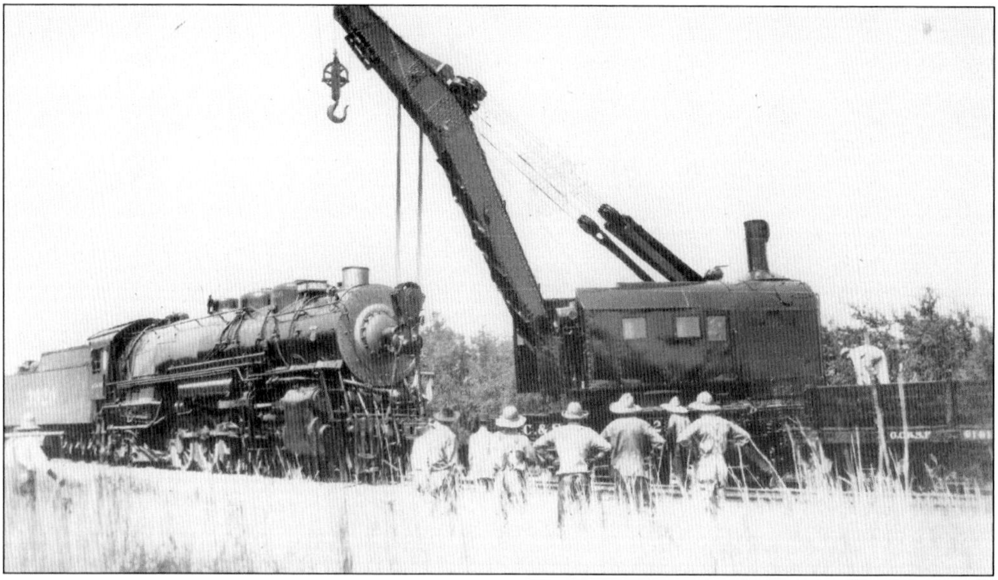

Santa Fe Wreck, c. 1927. Cowboys watch as a railroad crane is used to set the locomotive back on the tracks following an apparent derailment. The crane was mounted on a railcar and hauled to the scene for accident recovery. Several photographic records exist of accidents involving the Santa Fe Railway, but this mishap involving train No. 3920 was photographed in stunning detail by an amateur for a personal album.

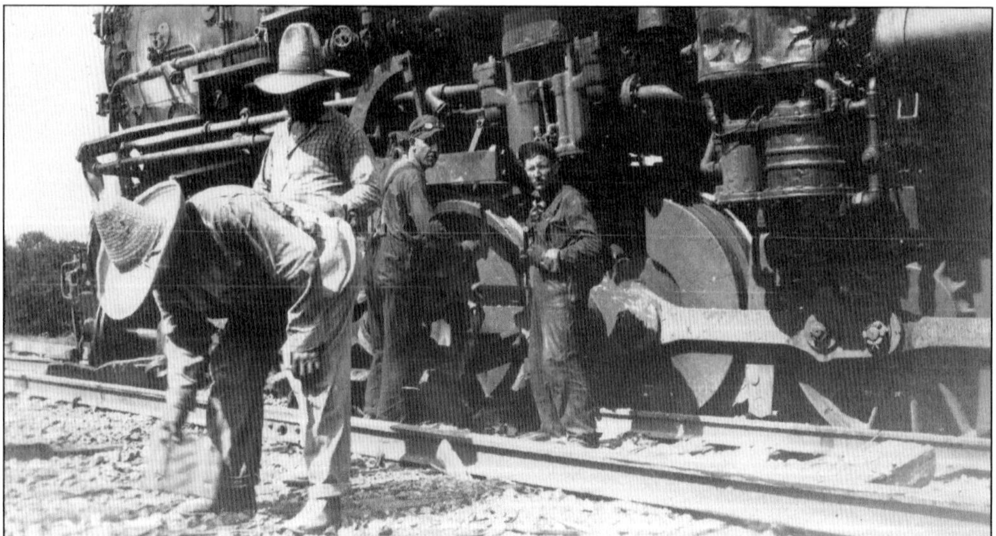

Santa Fe Wreck, c. 1927. Train wrecks doubtless could be heard from quite a distance and would attract a crowd in all but the most desolate country. Crewmen watch a spectator who has evidently spied something of interest on the ground near the rails.

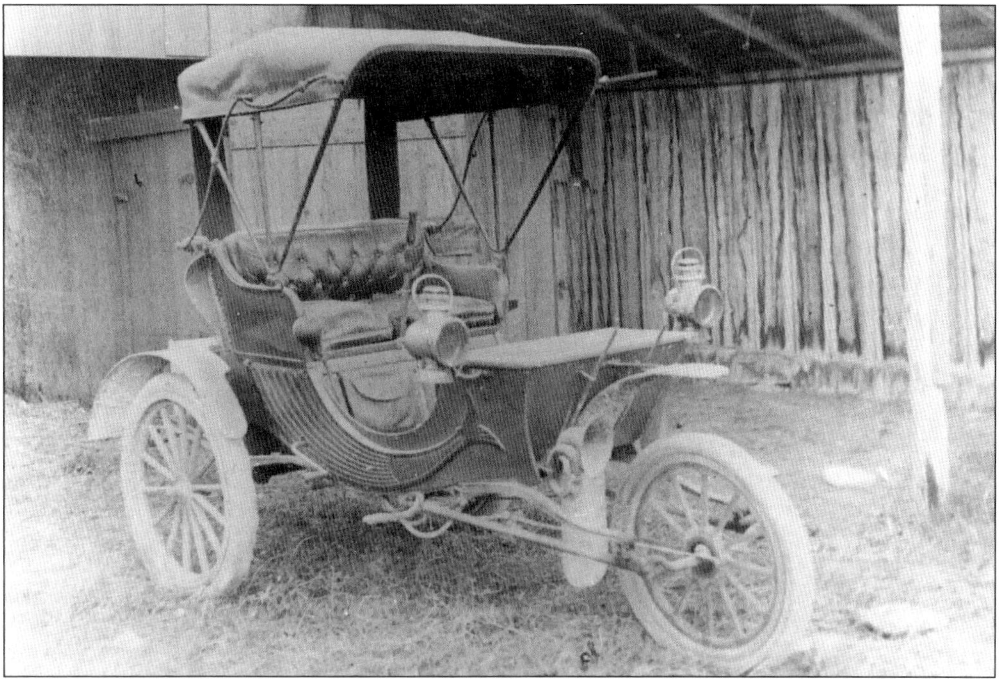

THE FIRST CAR IN LAMPASAS, C. 1906. Thomas Huling (1877–1947) owned the first car in Lampasas. It was a three-wheeled touring car manufactured by American Charles Duryea (1861–1938). A three-cylinder automobile made between 1898 and 1907, it was a novelty in Lampasas.

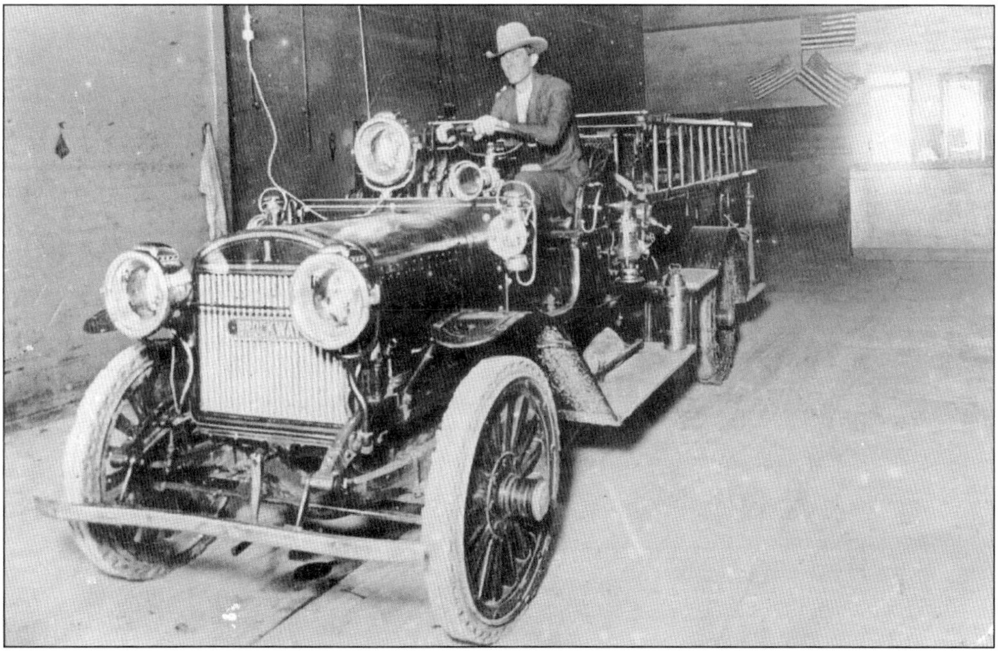

WILL STANDARD IN THE FIRST MOTORIZED FIRE VEHICLE IN LAMPASAS. In 1915, the Lampasas Volunteer Fire Department purchased this Brockway fire engine, with an ALF brand hose and chemical equipment, and a 100-gallon soda-acid tank. Will Standard was head of the fire department from 1918 until his death in 1943. (Photograph by Lucile Standard.)

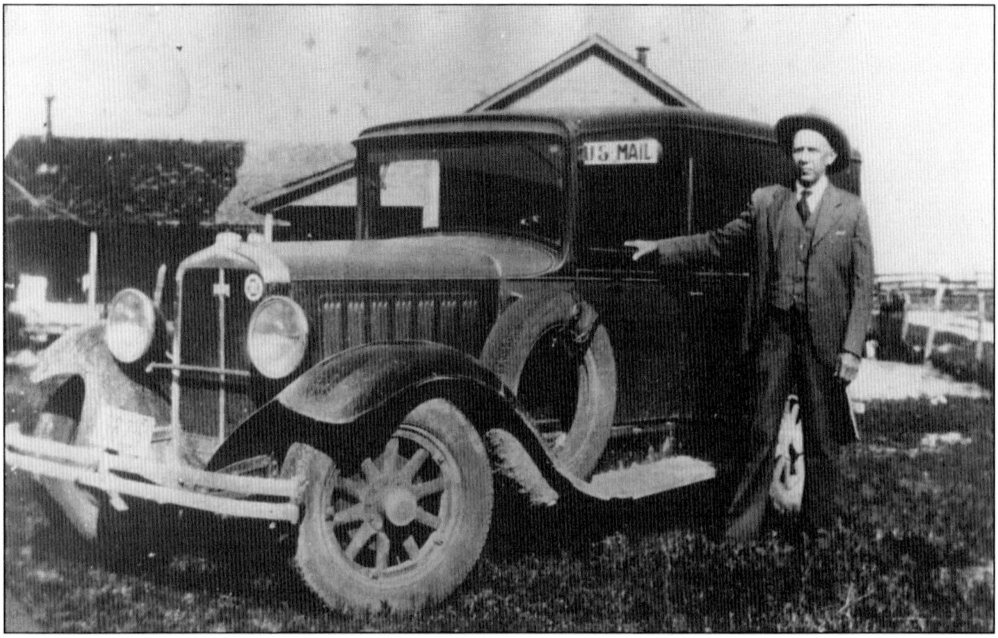

U.S. Mail Truck, 1920s. William Chambers drove this 1927 Dodge on the mail route to Izoro and Rumley in Lampasas County. Izoro and Rumley were small settlements in the northeast part of the county.

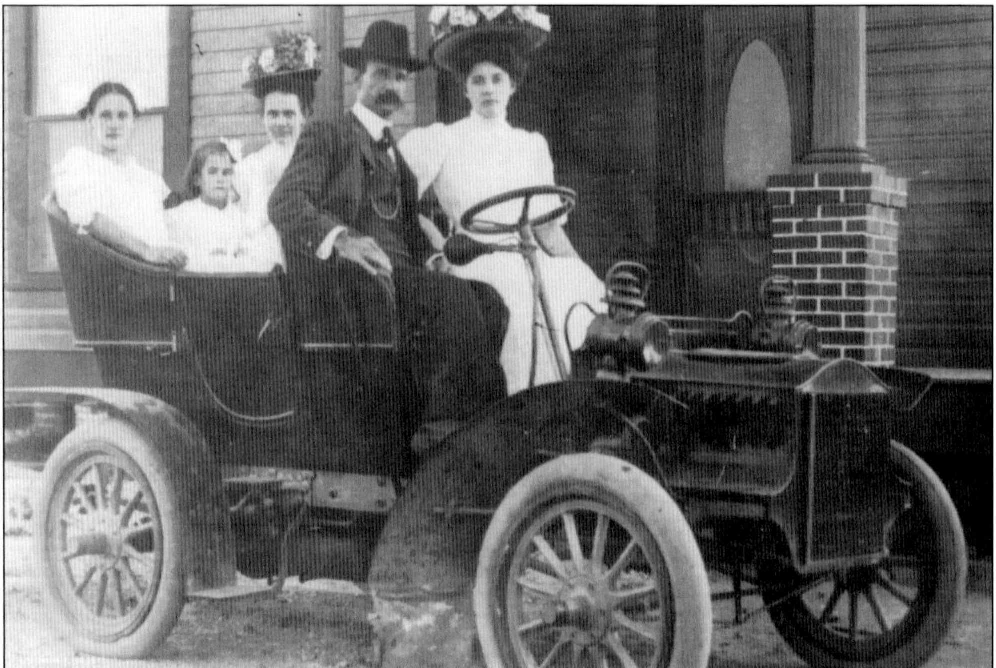

In front of the Haby House at 108 North Chestnut, Lampasas. A well-to-do family in Lampasas, the Haby family traveled in style. Pictured here in the front seat is Emil Haby, who came to Lampasas in the early 1900s to start the town's first electric company. Note the wooden spokes on the wheels of the car. (Courtesy of Ellen McFarland.)

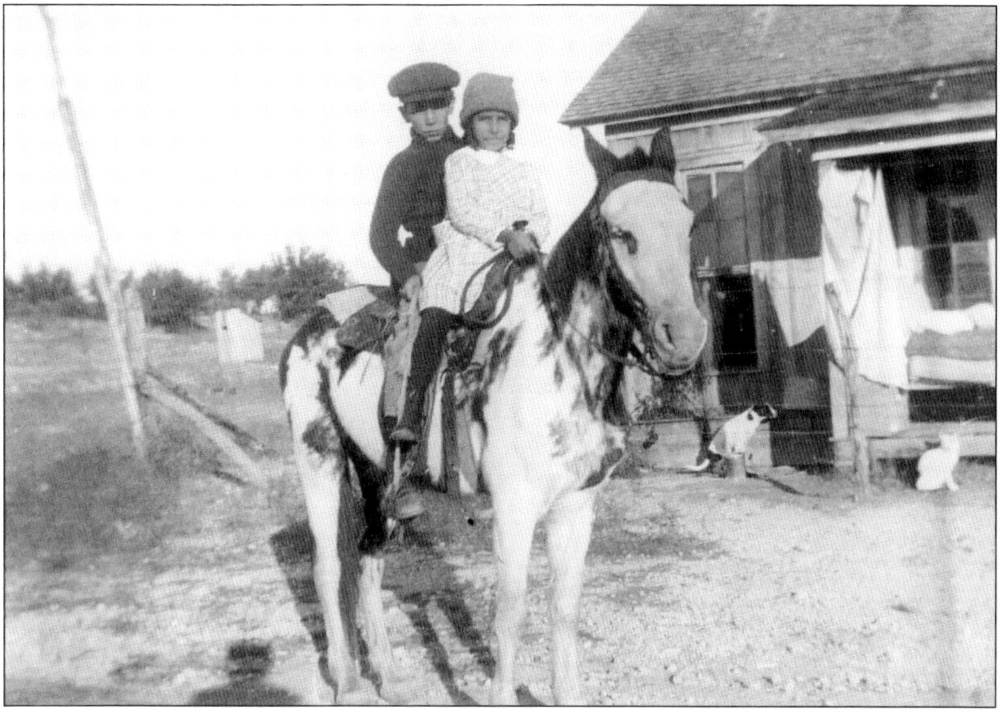

GOING TO CLAY ROCK SCHOOL. Carl Lang and Pauline Lang traveled to school on their horse, Paint. Many schoolchildren traveled this way to school in rural Lampasas. Clay Rock School was built in 1917 and was located between the city of Lampasas and Rumley off present-day Texas Farm to Market 580 East. (Courtesy of Kay Pearce Bailey.)

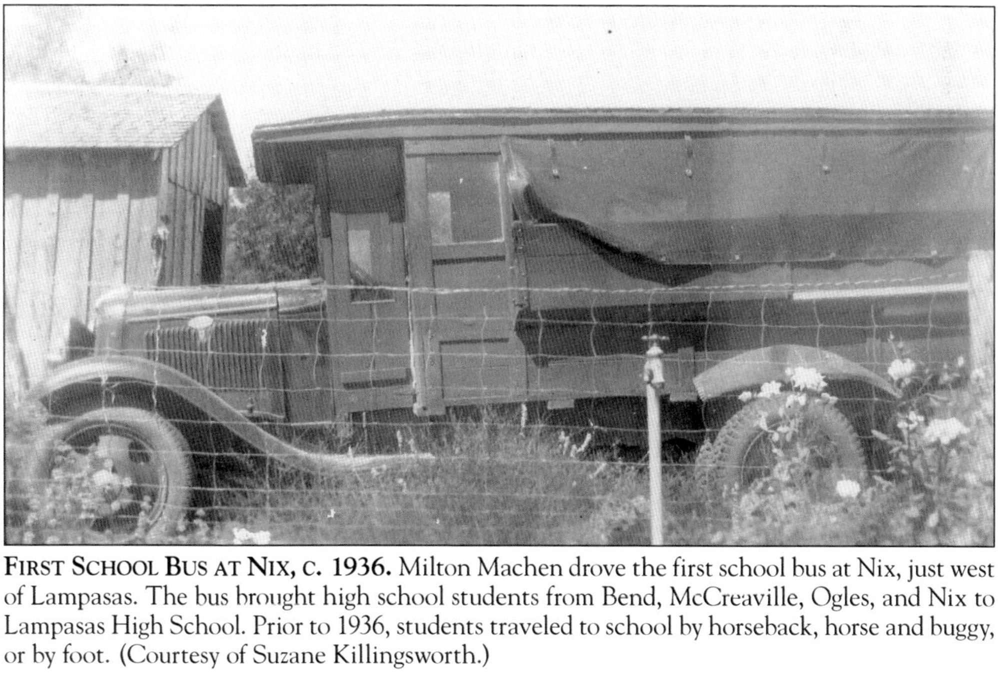

FIRST SCHOOL BUS AT NIX, C. 1936. Milton Machen drove the first school bus at Nix, just west of Lampasas. The bus brought high school students from Bend, McCreaville, Ogles, and Nix to Lampasas High School. Prior to 1936, students traveled to school by horseback, horse and buggy, or by foot. (Courtesy of Suzane Killingsworth.)

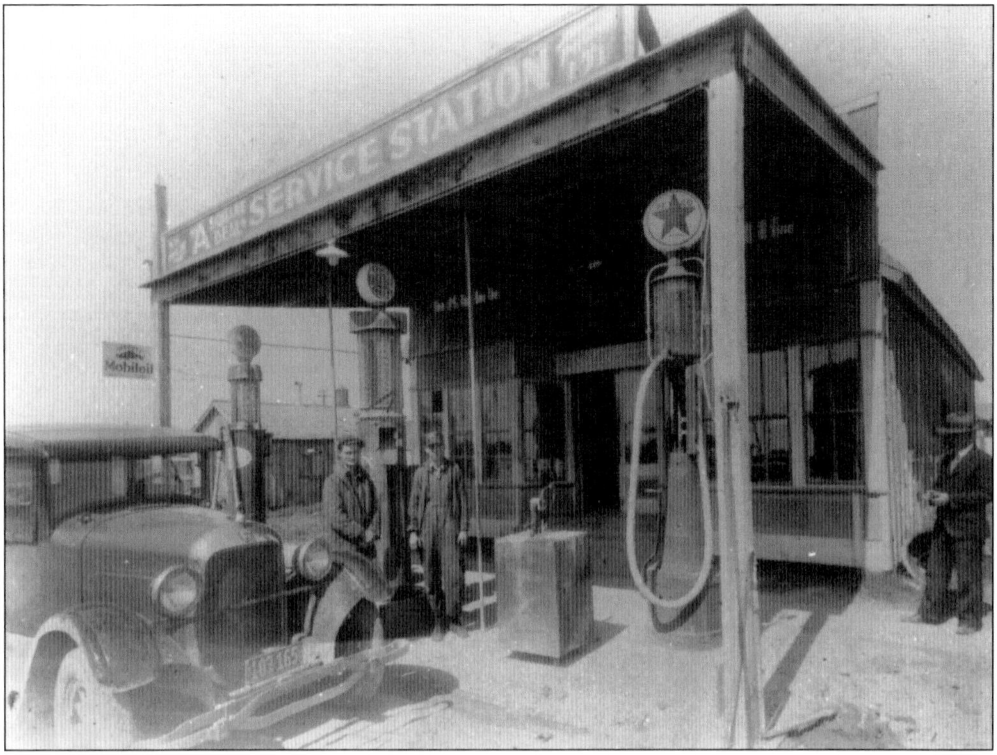

"A SQUARE DEAL" SERVICE STATION, C. 1929. This service station offered at least three brands of gasoline for sale: Mobil, Gulf, and Texaco. Note the oil pump at the center of the photograph. Pulled up for service is a 1929 Essex automobile.

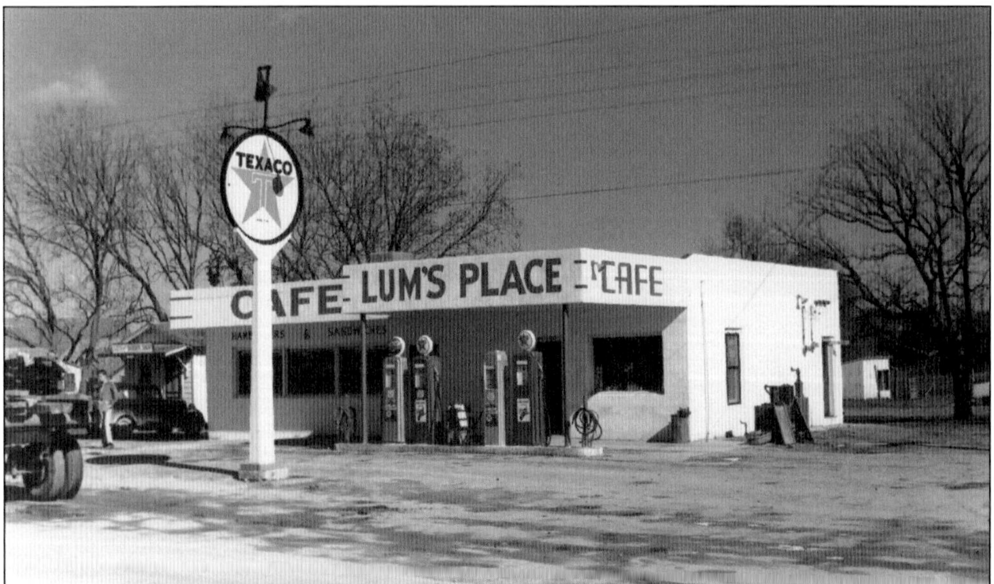

LUM'S PLACE, 1950S. Located on the north end of Key Avenue, Lum's was a gathering place for Lampasas teenagers in the 1950s. Hamburgers and Cokes were regular fare. Lum Scott owned the establishment. (Photograph by Virgil Wooten.)

Five

Silk Stocking Row and Beyond

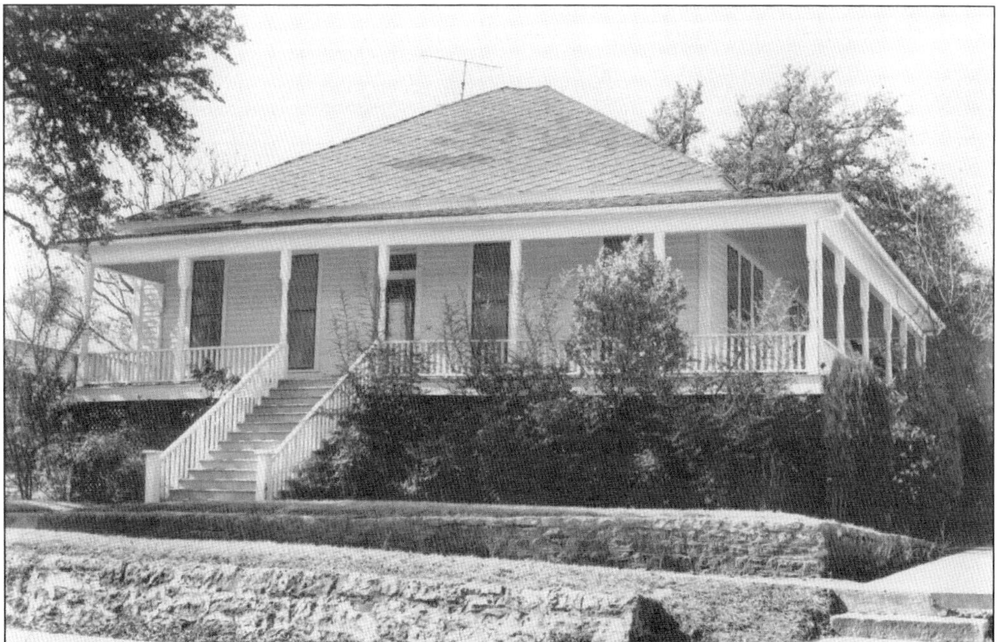

C. C. Abney Home. In 1883, banker P. M. Hargrave built this house in the Louisiana-raised-cottage style, unique in Lampasas. It was among the earliest houses built along West Third Street. Due to the many fine homes built there by prosperous businessmen, the street became known as "Silk Stocking Row." Banker Carleton C. Abney and his wife, Florence, resided there for 50 years. (Courtesy of Sue Zane M. Faulkner.)

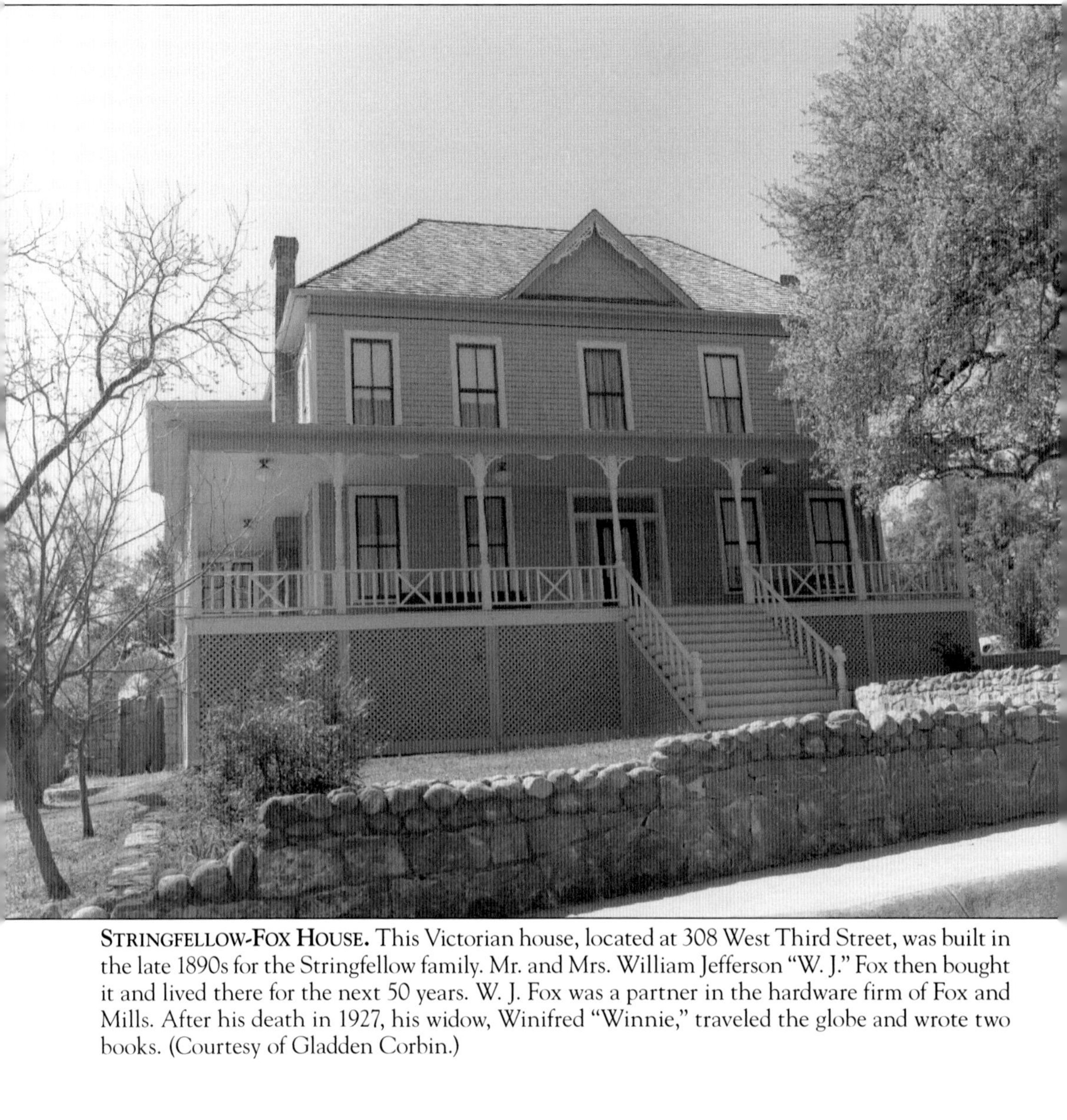

STRINGFELLOW-FOX HOUSE. This Victorian house, located at 308 West Third Street, was built in the late 1890s for the Stringfellow family. Mr. and Mrs. William Jefferson "W. J." Fox then bought it and lived there for the next 50 years. W. J. Fox was a partner in the hardware firm of Fox and Mills. After his death in 1927, his widow, Winifred "Winnie," traveled the globe and wrote two books. (Courtesy of Gladden Corbin.)

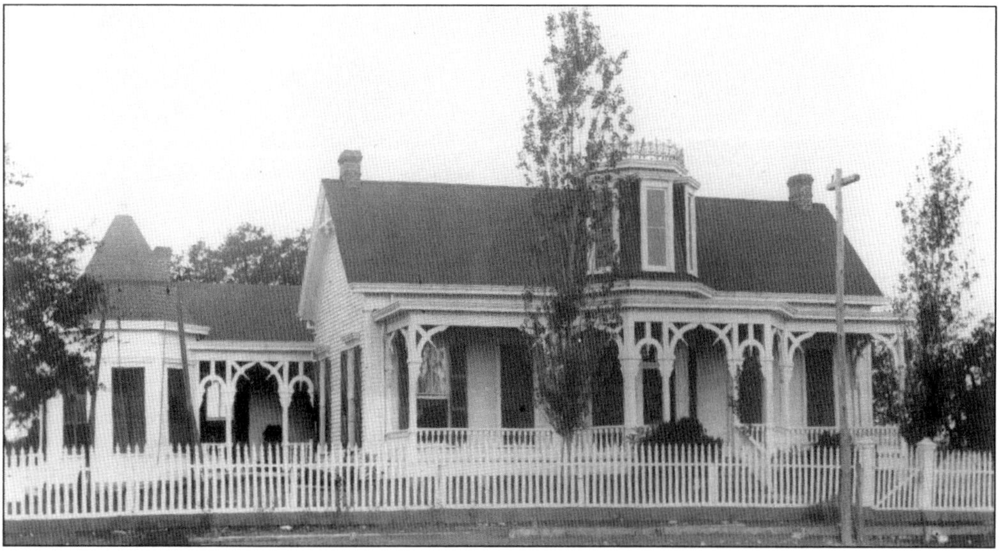

J. R. KEY HOME. Shown here is J. R. Key's ornate Victorian home as it originally was built in the 1880s at 402 South Ridge Street. Five generations of the family have lived there. For Key's many civic contributions, the town's main thoroughfare, Grand Avenue, was changed to Key Avenue in 1937. (Courtesy of Cornelia and Newton Key.)

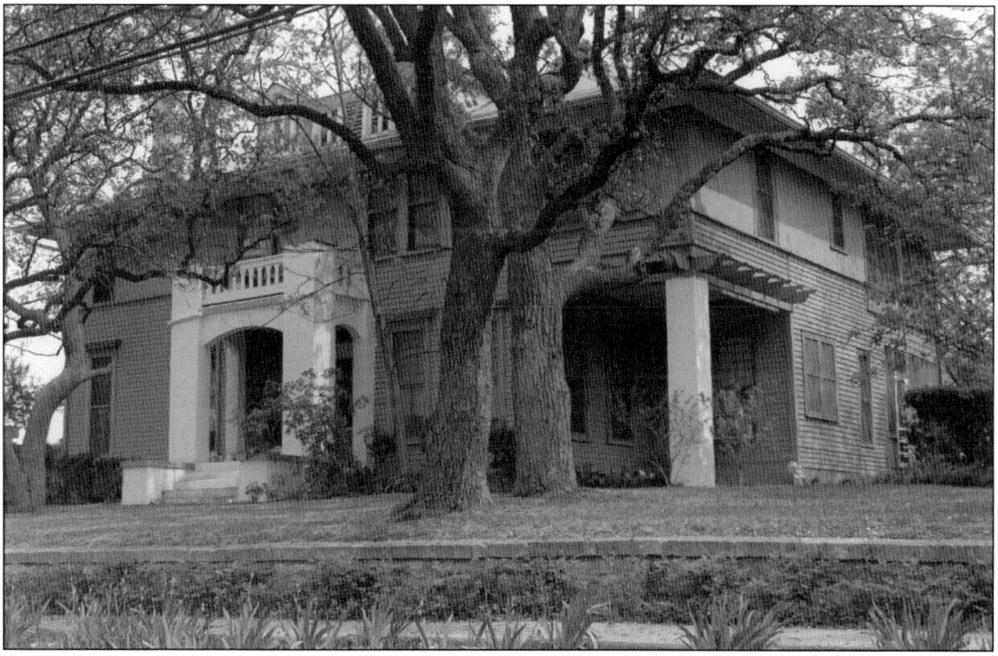

J. R. KEY HOUSE TRANSFORMED. Around 1910, the Keys remodeled their house, adding a second story and updating its style. The hexagonal structure, visible in the photograph above, was made a free-standing building and used variously as servants' quarters and for storage. It can still be seen today near the home's southwest corner. (Courtesy of Gladden Corbin.)

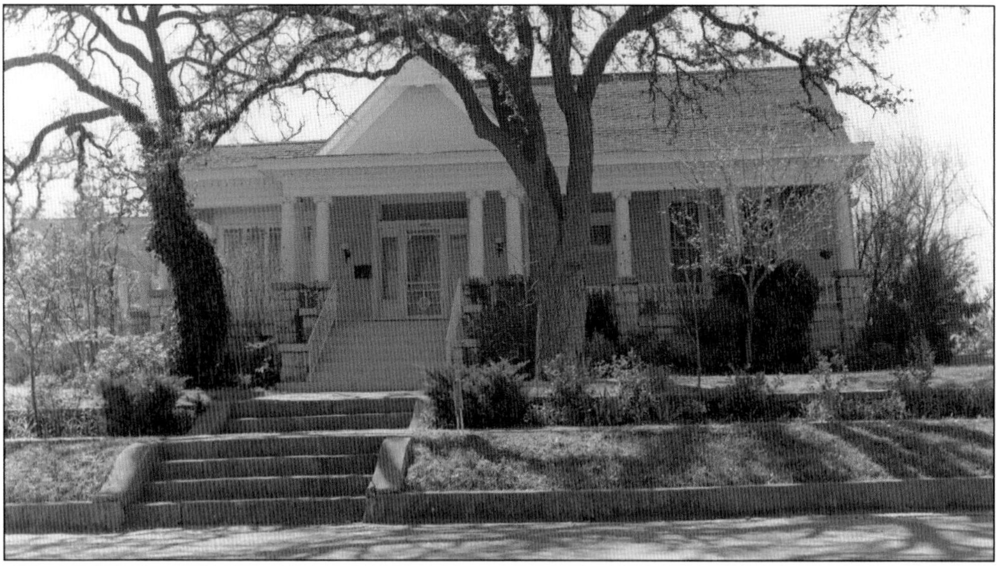

HIGDON HOUSE. This 1886 home, located at 408 West Third Street, was built by E. M. Longcope, a prominent banker. About 1902, A. L. and Adelaide Higdon bought the house. Higdon was a prosperous merchant and a partner in one of Lampasas's largest mercantile houses. Although Higdon died in 1943, his wife continued to live in the house until her death in 1956. (Courtesy of Gladden Corbin.)

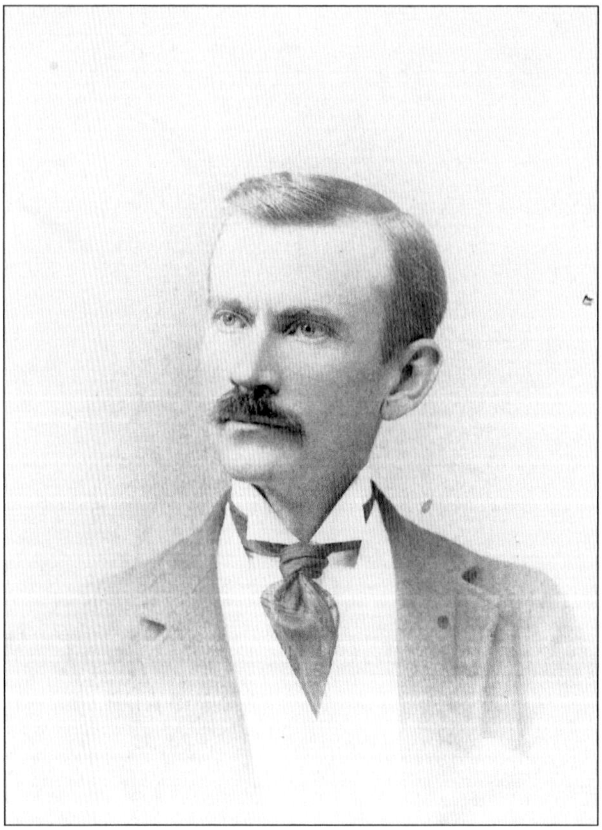

FRANK MALONE. Among the original officers of the First National Bank of Lampasas were F. R. "Frank" Malone (pictured here) and E. M. Longcope. Not only were they professional colleagues, they were also neighbors on Silk Stocking Row, just south of the intersection of Third and Park Streets. Besides serving as officers of the town's first incorporated bank, Malone and Longcope were instrumental in founding the Texas Bankers Association in 1886.

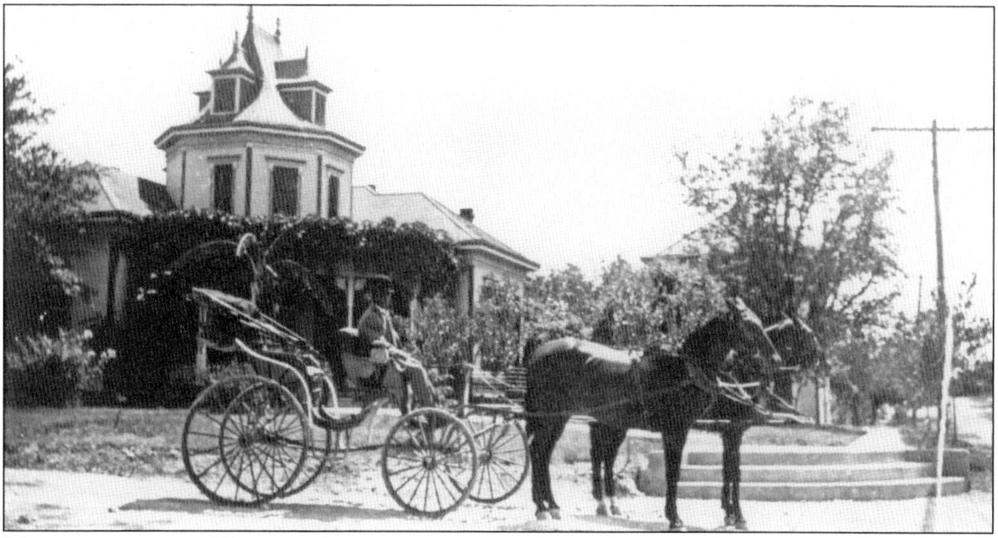

MALONE-MANUEL HOUSE. This Victorian-era Queen Ann–style house, located at 502 West Third Street, was built in 1883 for banker Frank Malone and his family. In 1891, the property sold to John N. and Harriet Manuel, owners of a hardware company. The home remained in the Manuel family until 1972. Restoration of the house, carriage house, and garage (which had once been stables) began in 1984. (Courtesy of Jim Anderson.)

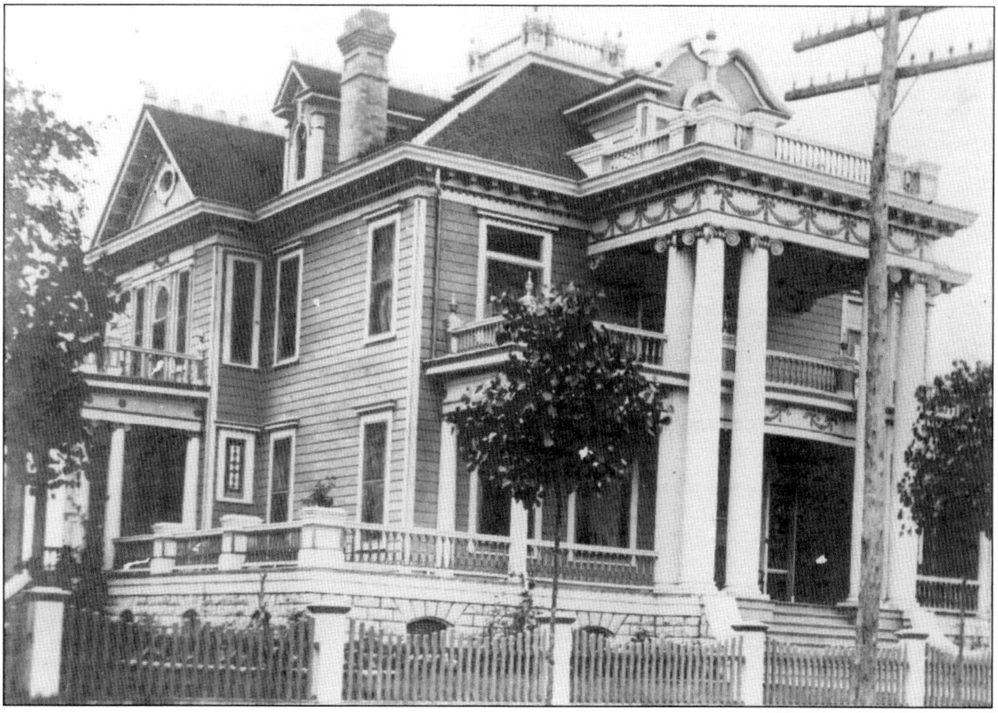

OLD BARNES HOME. This grand Victorian home that once stood at 602 West Third Street belonged to W. F. Barnes, who in 1912 partnered with his son J. F. in the lumberyard business. After the old home was destroyed by fire in 1919, a smaller, one-story Spanish-style house was built in its place about 1920. This later house was the home of Alice Barnes, W. F.'s widow, until she died in 1958.

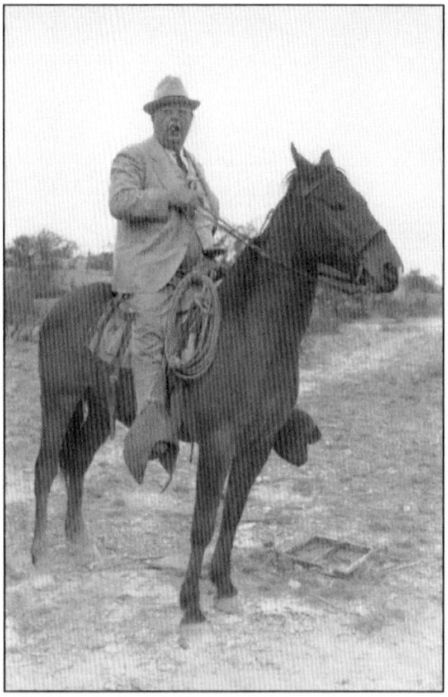

C. D. STOKES ON HORSEBACK, 1920S. Charles Diskin "C. D." Stokes and his older brother, M. Y., came to Lampasas in 1880. In time, they built a financial empire that started with a produce operation and eventually included wholesale and retail grocery businesses, a bank, and a department store. Their wool-buying enterprise put Lampasas on the map.

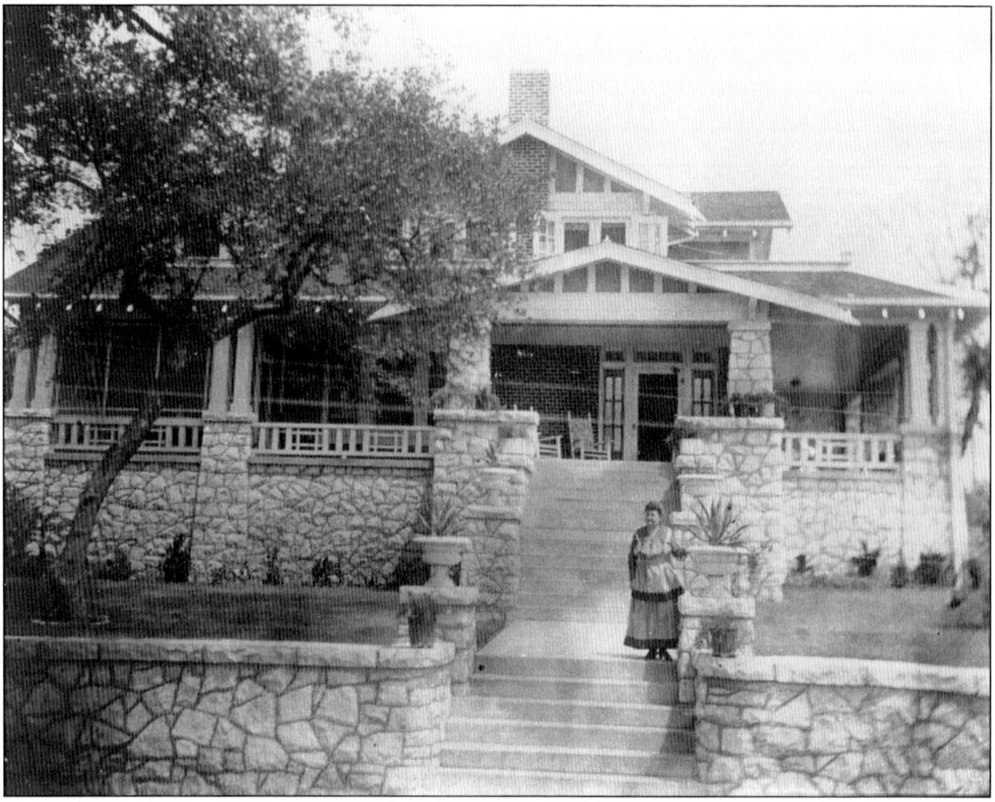

C. D. STOKES HOUSE. It is said that C. D. Stokes built this World War I–era house at the south end of Park Street as an anniversary present for his wife, Kate, pictured here. About 1922, the couple bought lots just south of their house for a private park and zoo. Some say the zoo contained mainly deer and peacocks, but others insist there were monkeys and at least one bear.

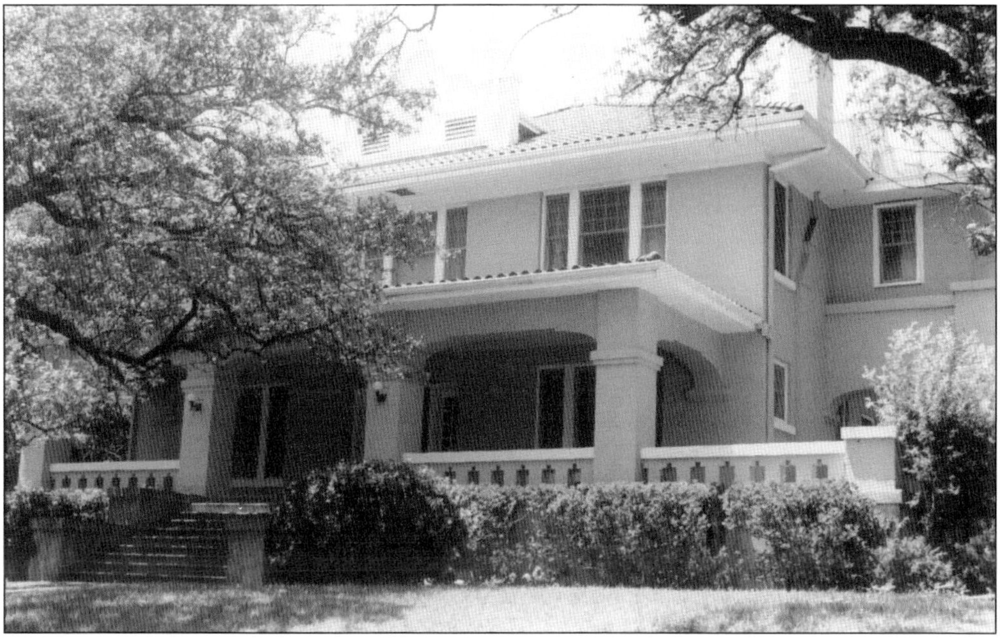

M. Y. STOKES HOUSE. After demolishing an older, three-story home at 401 West Fourth Street, Melmoth Young "M. Y." Stokes built this hilltop home during 1917 and 1918. It features a red, Spanish-clay, tile roof; 12-inch-thick masonry walls; beveled-glass windows; white oak floors; hardwood paneling and molding; and plaster moldings in the living room. (Courtesy of the *Lampasas Dispatch Record.*)

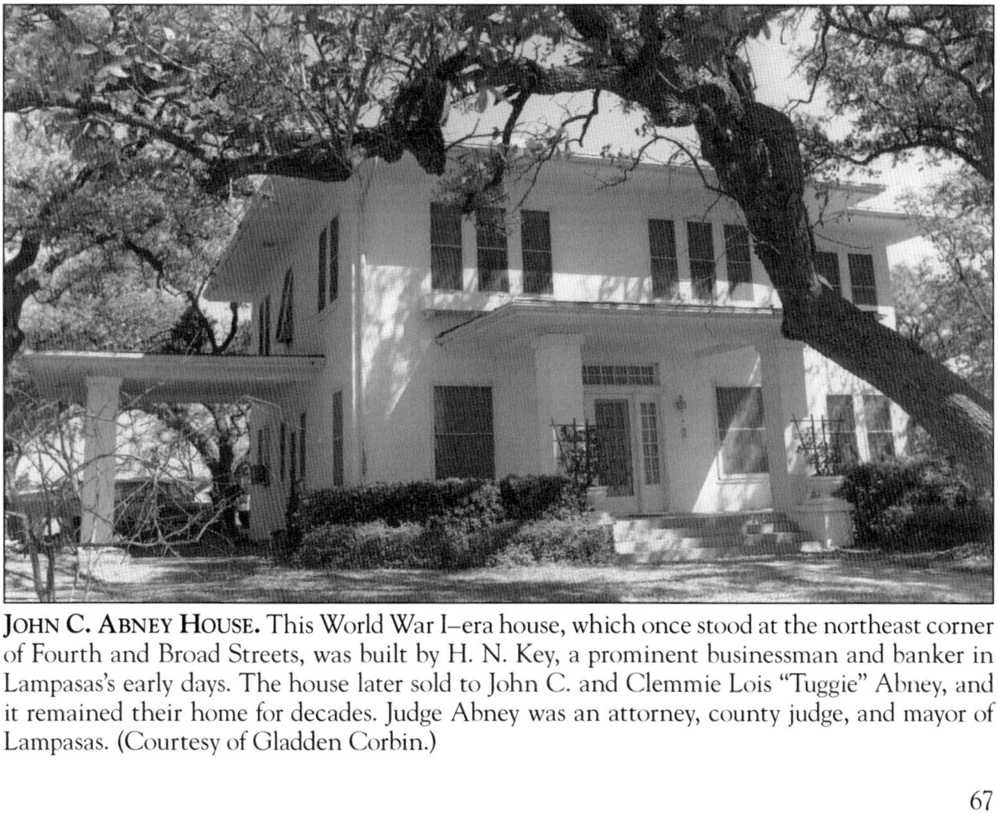

JOHN C. ABNEY HOUSE. This World War I–era house, which once stood at the northeast corner of Fourth and Broad Streets, was built by H. N. Key, a prominent businessman and banker in Lampasas's early days. The house later sold to John C. and Clemmie Lois "Tuggie" Abney, and it remained their home for decades. Judge Abney was an attorney, county judge, and mayor of Lampasas. (Courtesy of Gladden Corbin.)

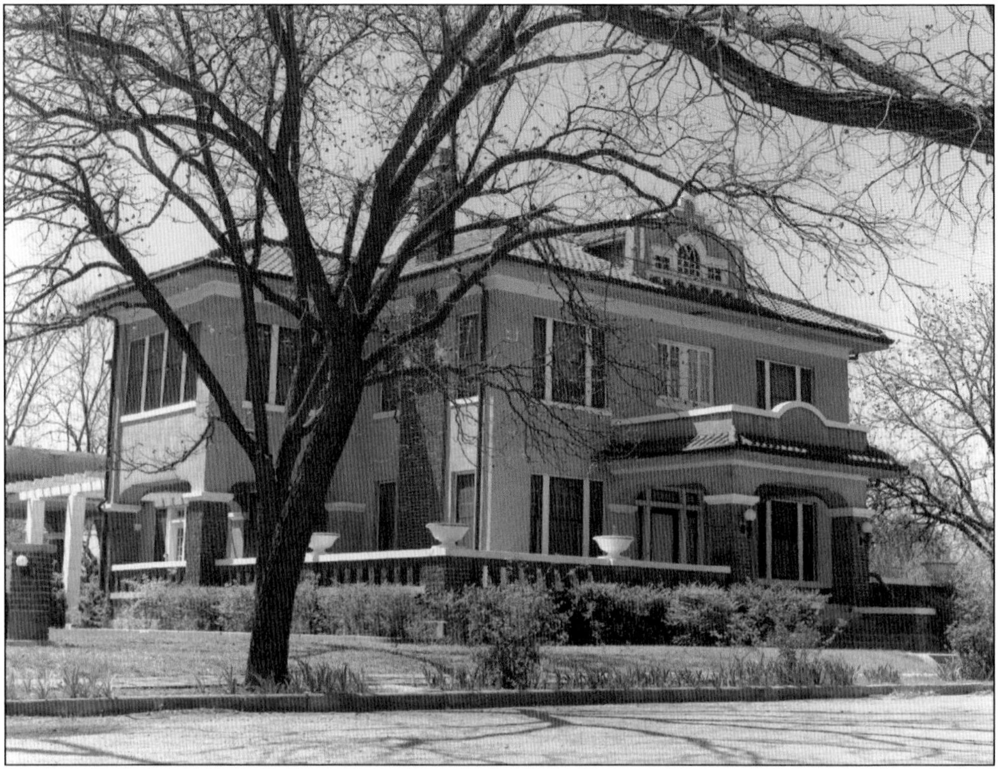

CAUTHEN HOUSE. Mrs. Jefferson H. (Cora Eha) Cauthen never got to live in her dream house. During the construction of the palatial house, she died. Her husband and children moved in during the spring of 1917. Jefferson Cauthen was a wool and mohair buyer. The house still stands at the northwest corner of Walnut and Second Streets. (Courtesy of Gladden Corbin.)

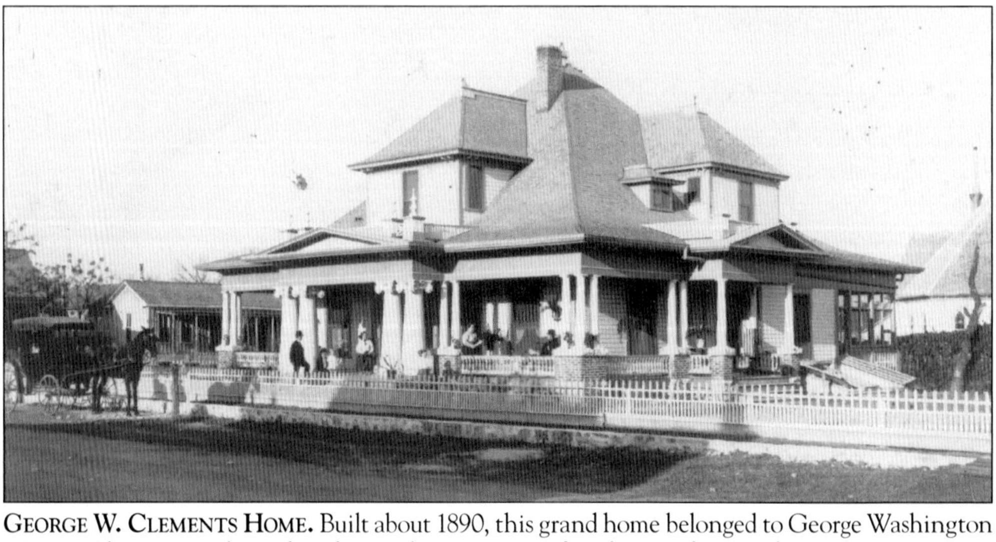

GEORGE W. CLEMENTS HOME. Built about 1890, this grand home belonged to George Washington "G. W." Clements and stood at the southeast corner of Walnut and Second Streets. G. W.'s son, Elbert, lived at the opposite end of the block, at Walnut and Third Streets. Both were successful businessmen, having invested in many different ventures, including G. W. Clements and Son grocery on the courthouse square. (Courtesy of Ann Richey Oliver and Robert Oliver.)

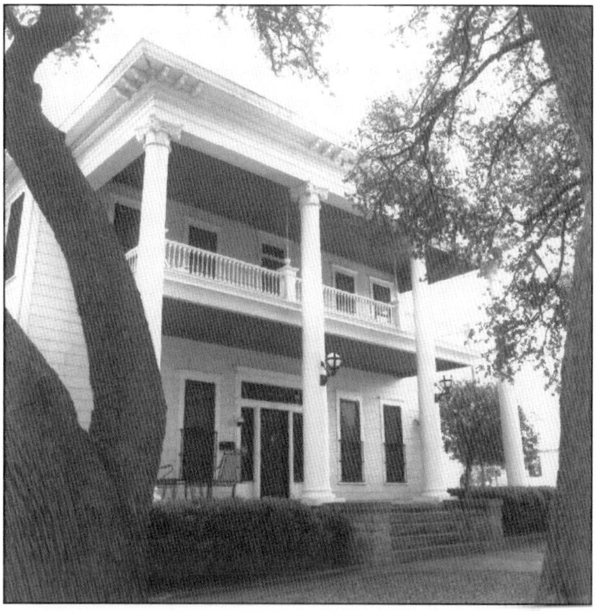

JERRY F. WHITE HOUSE. Still standing at 602 South Broad Street, this two-story home was built in the early 1900s by Jerry F. White, a founder and longtime president of the People's National Bank of Lampasas. The house features tall white columns in front and a second-story balcony suspended from the porch roof by four slender steel rods, rather than being supported by columns. (Courtesy of Gladden Corbin.)

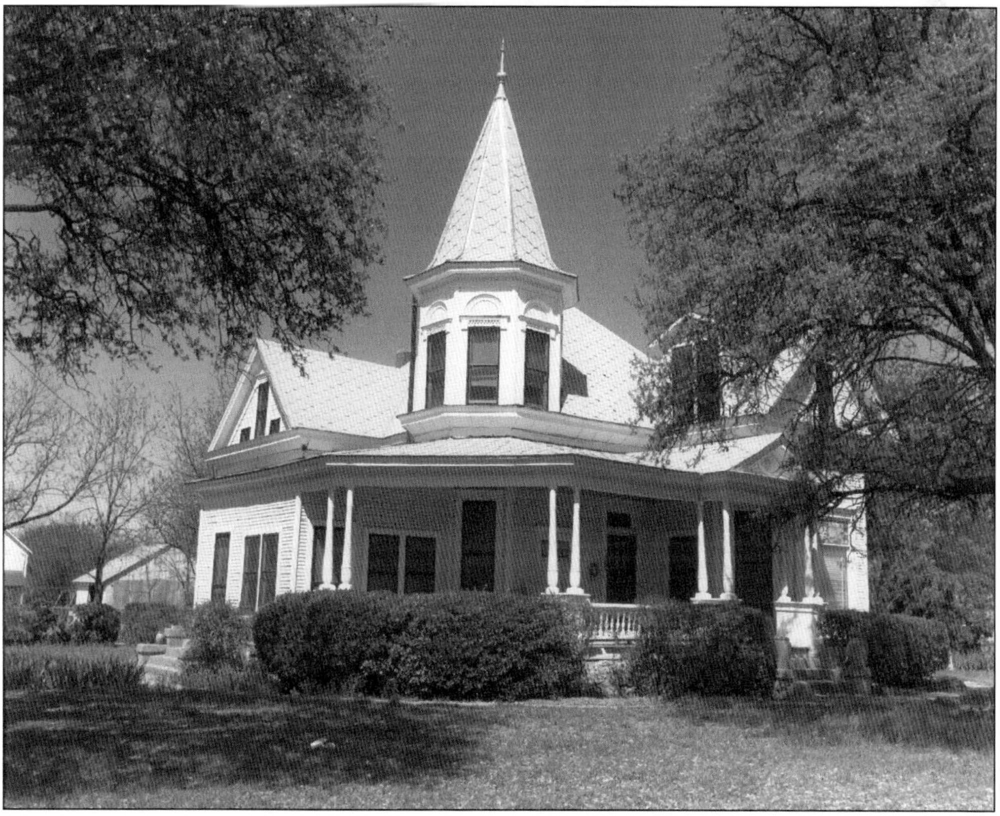

GILLEN HOUSE. This Victorian home at Key Avenue and Sixth Street was built in the early 1900s by Hosea Bailey for his bride, Ellen Mayo. During the 1930s, W. C. Gillen, knowing his wife, Kate, had long admired the house, bought it for her as a surprise. They lived there for the rest of their 67-year marriage. The house is still in the Gillen family. (Courtesy of Gladden Corbin.)

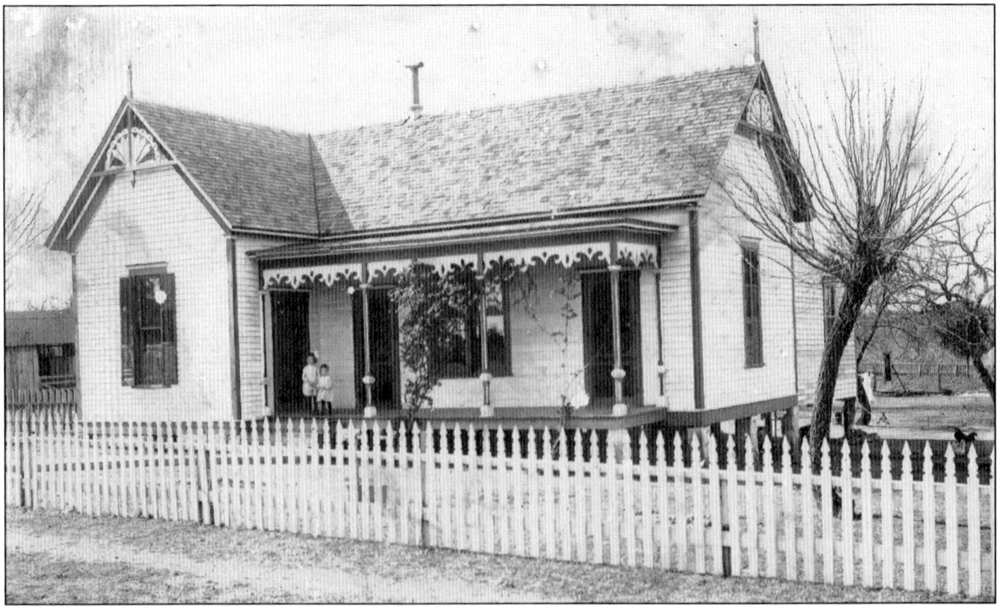

VALLIANT HOUSE. Maude Valliant and her brother James posed for this picture at a residence on Chestnut Street about a century ago. The house likely belonged to their grandfather, John M. Jones, who was listed in the 1910 census as a butcher by trade. He was named head of a household that included daughter Avis; daughter Pearl Valliant and her husband, James Leroy; and grandchildren Maude and James.

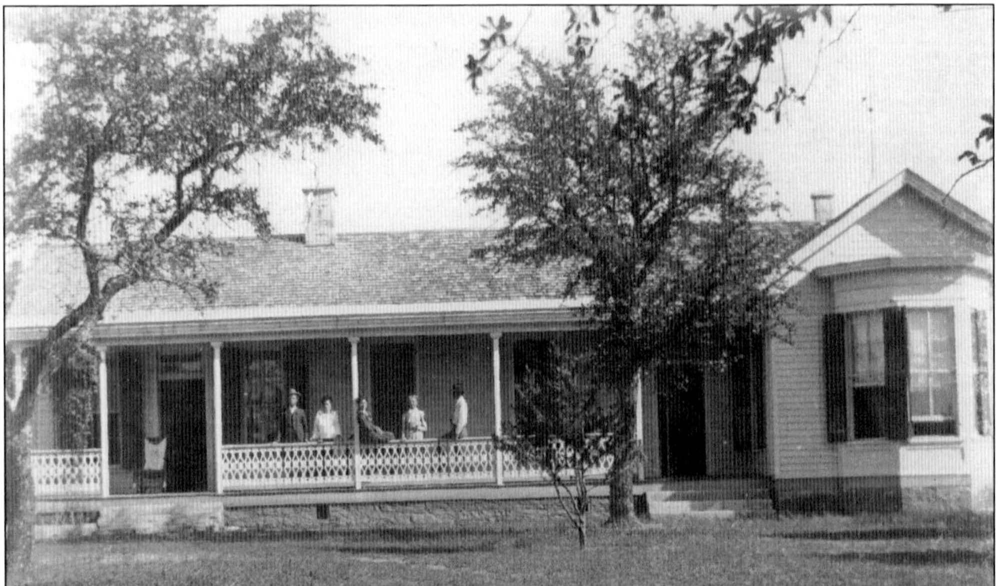

NORTHINGTON RANCH HOUSE, C. 1902. The 4,000-acre Alex J. Northington Ranch was located about four miles east of Lampasas. Pictured on the porch of the 1890s ranch house are, from left to right, Clyde Northington Jr.; Clyde's wife, Bessie; his sister Rachael; his mother, Maria Louisa; and his brother Ben. Northington ran a substantial cattle operation and also served as a state legislator and county commissioner. (Courtesy of Carol Northington Wright.)

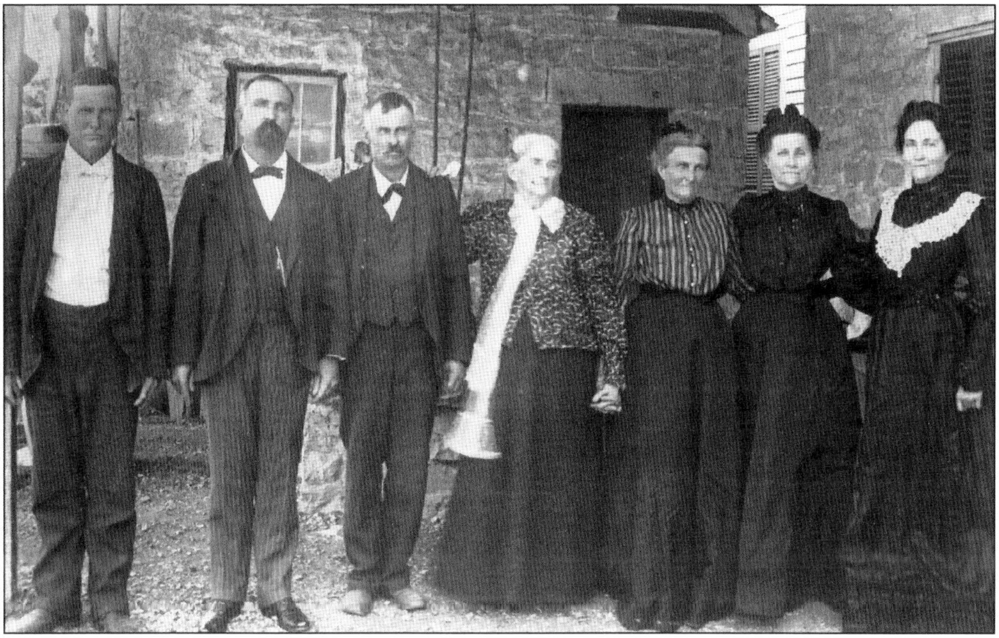

HULING FAMILY ON WELL PORCH, C. 1890. A veteran of the "Runaway Scrape" during the Texas War for Independence, Elizabeth Huling (fourth from the left) posed for this photograph with six of her seven grown children outside the Lampasas home she bought in 1872. Standing from left to right are Proctor, Mark Bean "Tat," William N. "Dick," Elizabeth, Isabella Victoria "Belle," Rebecca, and Almonte. (Courtesy of Charlene Nash.)

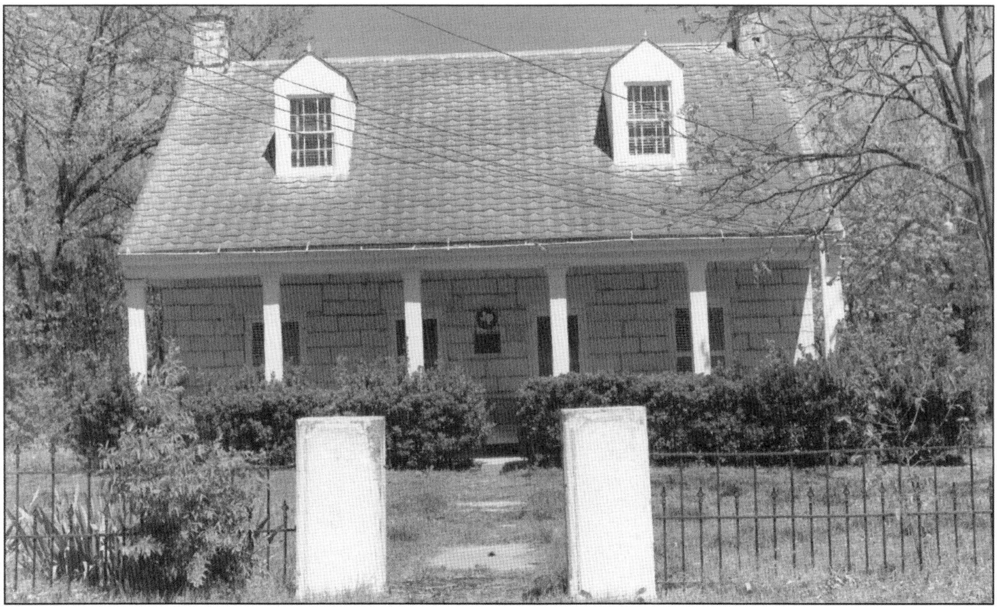

ELIZABETH HULING HOME. After her husband Thomas's death, Elizabeth left her country home and, in 1872, bought this stone house on Second Street for $3,000 in gold. The house of hand-hewn stone was built in 1860 by Ben Gooch. The preceding photograph was taken on the east side of the house pictured here, which still stands at 205 East Second Street. (Courtesy of Gladden Corbin.)

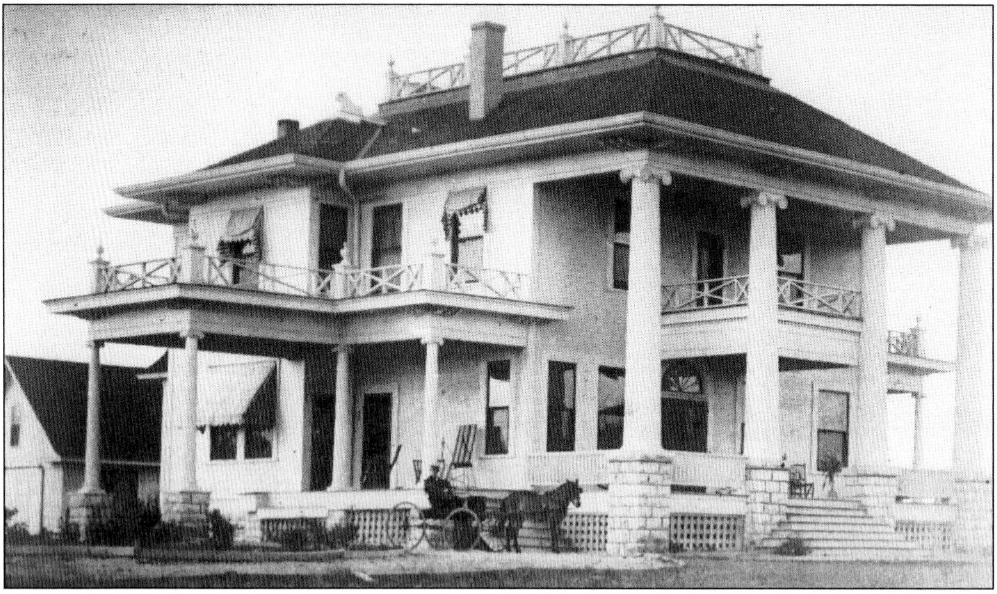

CAMPBELL MANSION AT ARGYLL HEIGHTS. Completed in 1904, this house was built by William Thomas Campbell, a Texaco founder, on Argyll Heights, his estate north of Hanna Springs. Campbell died less than three years later, but his wife, Sarah Jane, continued to live there, managing the family's various interests until her death in 1951. Fire destroyed the mansion in 1974. (Courtesy of Sarah Campbell McElwain.)

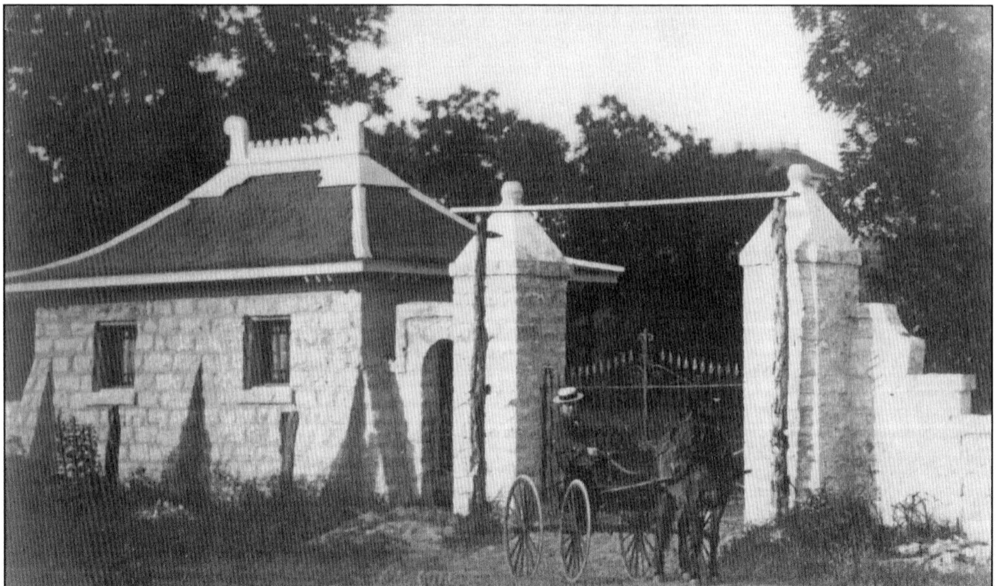

GATEWAY TO ARGYLL HEIGHTS. Pictured is W. T. Campbell, youngest child of Sarah Jane and William Thomas Campbell, at the main gate to Argyll Heights. Behind the wall is the gatekeeper's residence. Today all that remains is a World War I–era house built by the Campbells' other son, Villard, and a section of the rock wall that enclosed the once grand estate. (Courtesy of Sarah Campbell McElwain.)

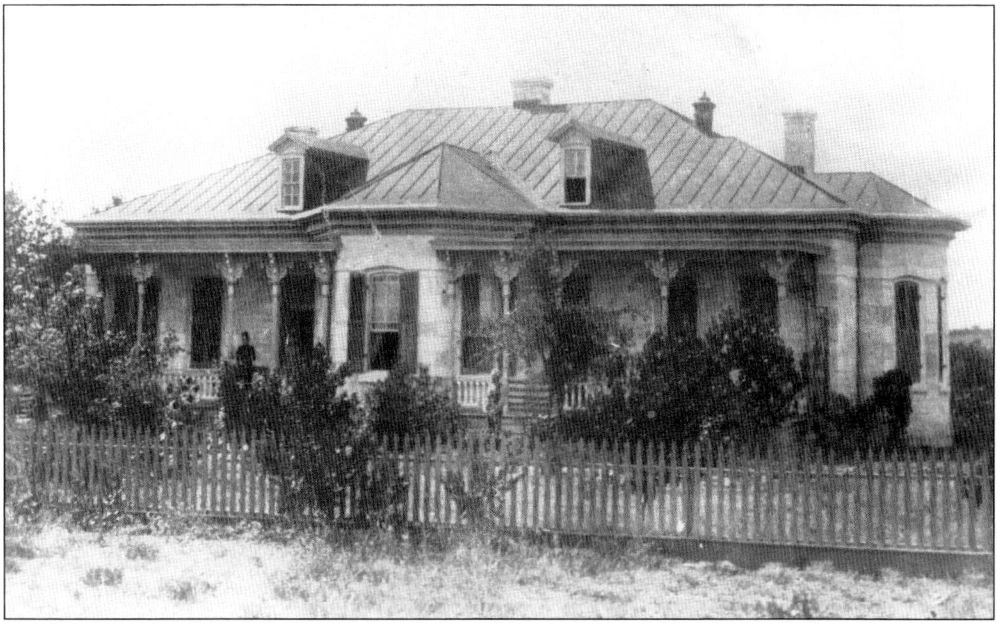

JOHN MARKWARD HOUSE. Several miles from town, off Texas Farm to Market 580 East, is the 1875 home of John Markward, an outstanding businessman and civic leader of early Lampasas. Hand-cut stone was used by builder Theo Barfine. A native of Prussia, Markward arrived in Lampasas in 1857 and later married the daughter of early Lampasas educator Major Martin White. All are buried in the White-Markward Cemetery near the house.

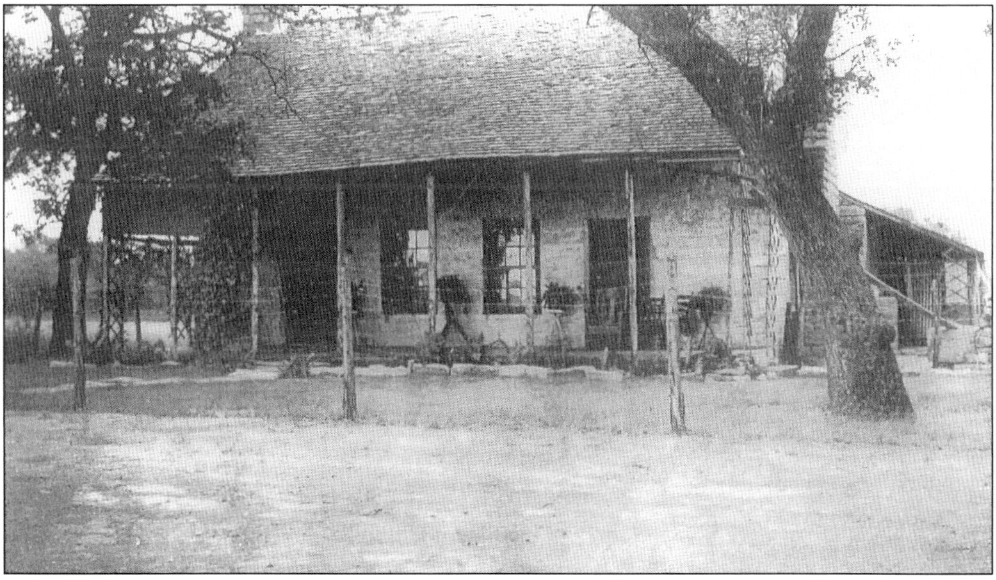

PHILLIP SMITH HOUSE. The Smith family emigrated from Germany when their son Phillip was a child, arriving in Texas in 1832. By 1854, Phillip and his wife, Caroline, had settled on the Lampasas River. An earlier log home was replaced by this two-story stone house in 1870 and is still occupied today. The Smiths donated land for a school and cemetery, which still bear their name. (Courtesy of Alicia Straley.)

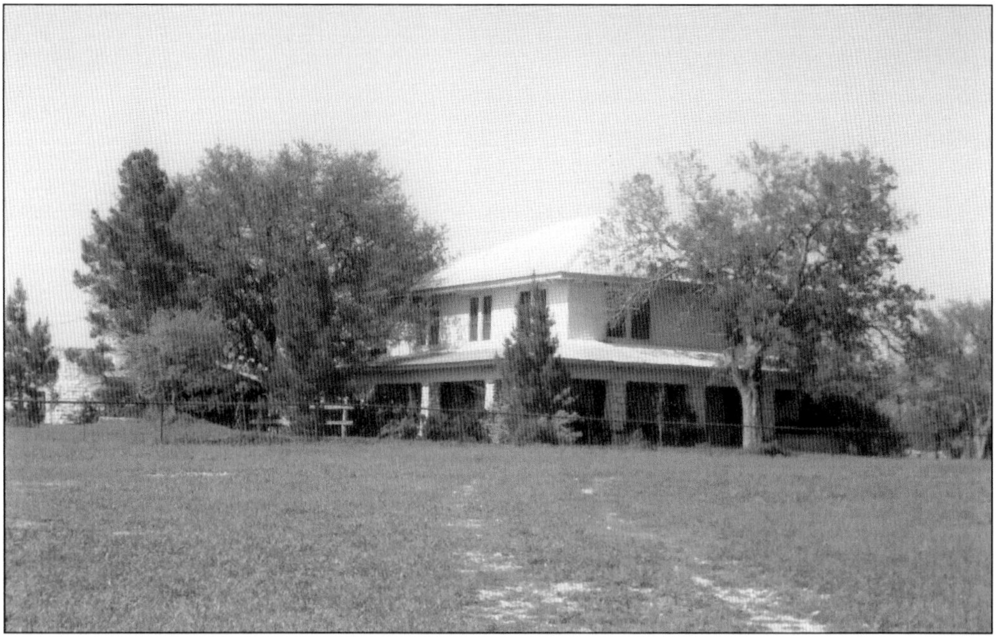

FRANK HOME PLACE, ADAMSVILLE. Frederick Bernhardt "Ben" Frank and his wife, Henrietta, moved to the Adamsville area about 1897. They bought 320 acres and a house on the west side of Sims Creek. Eventually, the house was enlarged, and a concrete fence was added. In 1923, the Franks replaced it with the two-story home pictured here. The house is still standing. (Courtesy of private collector.)

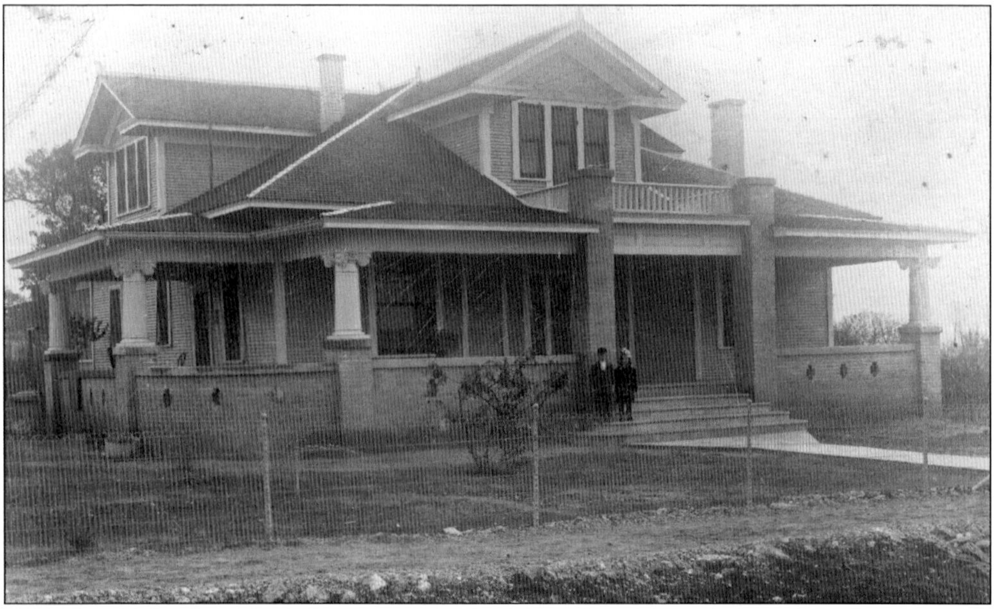

STEPHENS-STALLINGS HOUSE, LOMETA. Main Street in Lometa was once the address of grand homes, such as the one pictured above. It is now known as the Stephens House, after Lometa settler John Warrick Stephens. At one time it belonged to his son-in-law, Henry Stallings. The partnership of Stallings; his brother-in-law, Lucius M. "Mickey" Stephens; and later Gordon McCann helped make wool and mohair big business in Lampasas County. (Courtesy of Jane McMillin.)

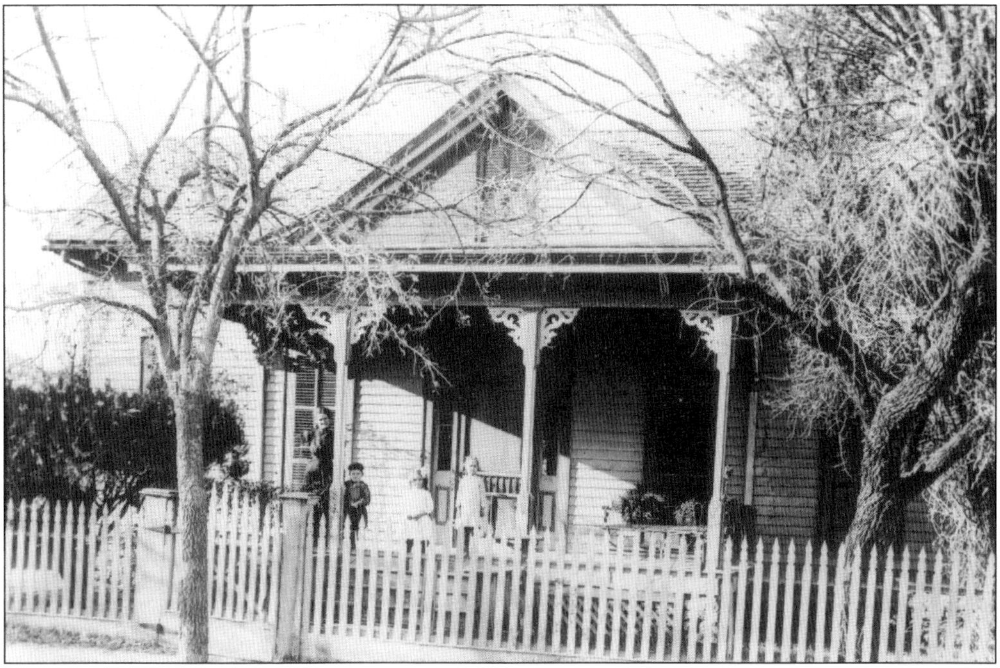

Emma Stokes House. After his wife, Elizabeth, died in 1900, Richard Stokes married Emma Woody Fulton of the Long Cove Community, north of Lometa. At age 73, Stokes dived into the raging floodwaters of the Colorado at Chadwick's Mill and saved three people from drowning. For his heroism, Stokes was awarded a Carnegie Medal.

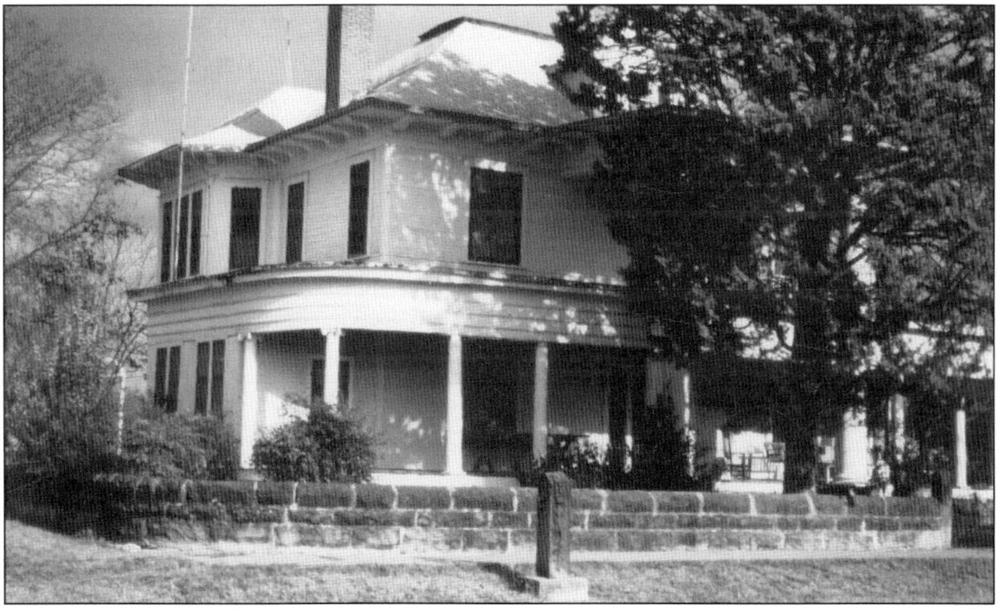

Dr. Biggs's House, Lometa. The beloved Dr. W. D. Biggs practiced medicine in the Lometa area for more than 40 years, from 1903 to 1945. By his own estimate, he delivered more than 3,000 babies, many by kerosene lamplight. His two-story house at Main and Sixth Streets was built in 1912 by William Watson, a cattleman who lived in the area during the early 1900s. (Courtesy of Ruth Gadbury.)

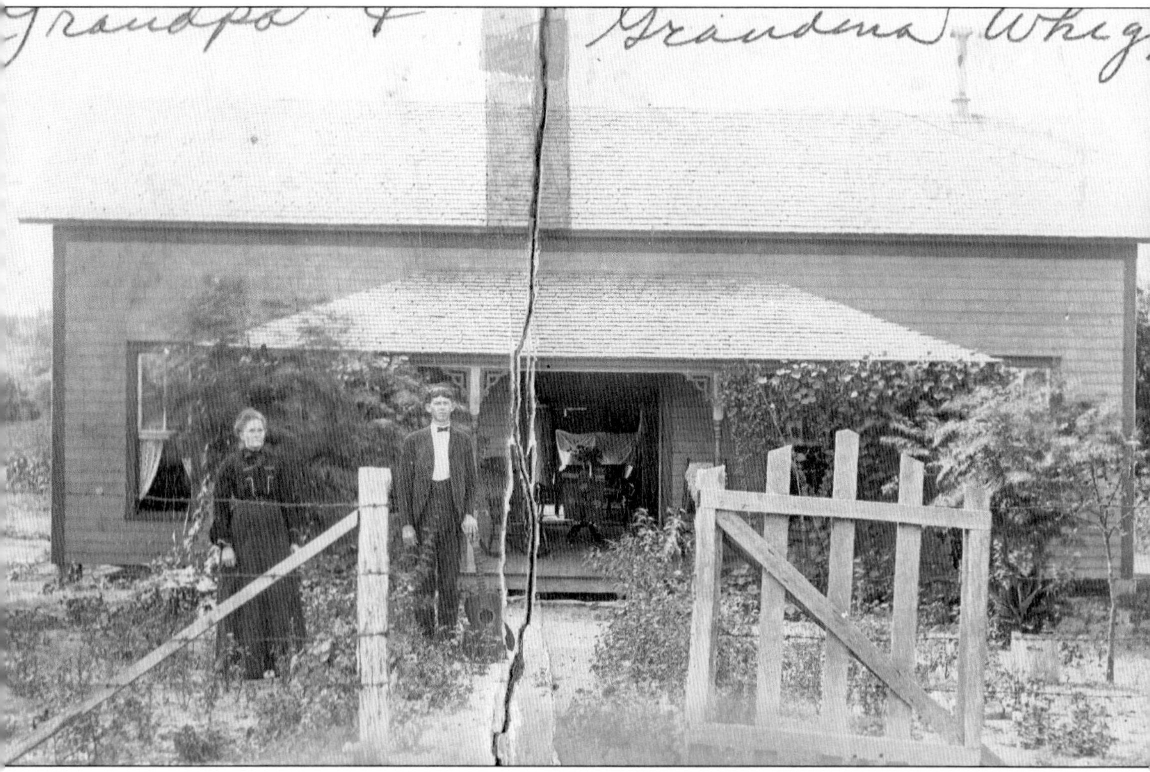

WHIGHAM HOUSE AT KEMPNER. After the Civil War, the Thomas Whigham family moved to Texas from Alabama. They lived in the eastern portion of Lampasas County near the present site of Kempner. The Whighams had 11 children, 5 of whom died of typhoid fever. Lacking the drugs and vaccines available today, many infectious diseases were deadly to early settlers and devastated many families. (Courtesy of Kay Briggs.)

Six

Reading, 'Riting, and 'Rithmatic

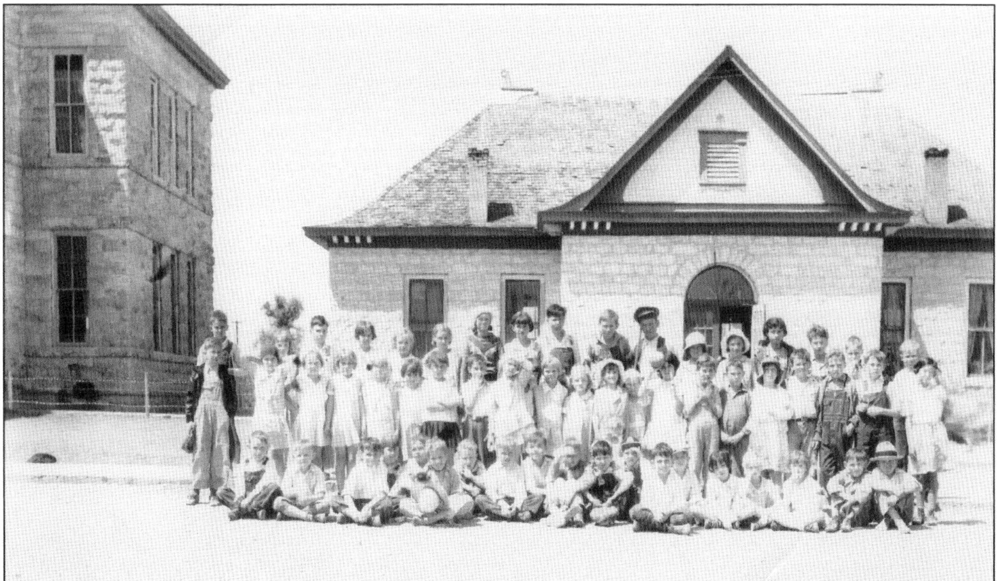

Lampasas Grammar School, 1934. When scholastic enrollment exceeded the capacity of Lampasas's first public school building, this two-room rock structure was constructed in 1910 to house two classes of the grammar school. One- and two-room schools dotted the countryside for decades, often providing space for other community activities and becoming the heart of the community. Consolidations, which began in the 1930s, left few, if any, country schools.

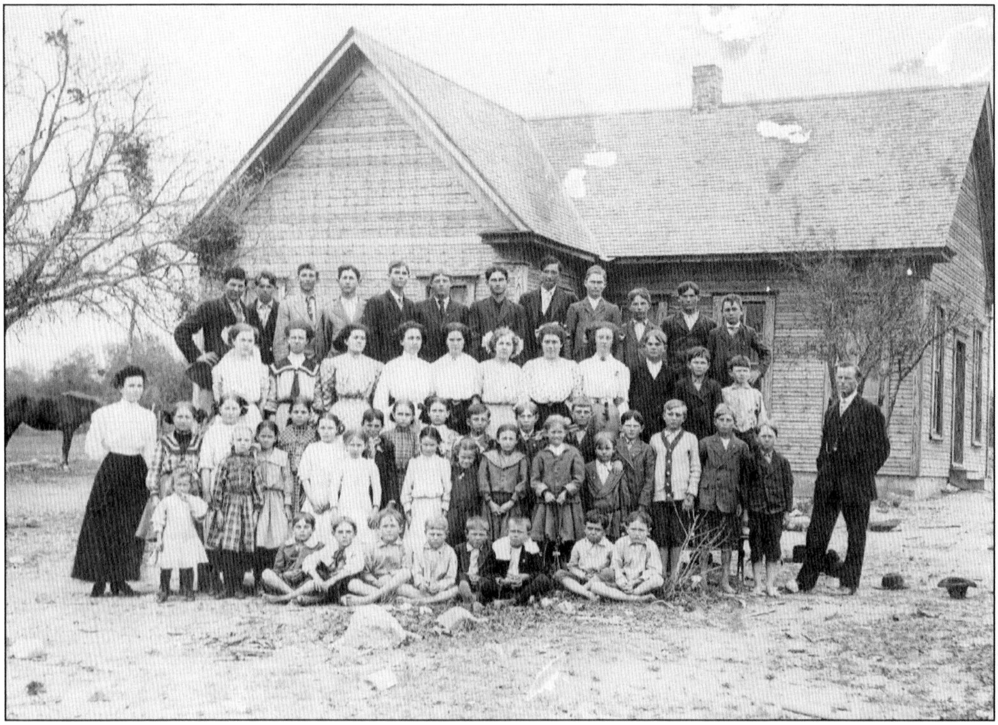

THE STRALEY SCHOOL IN ADAMSVILLE, 1910. This school was named for Joseph Leland Straley, who donated the land for the school, a Baptist church, and a cemetery in Adamsville. It was located southeast of the present-day Adamsville Baptist Church on U.S. Highway 281. The lumber from the school was used to build the Baptist parsonage in 1947.

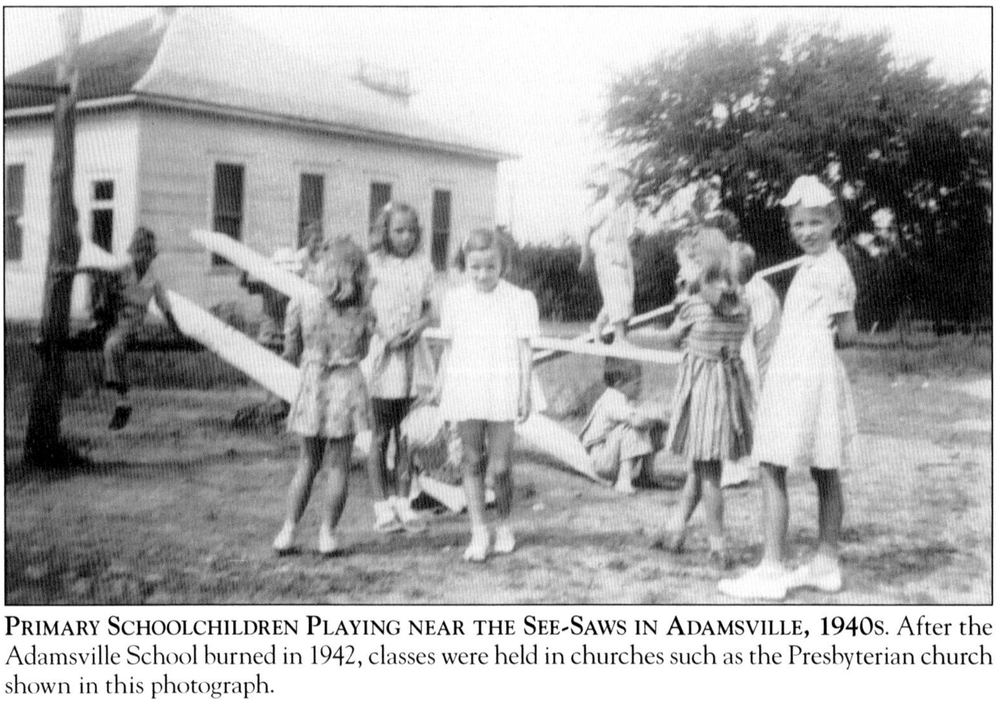

PRIMARY SCHOOLCHILDREN PLAYING NEAR THE SEE-SAWS IN ADAMSVILLE, 1940S. After the Adamsville School burned in 1942, classes were held in churches such as the Presbyterian church shown in this photograph.

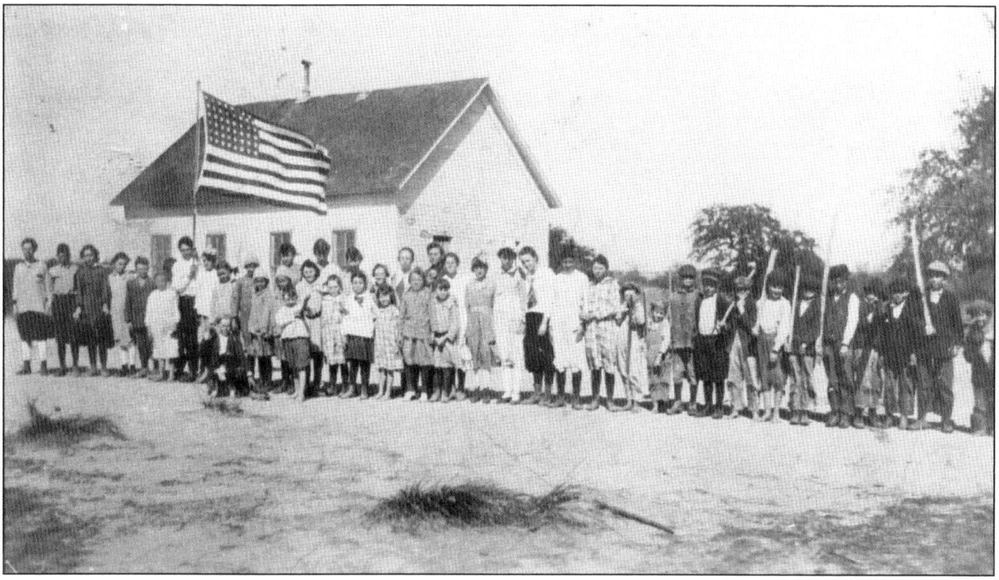

LITTLEFIELD SCHOOL, MID-1920S. Littlefield was on the boundary between Lampasas and Coryell Counties. This schoolhouse was a center for educational and social activities. A contemporary note on the back of the photograph draws the viewer's attention to the girls' basketball uniforms: "3 yards for black bloomers, plus middie blouse and tie."

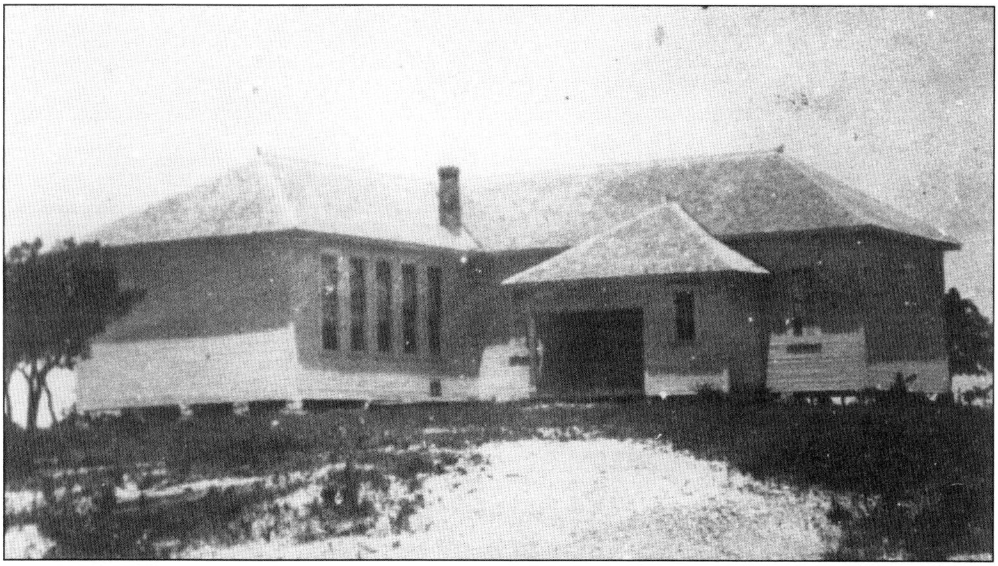

MOLINE SCHOOL, C. 1925. Settled in the 1880s, Moline was located on the north central edge of Lampasas County. In 1916, the Moline School was built by G. C. O'Neal and others on five acres of land on a hilltop donated by Kenneth and Olive Patterson. In the early 1920s, the school employed three teachers. In the 1930s, Moline was the largest rural school in the county. It closed in 1943.

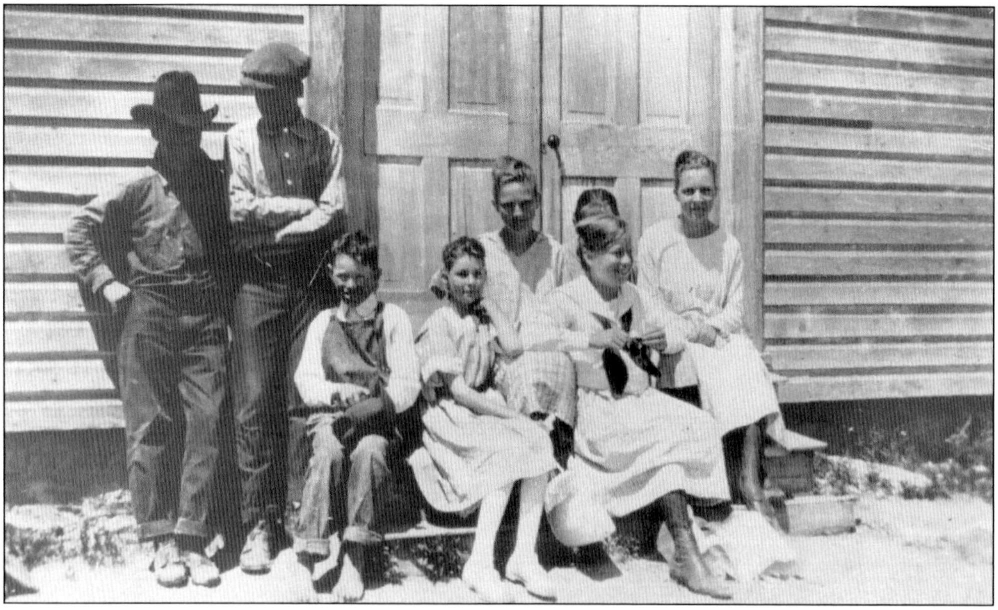

FRIENDSHIP SCHOOL, 1921. The Friendship School was southwest of Adamsville on the west side of Simms Creek, near U.S. Highway 281. Pictured from left to right are Howard Spivey, Walter Frank, Arthur Harrell, Jewel Petrey, Laura Frank, Letha Spivey, and Iris Harris. This one-room schoolhouse had long seats that also served as church pews every Sunday.

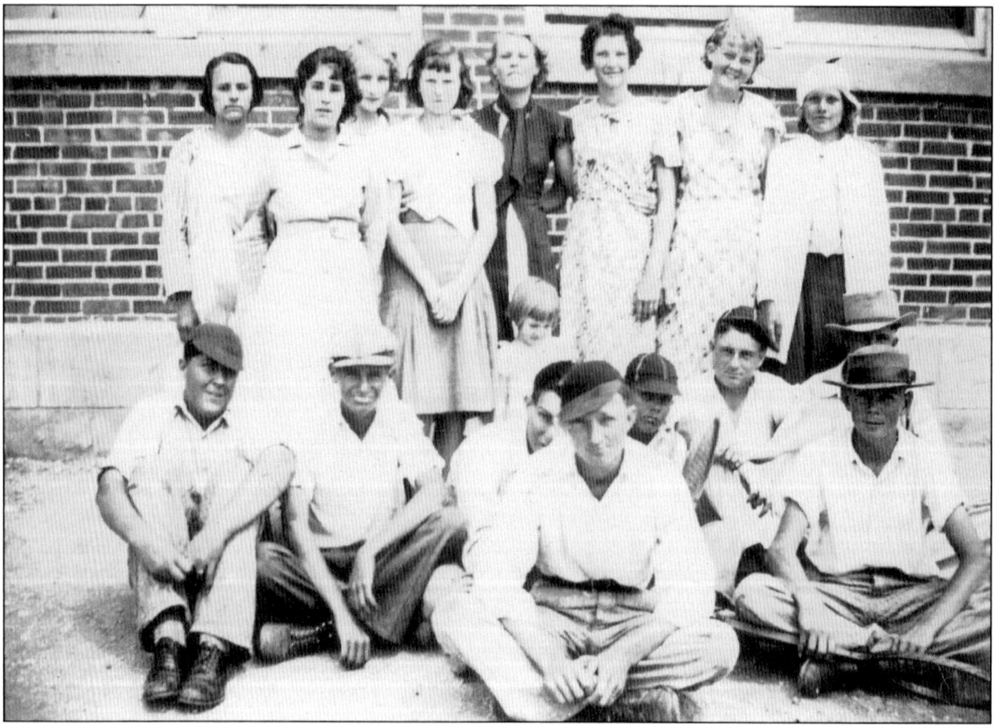

STUDENTS IN KEMPNER, 1933–1934. By 1884, the village of Kempner had established a school. The country school remained independent until the 1960s, when it consolidated with the Lampasas school district. (Courtesy of Maudie Estelle Trousdale Walker)

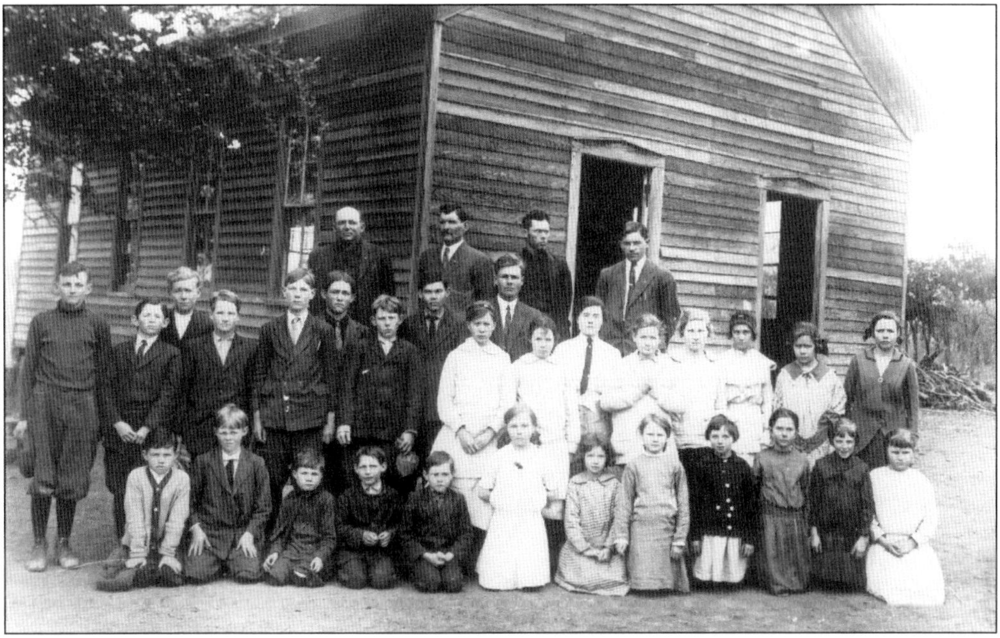

ATHERTON SCHOOL, 1915. This clapboard school building was in Atherton, northeast of Lometa. The first school in Atherton was a boarding school for boys built in the 1880s. The early school also served as a community center and meeting place for church groups. This more modern school was probably built in 1904. The school and the community were named for early educator and postmistress Abbie Atherton.

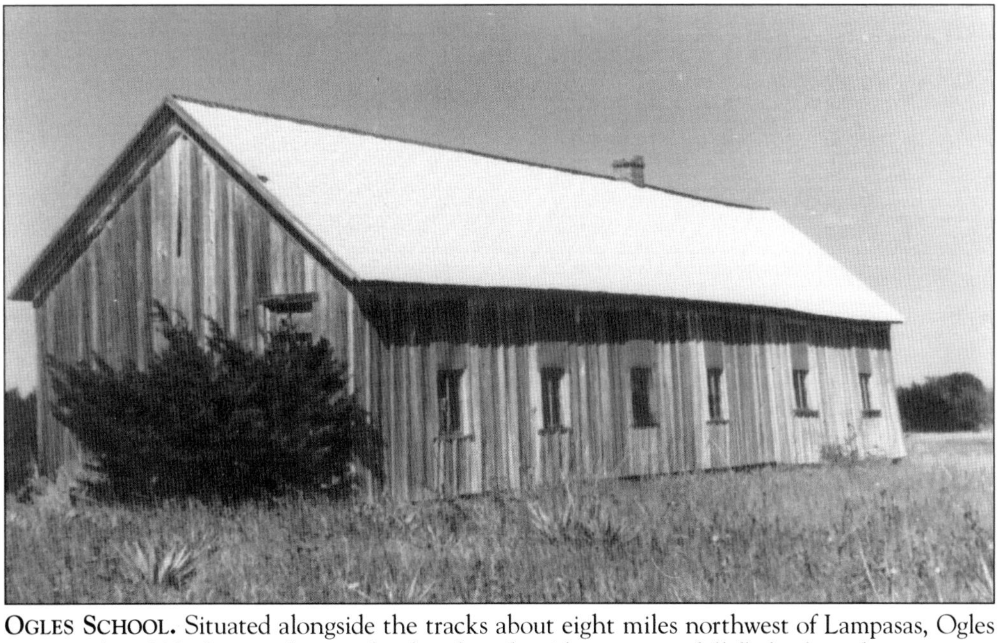

OGLES SCHOOL. Situated alongside the tracks about eight miles northwest of Lampasas, Ogles grew in the 1880s from a cluster of railroad workers' houses to a full-fledged rural community with a school and other amenities. The school was held in the barn-like structure pictured here: one long room with a wood stove and a bookcase. Until the early 1920s, the Ogles Methodist Church held services in the building.

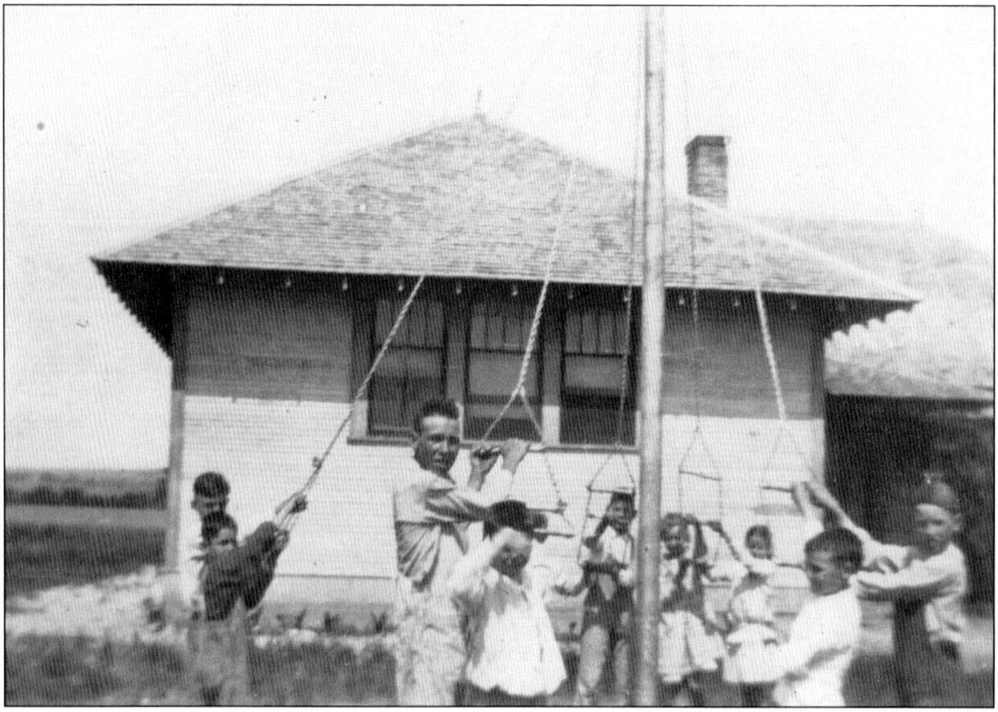

Playing on the Swings at Unity School. Swinging was a popular recess game. Each child held onto a triangular handle and ran around the pole until the force of the group carried individuals off their feet. Other activities included playing marbles (for the boys) and jacks (for the girls), particularly when the school did not have playground equipment.

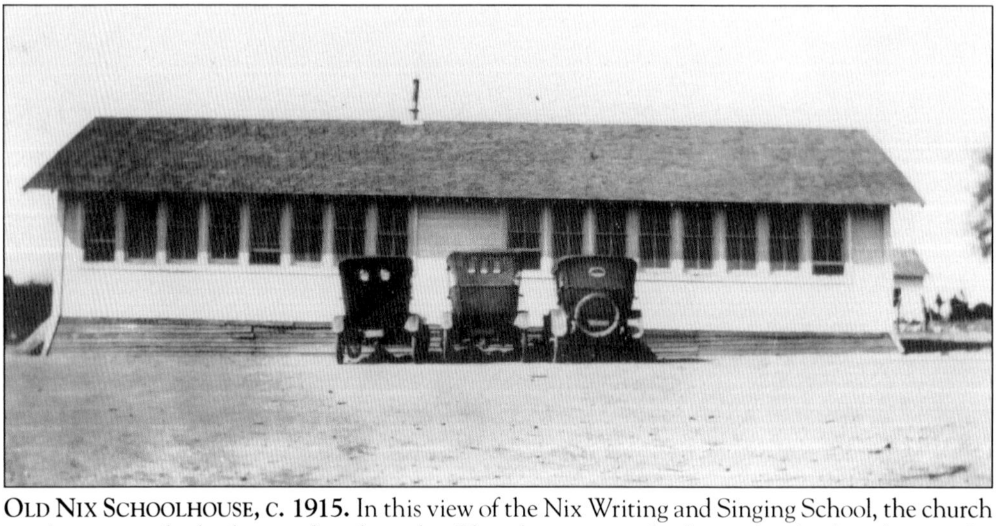

Old Nix Schoolhouse, c. 1915. In this view of the Nix Writing and Singing School, the church can be seen in the background to the right. Church was never far from school, often sharing the same building in the county's early years.

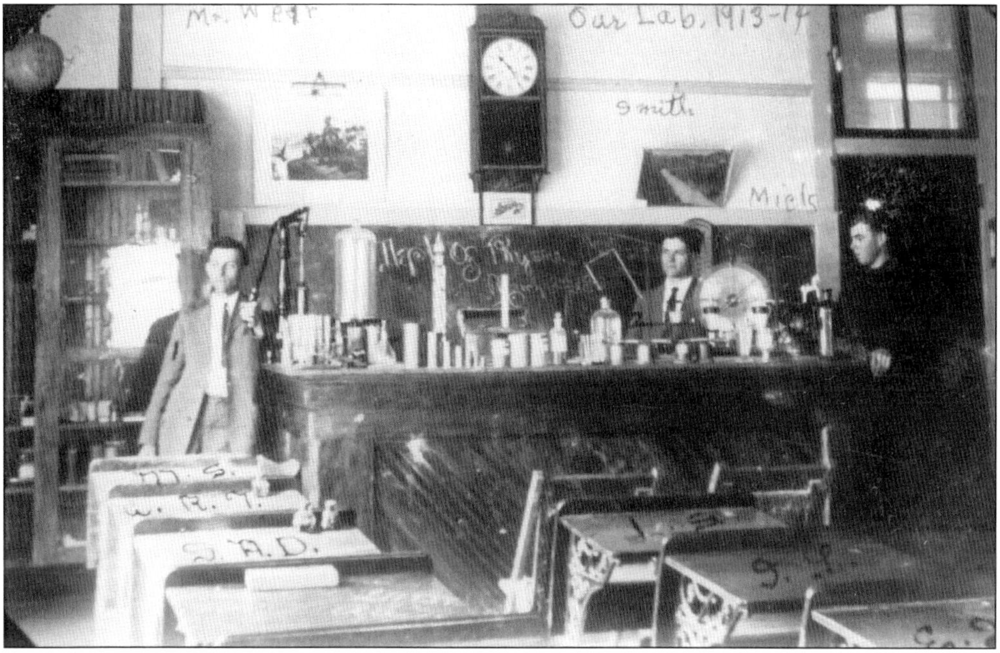

LOMETA HIGH SCHOOL SCIENCE LABORATORY, 1913–1914. Prof. Jessie Weir, superintendent, taught science, among other subjects, at Lometa High School. The school had its own lab, shown here, outfitted with test tubes, microscopes, and other learning tools for the students. Note the wooden desks with ink stands. (Courtesy of Ruth Gadbury and Mrs. O. S. Davis.)

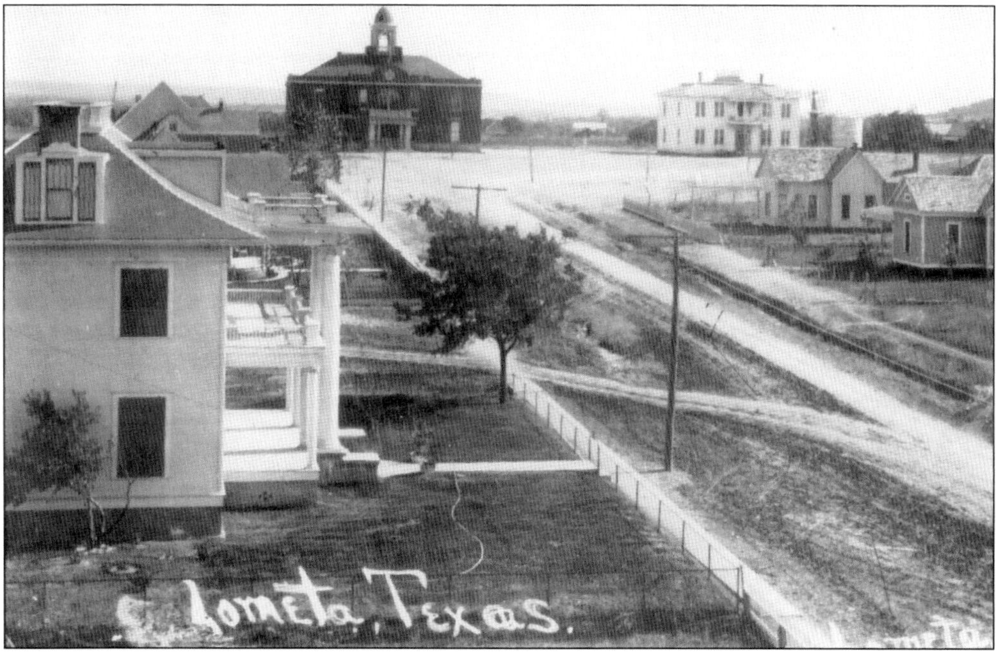

LOMETA SCHOOL BUILDINGS, C. 1911. In 1906, when the Lometa Independent School District was created, a redbrick building was built for the high school, the focal point of this photograph. The former Lometa Educational Association (LEA) College building, visible here at the upper right, was newly dedicated to the lower grades. (Courtesy of Ruth Gadbury and Opal McMahan.)

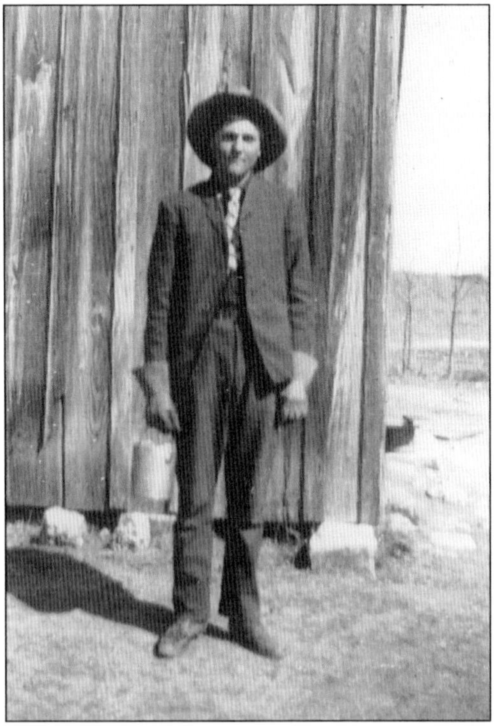

Bringing Lunch to School, Pecan Grove. Alvie, A. G. and J. H. Hodges's father, is shown here carrying a metal lunch pail. Students carried their lunch to school in syrup buckets or brown paper sacks. Lunch usually consisted of leftovers, sometimes a cold biscuit and sausage, fried potatoes, or a fried pie. A piece of fruit was a treat. Pecan Grove was near Unity, in the northeastern part of the county.

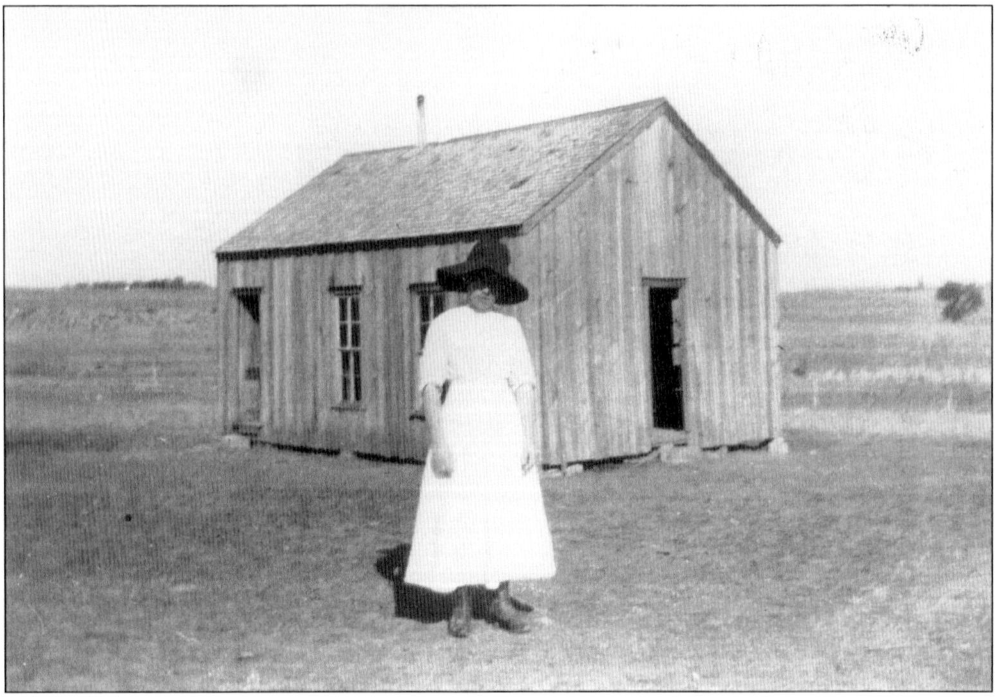

Ollie Lloyd in front of the Smokehouse School in Andersonville, c. 1918. Lloyd taught school in this converted smokehouse located eight to nine miles north of the city of Lampasas, near Lucy Creek. One-room schoolhouses were common in small communities, and school was often held in buildings that at one time served another purpose.

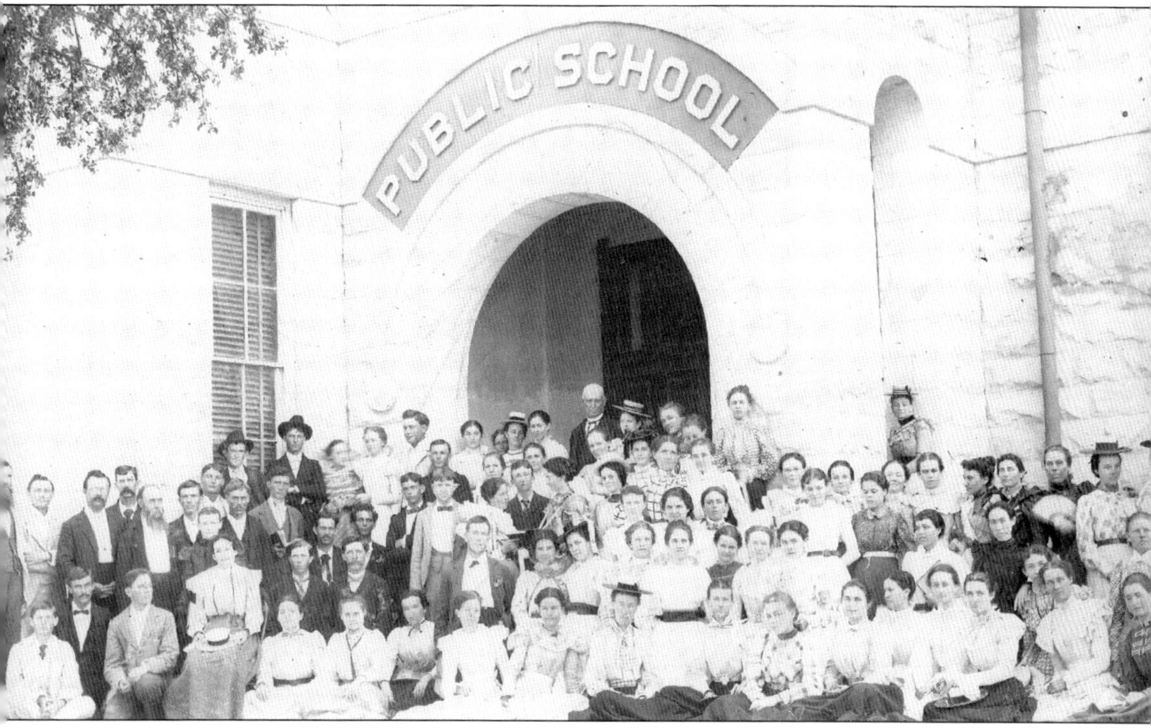

SUMMER NORMAL SCHOOL, LAMPASAS, 1920S. In summer, a normal school was held in the Lampasas public school building for the continuing education of teachers. Teacher training sessions in Texas lasted 10 weeks in the 1920s. During that time, teachers reviewed the subjects that they planned to teach and to prepare for exams to earn certification.

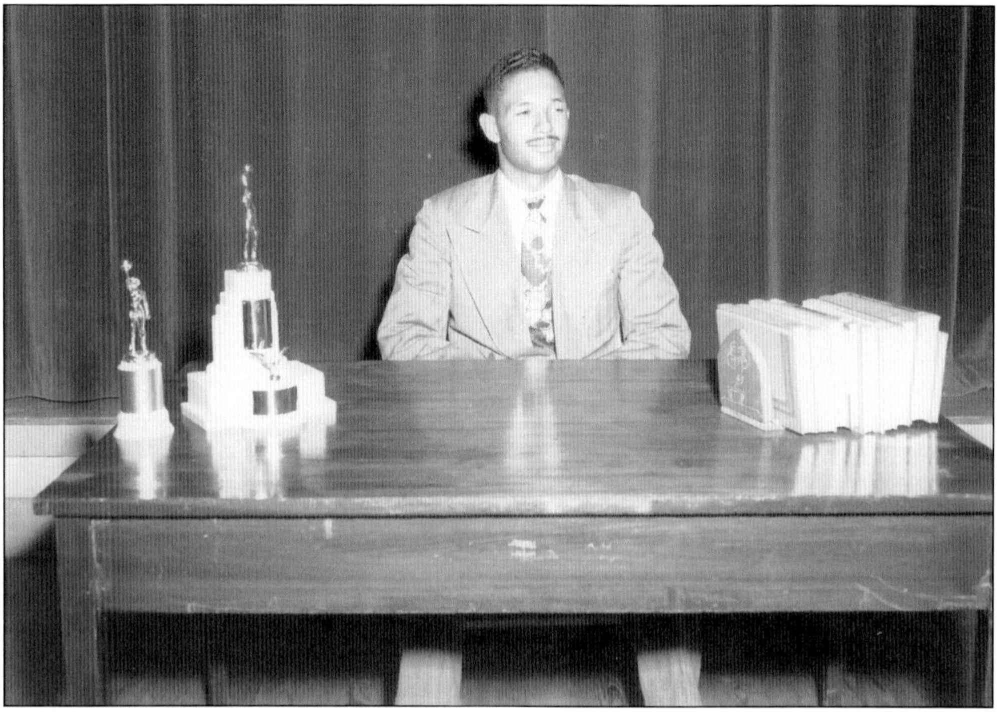

BILLIE ORMAN, 1950S. Orman was appointed principal of the Lampasas Colored School in 1953. He came to Lampasas from Brownwood to take the job. Here Orman sits in front of the stage at the school. The Lampasas Independent School District integrated in 1963, and the Lampasas Colored School closed. Orman later earned his Ph.D. (Photograph by Virgil Wooten.)

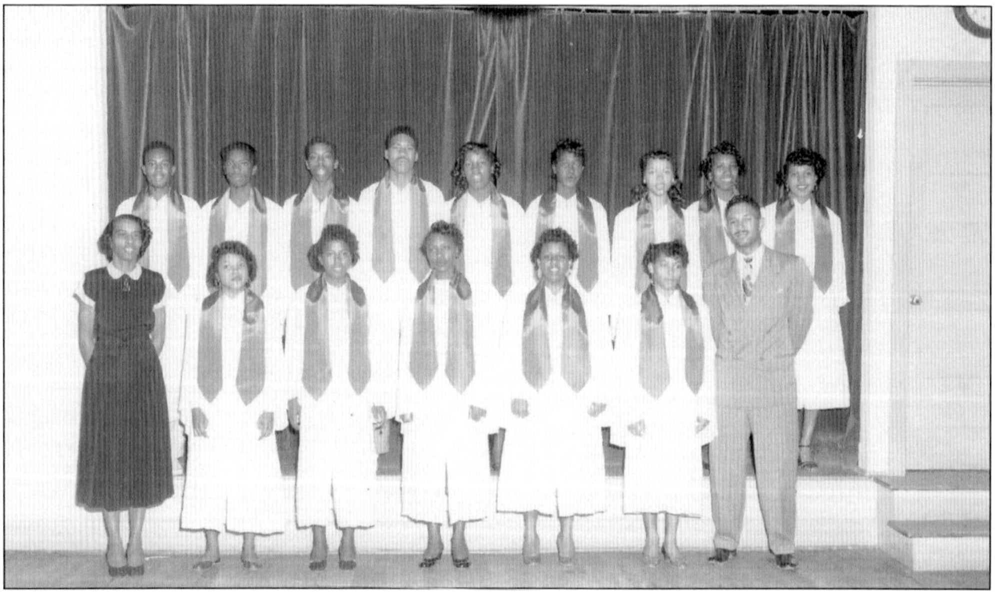

THE LAMPASAS COLORED SCHOOL CHOIR, 1950S. The Lampasas Colored School had two teachers in the 1950s, Billie Orman, the principal, and Ernestine Patrick, both pictured in the front row here. In addition, Patrick directed the Lampasas Colored School choir. (Photograph by Virgil Wooten.)

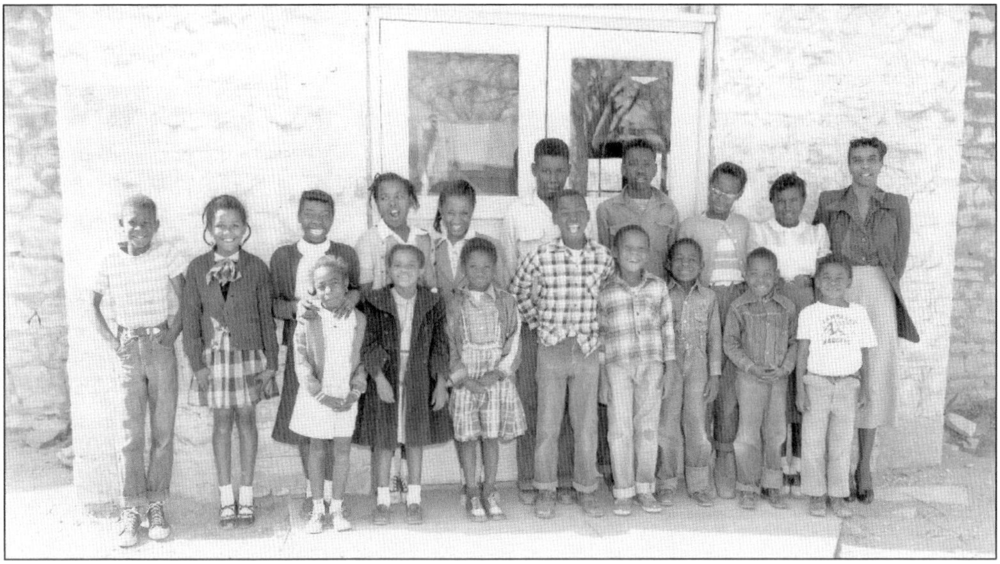

THE LAMPASAS COLORED SCHOOL, ELEMENTARY CLASS, 1950S. Both the elementary and upper grades of the Lampasas Colored School were held in a limestone building located on the east side of the city. Ernestine Patrick taught elementary students at the Lampasas Colored School. She stands here with her students. (Photograph by Virgil Wooten.)

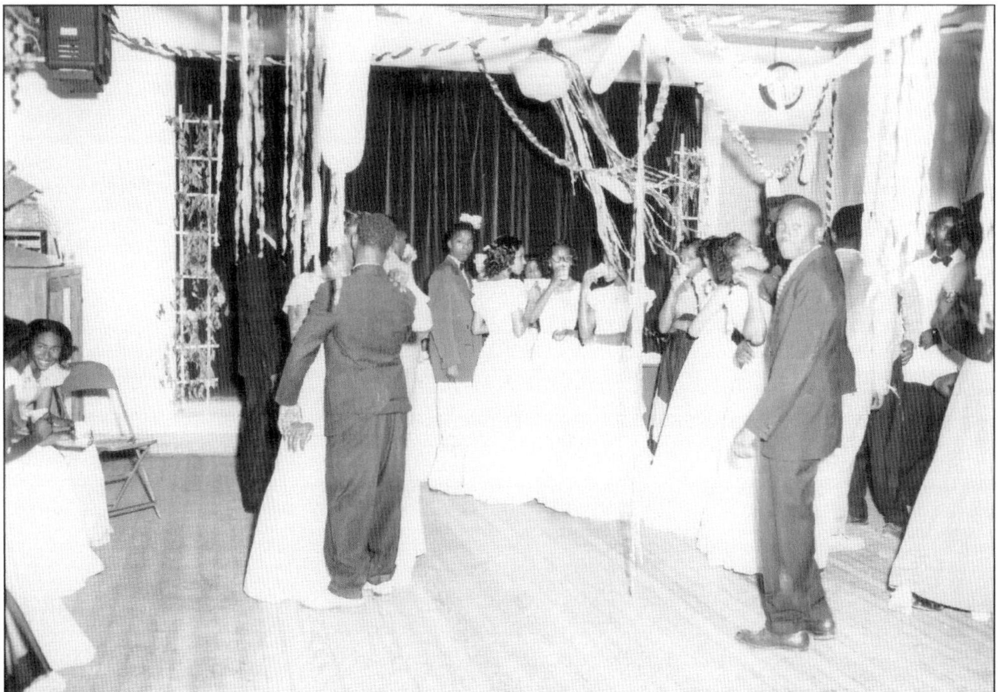

THE PROM AT THE LAMPASAS COLORED SCHOOL. There was a stage at one end of the large room that was the Lampasas Colored School where the choir performed and where the prom was held. The stage is visible in this photograph. Students are dressed in suits and long dresses, and dance or sip punch as they enjoy this traditional end-of-year school event. (Photograph by Virgil Wooten.)

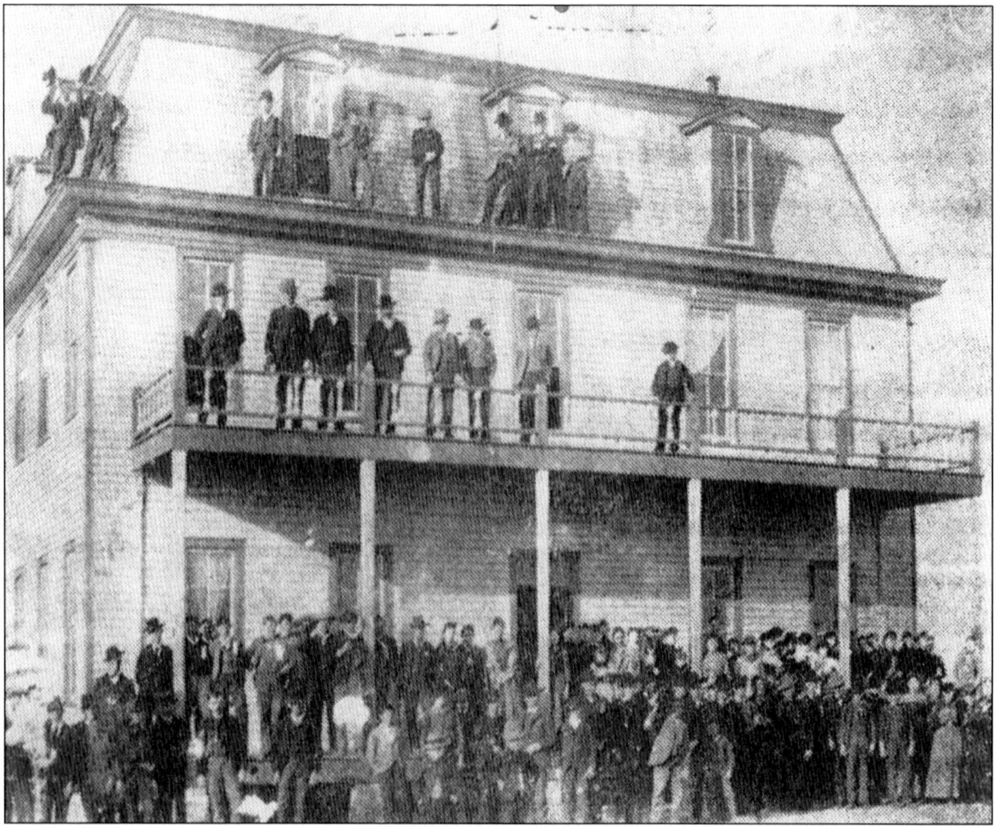

THE BOYS' DORMITORY AT CENTENARY COLLEGE, 1889. Centenary College was a coeducational preparatory school founded in 1883 in honor of 100 years of the Methodist church in the United States. Courses taught by eight professors included mathematics, ancient languages, mental and moral studies, elocution and literature, and hygiene and physiology. The school moved to the Park Hotel in 1894 and closed when the hotel burned in 1895.

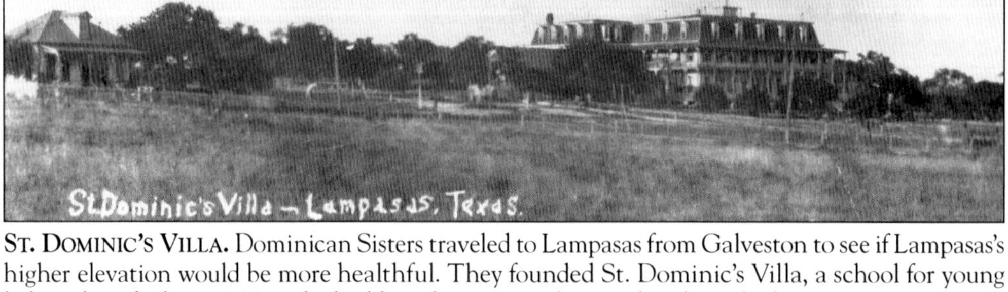

ST. DOMINIC'S VILLA. Dominican Sisters traveled to Lampasas from Galveston to see if Lampasas's higher elevation would be more healthful. They founded St. Dominic's Villa, a school for young ladies of any faith, in 1900 in the building that previously served as the girls' dormitory at Centenary College. The school closed in 1925, due in part to the anti-Catholicism of the Ku Klux Klan.

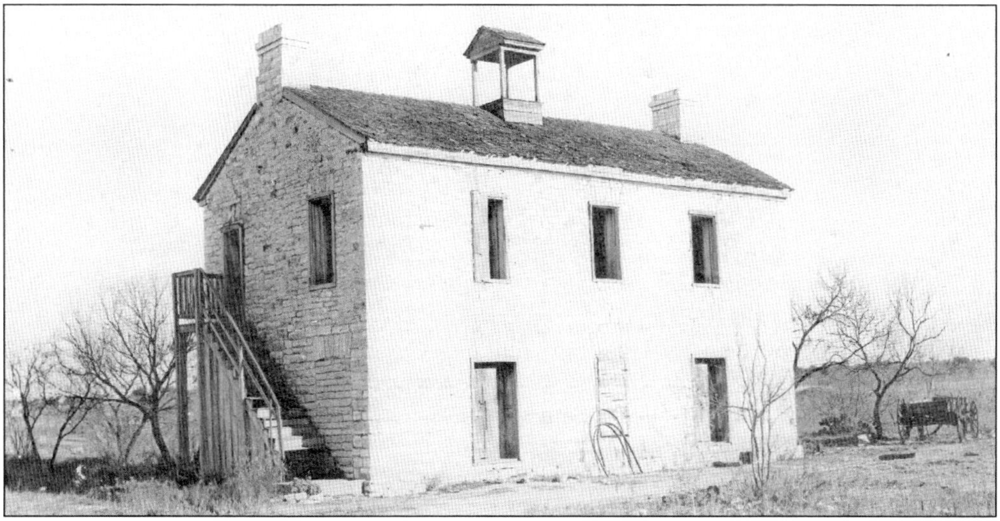

ATEN COLLEGE, 1876. The building that later housed Aten College was erected in 1869 along Sulphur Creek between Pecan and Elm Streets. The college was named for Mr. and Mrs. A. V. Aten after they purchased the school in the 1870s. The college conferred its first bachelor of arts degrees in 1884. Two years later, the Atens sold the school.

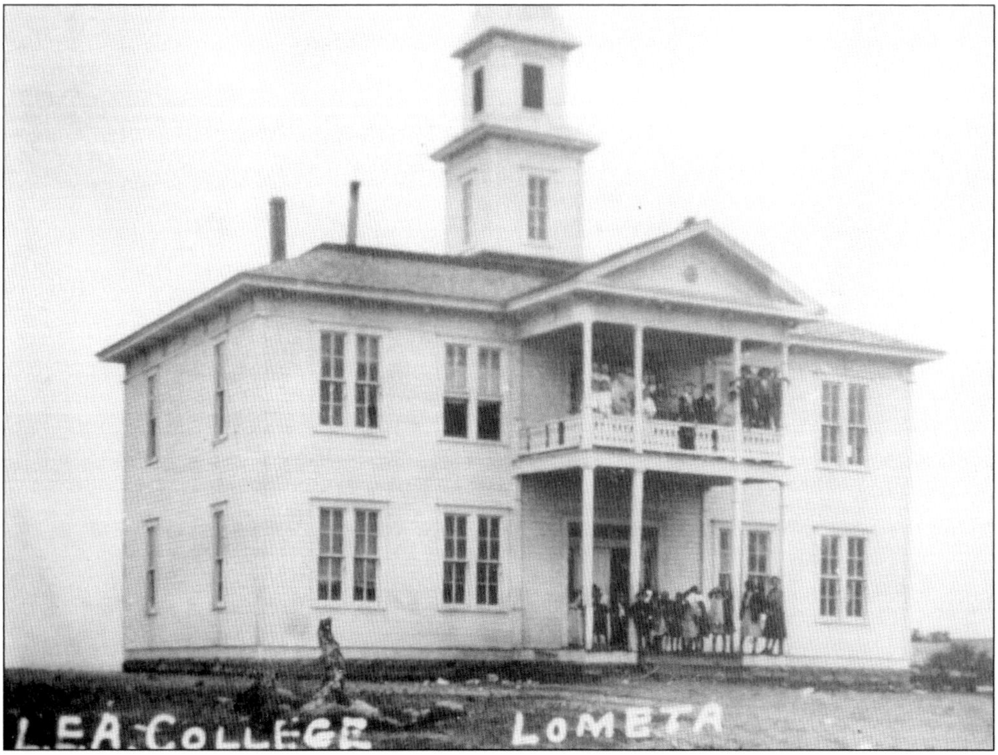

L.E.A. COLLEGE, LOMETA. Lometa Educational Association College, or L.E.A. College, as it became known, was erected in 1894–1895. Prof. M. L. Stallings was the administrator. The building had four large rooms and a cupola, which held a large brass bell. The college was comparable to high school and operated as such until 1906, when it lost its charter. (Courtesy of Ruth Gadbury and Joyce Hightower.)

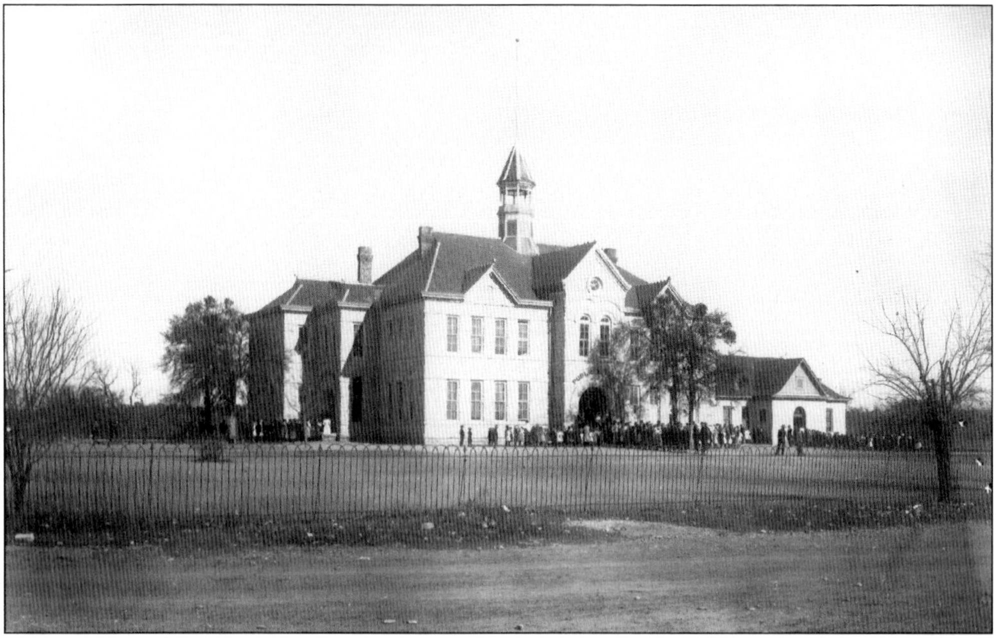

THE FIRST PUBLIC SCHOOL BUILDING IN LAMPASAS, LATE 1890S. The first public school in Lampasas was built of natural limestone at the north end of Main Street in 1895. Eleven grades were held there, and it was heated by wood stoves kept going by a custodian. The school burned in 1977. Note the cupola on top and the wrought iron fence that surrounds the building.

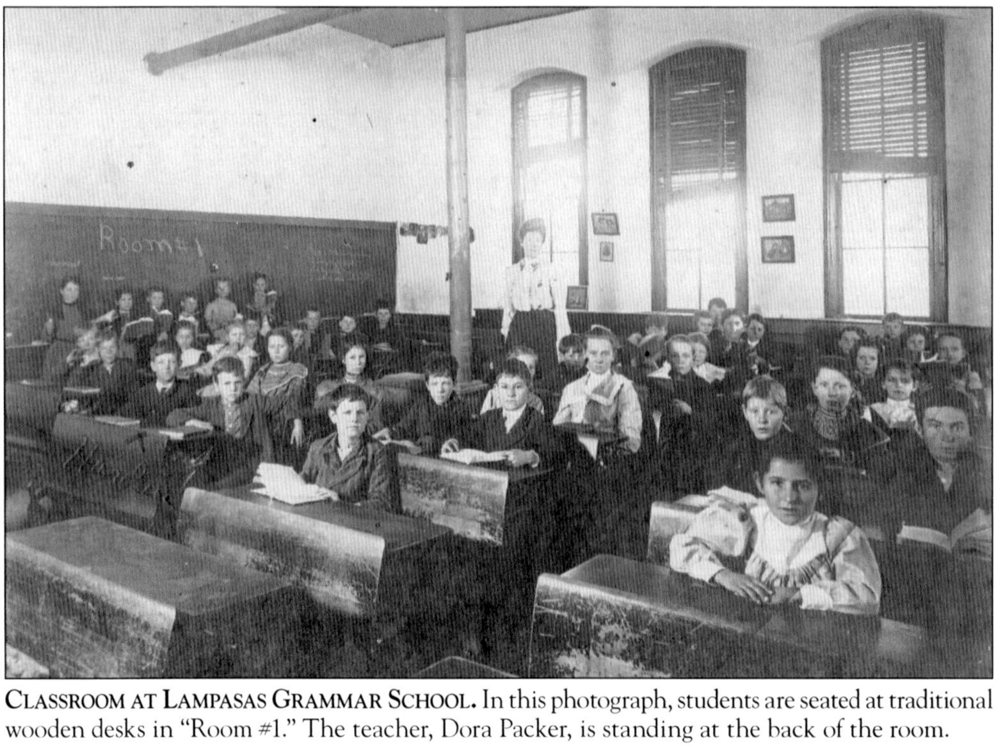

CLASSROOM AT LAMPASAS GRAMMAR SCHOOL. In this photograph, students are seated at traditional wooden desks in "Room #1." The teacher, Dora Packer, is standing at the back of the room.

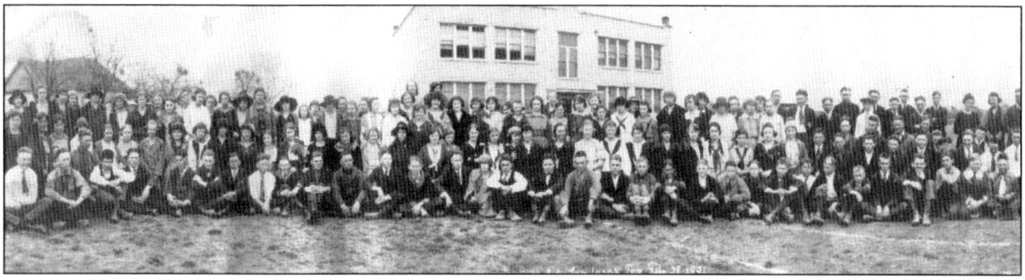

LAMPASAS HIGH SCHOOL, 1921. The first high school was built in 1917. It was a two-story structure and had eight rooms. The south wing was added in 1922. This photograph shows the building that became the north wing once additions were made to the structure.

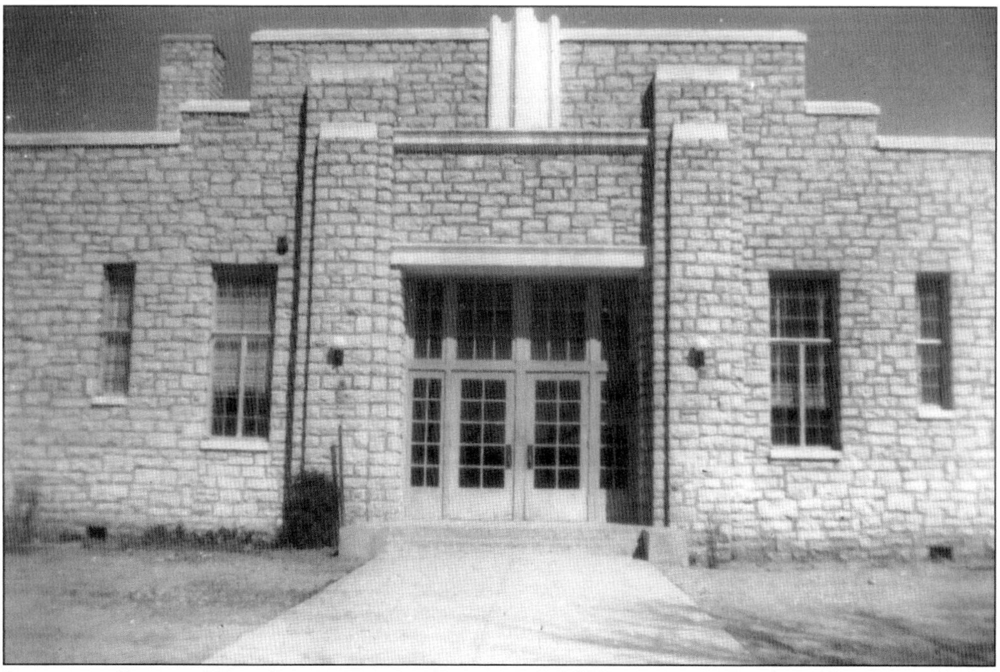

LAMPASAS JUNIOR HIGH SCHOOL, 1943. During World War II, many local children contributed to the war effort by buying U.S. Savings Stamps at school. A full stamp book could be redeemed for a war bond. During its long history, the rock structure pictured above served also as an elementary school. The main entrance is one of the city's few surviving examples of art deco. It was built in 1938.

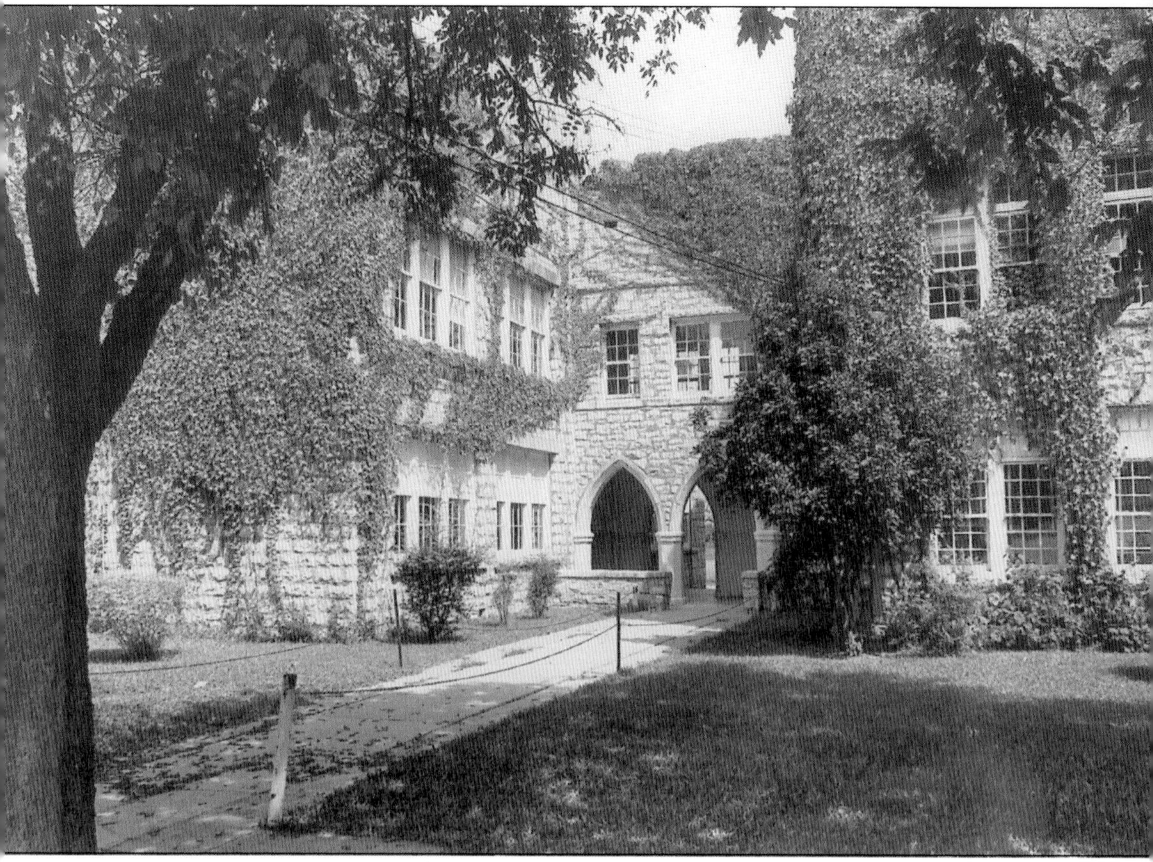

IVY-COVERED HIGH SCHOOL. The north and south wings of Lampasas High School were connected by arches, shown here. The image of the ivy-covered high school remains in the school song to this day, although the building itself no longer stands. (Courtesy of Gladden Corbin.)

Seven

The Badgers, the Hornets, and the Eagles

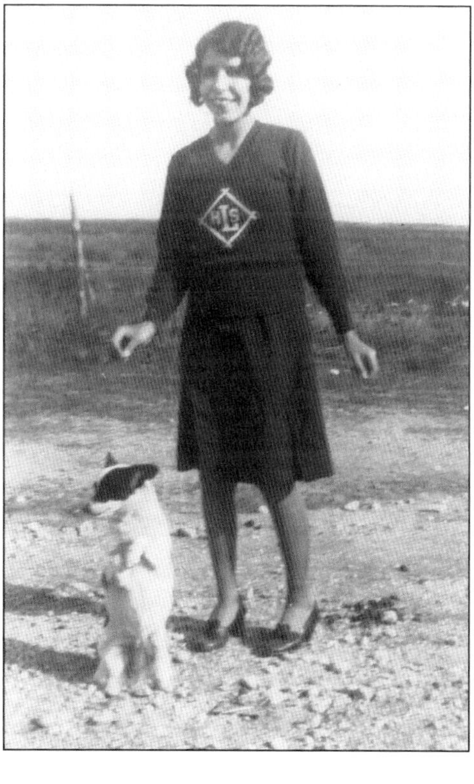

Sportsman's Paradise. Like most places in Texas, sports fans in Lampasas County are legion. Pauline Lang, the high school coed pictured here, supports the Lampasas Badgers. The Lometa school's mascot is the hornet. Prior to 1963, when public schools were integrated, the Lampasas Colored School adopted the eagle as its mascot. Hunting, fishing, and swimming also have a long history in Lampasas. And golf has been a mainstay since the city built a course in Hancock Park in the late 1940s. (Courtesy of Kay Pearce Bailey.)

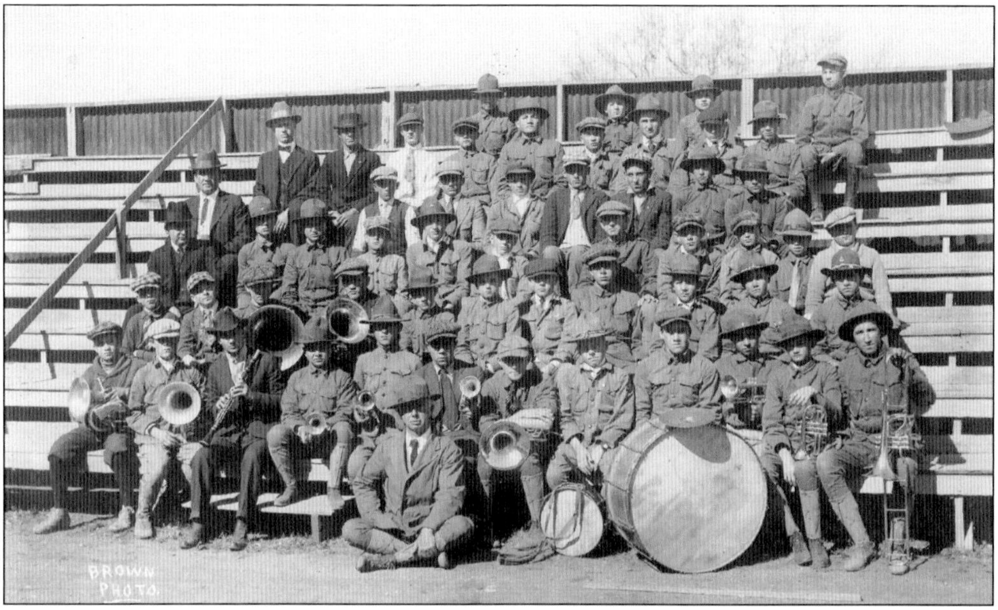

THE BOY SCOUT BAND, C. WORLD WAR I. The Boy Scout Band played at various events in Lampasas County, including a registration day event held in 1917 for the U.S. Army. The band also played at athletic events in the county. Lampasas schools may have had orchestras, glee clubs, or choral clubs, but they did not have school bands at this time.

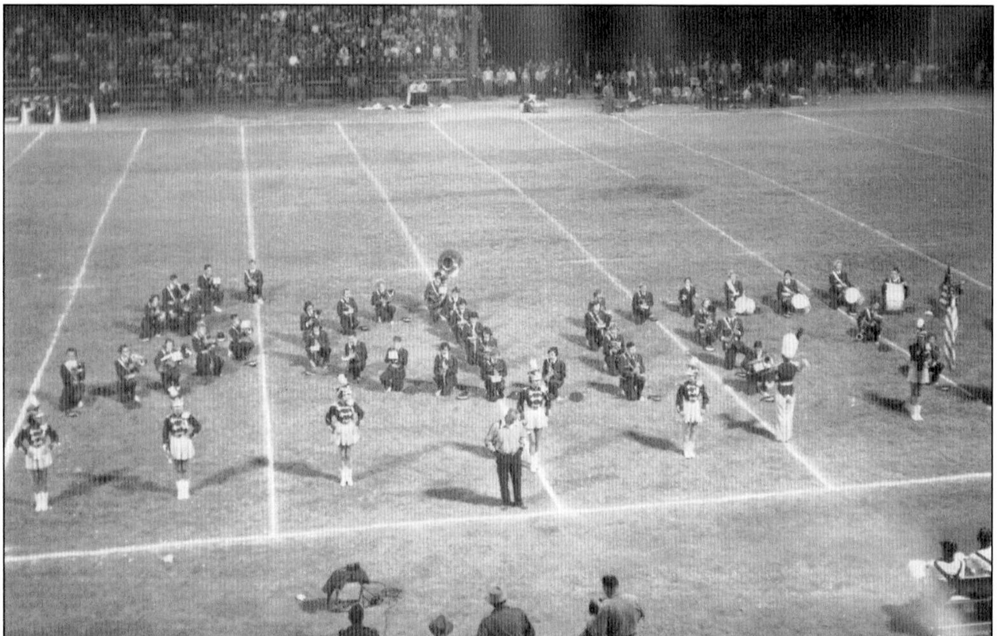

HALFTIME AT THE LAMPASAS-HAMILTON GAME, OCTOBER 22, 1954. The Lampasas High School band spells out "Sam" in honor of coach Sam Fowler at halftime. The photograph is inscribed to Coach Fowler, "with all our love and respect forever," and signed "L.T.P." or the Lucky Thirteen Peppers, a school pep club. Fowler and Curtis Bozarth were two of the most beloved coaches and teachers in the history of Lampasas schools.

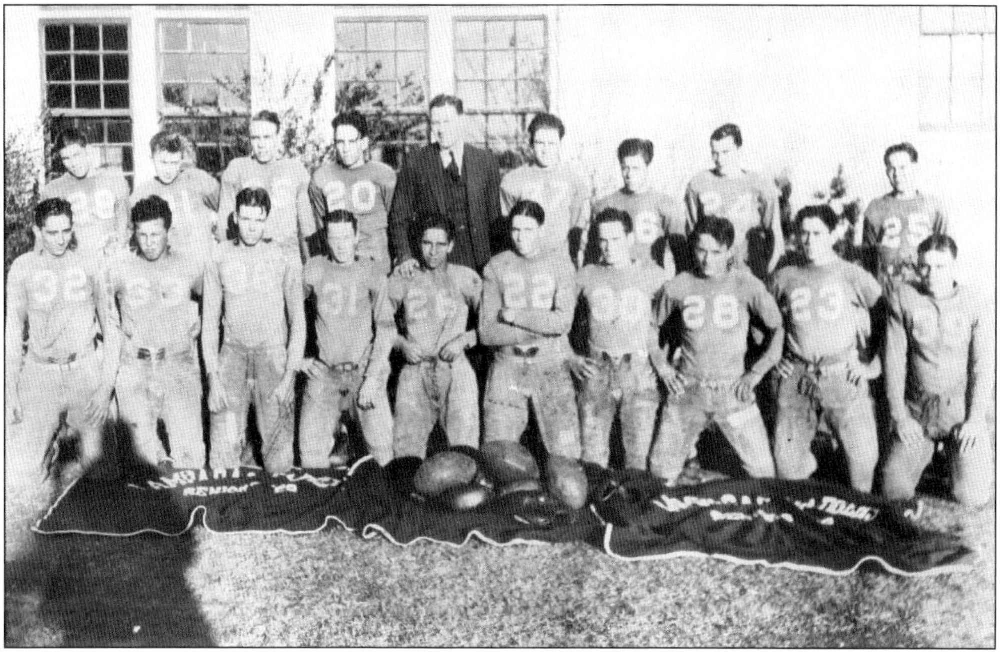

REGIONAL CHAMPIONSHIP CONTENDERS, 1930. This Lampasas High School football team garnered significant accolades. It was named Eastern Division Champion, East and West District Champion, and Bi-District Champion. It was a contender for the regional championship. Pictured here with Coach John Rowntree is the team that won 303 points that season. (Photograph by Virgil Wooten.)

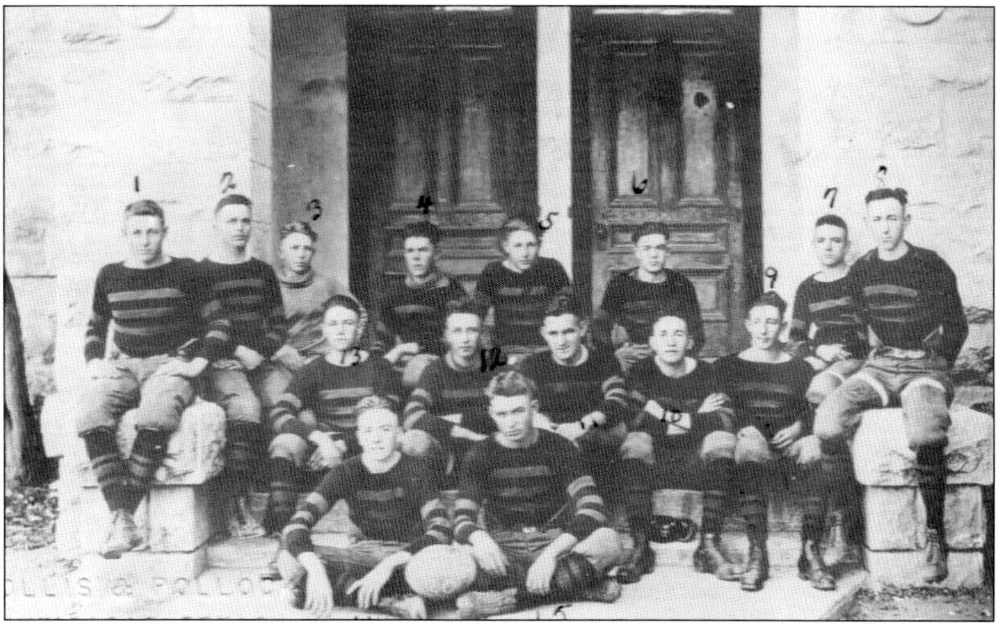

LAMPASAS HIGH SCHOOL FOOTBALL TEAM, 1920. The Lampasas High School Badgers are shown here in front of the entrance to the 1917 Lampasas High School building. The football rests between the right end and the fullback, as identified on the back of this picture postcard.

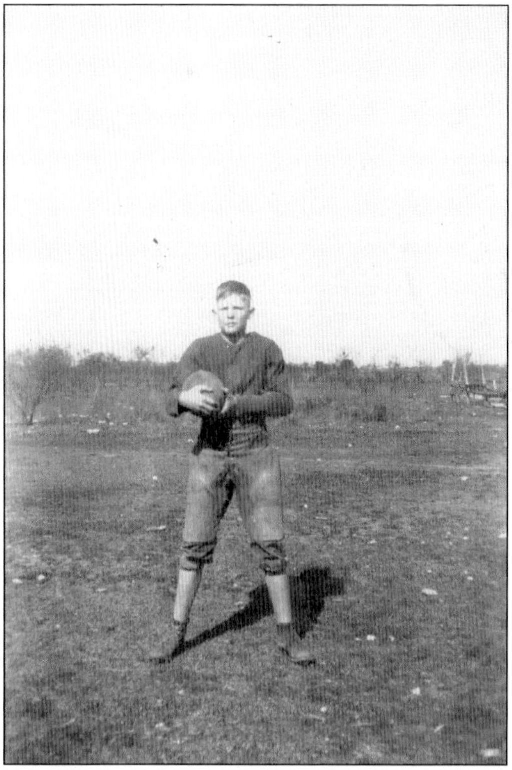

Willard Potts in Uniform, c. 1934. Willard Potts played both offense and defense for the Lometa Hornets. During the Depression, use of school buses was limited, so for out-of-town games, Frank Lee drove the team and what equipment it had on the back of his flatbed truck. (Courtesy of Janie Potts.)

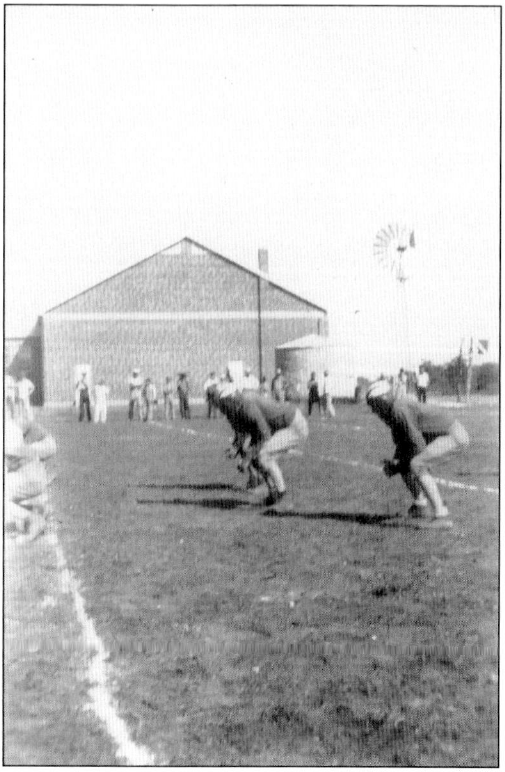

The Lometa Hornets on the Field, c. 1934. The Hornets are in the middle of a game in this photograph. Note the spectators standing alongside the field. They did not have bleachers or a grandstand. (Courtesy of Janie Potts.)

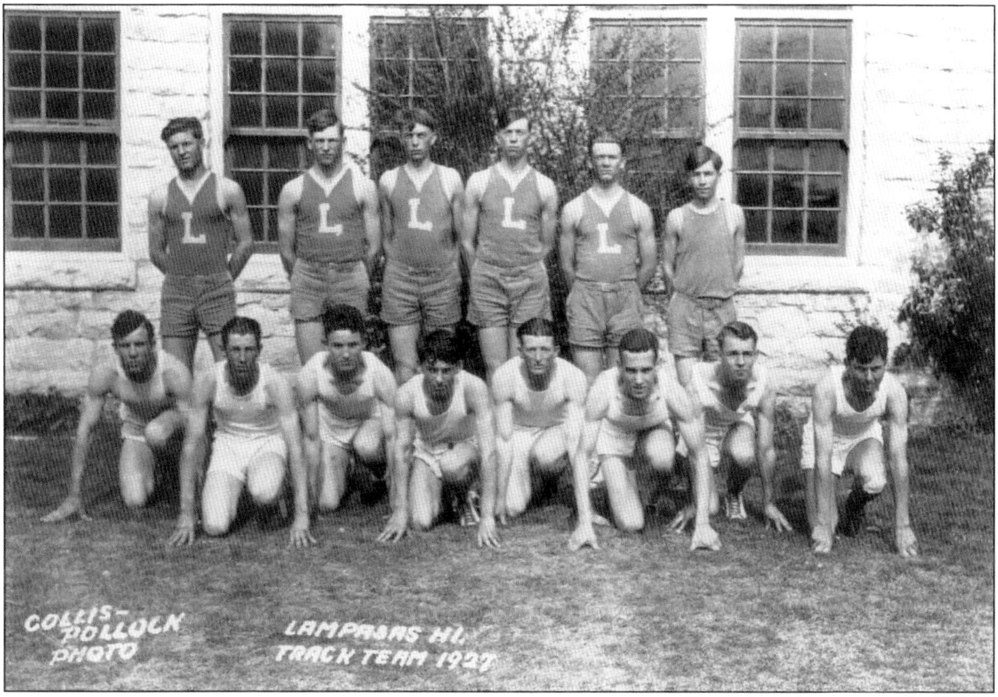

LAMPASAS HIGH SCHOOL TRACK TEAM, 1927. Winners on this team were Roy Cook, fourth from left top, who took second in the 880-yard run, and Olan Gamel, third from the left bottom, who achieved second in the 100-yard dash at the Texas Relays.

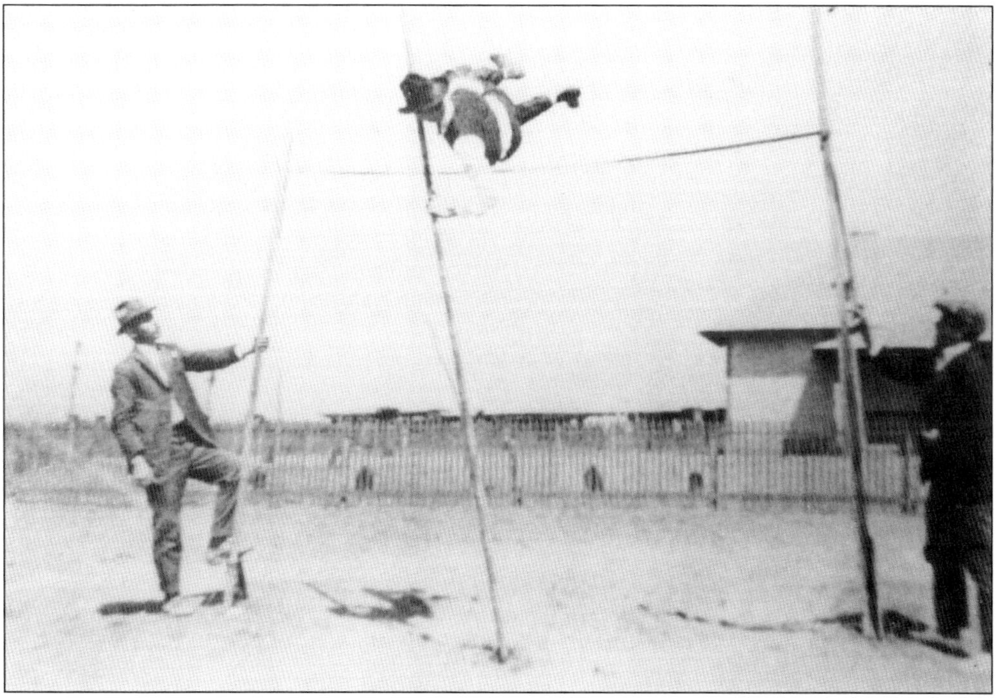

POLE VAULTING IN UNITY. Street clothing was worn for pole-vaulting practice in Unity.

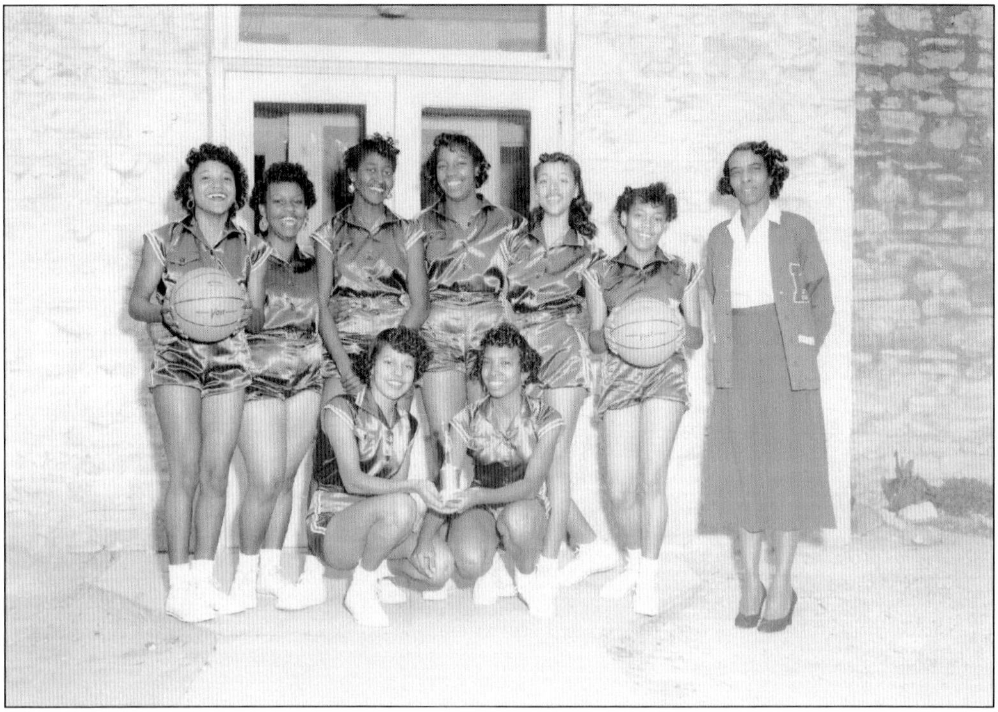

The Lampasas Colored School Basketball Team, Early 1950s. The Lampasas Colored School had its own teams and mascot, the eagle. The girls' basketball team is shown here with Ernestine Patrick, who taught at the school. Principal Billie Orman coached both the boys' and the girls' teams. The team proudly displays the trophy that it won. (Photograph by Virgil Wooten.)

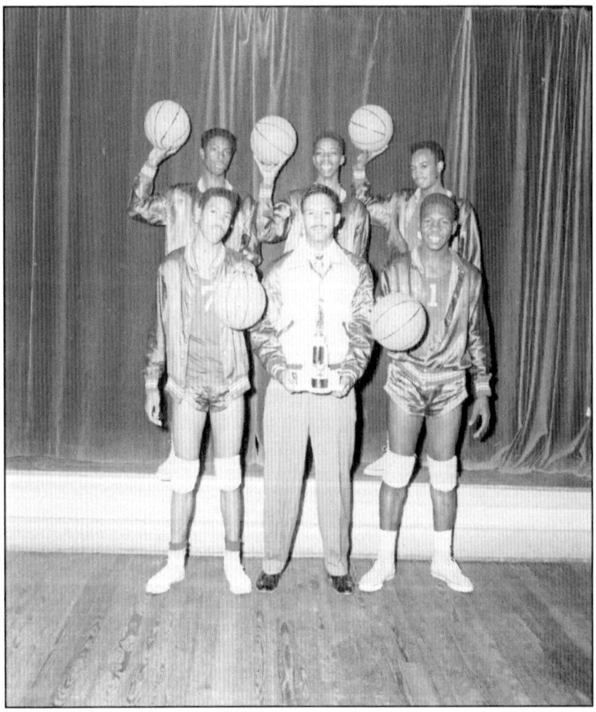

The Lampasas Colored School Basketball Team, Early 1950s. Pictured here with a trophy are some of the members of the boys' basketball team with their coach and the school principal Billie Orman. Lampasas Colored School teams played rivals only on Saturdays. The white teams reserved the gym on the weekdays. (Photograph by Virgil Wooten.)

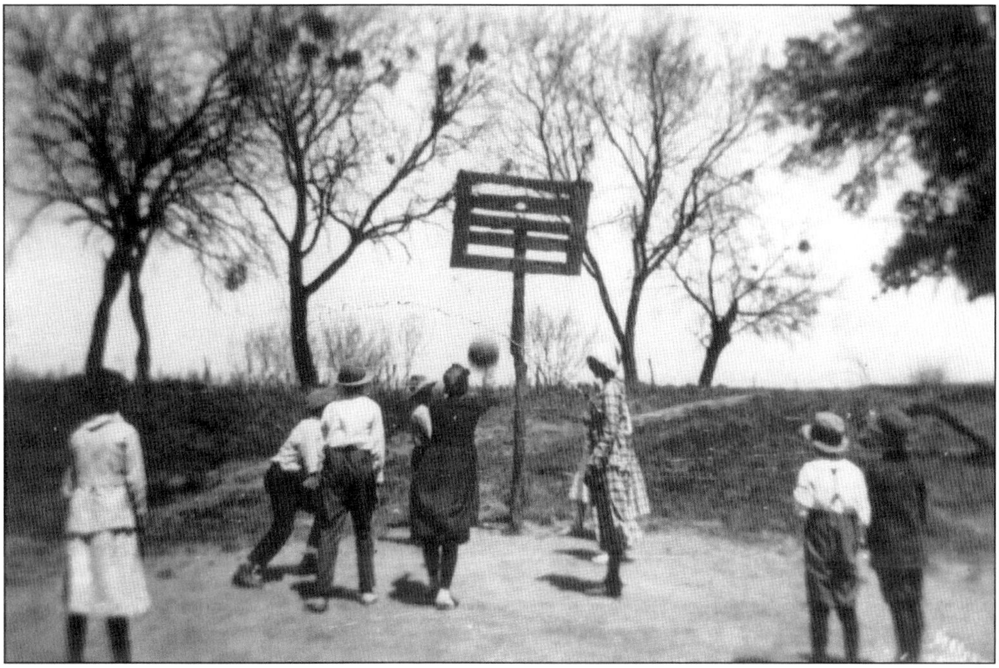

BASKETBALL GAME IN LITTLE BEND, C. 1918. Pick-up games in the playground occurred at recess, on weekends, or during other free time. Formal games were played outside too, until modern gymnasiums were built.

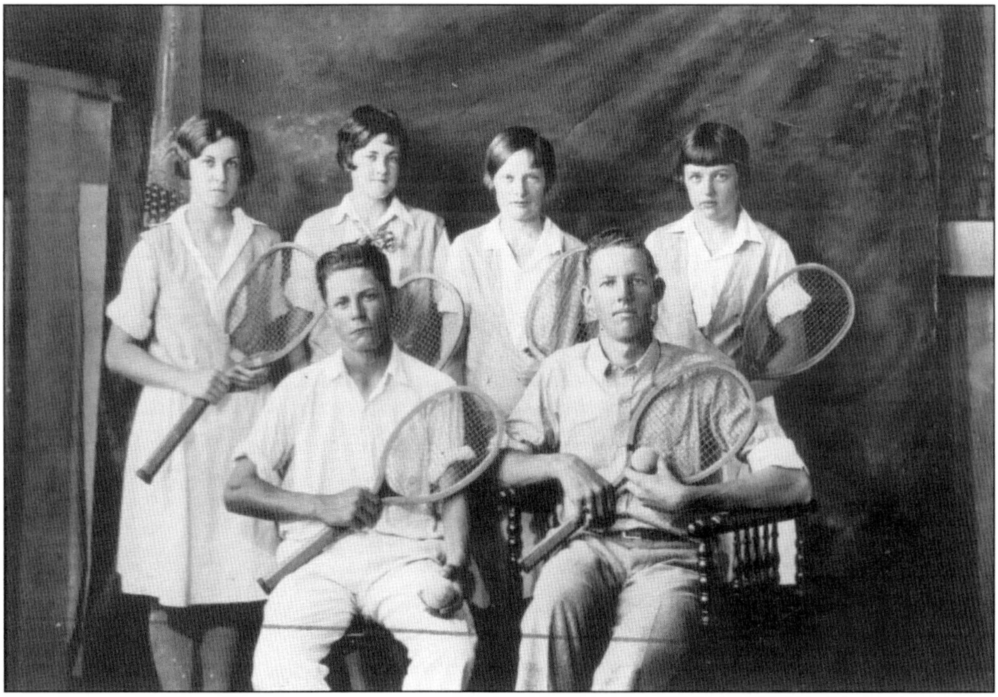

LAMPASAS TENNIS TEAM, 1927. Cliff Whigham, bottom right, placed first in doubles at the county meet. Notice the wooden tennis rackets.

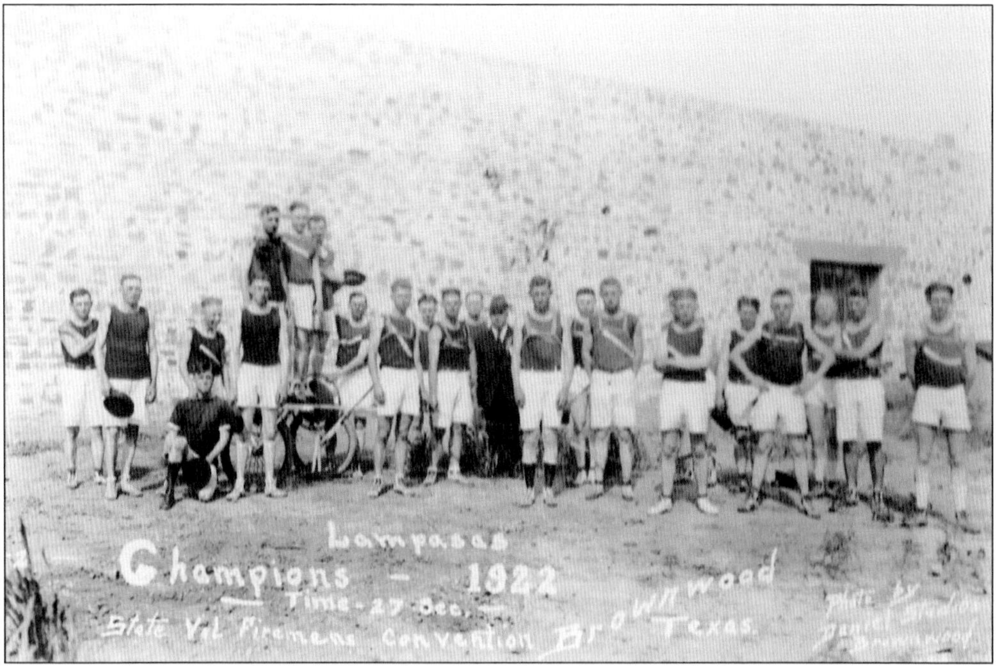

LAMPASAS VOLUNTEER FIRE DEPARTMENT CHAMPIONS, 1922. The Lampasas Volunteer Firemen were champions in the cart race at the State Volunteer Firemen's Convention in Brownwood, Texas, in 1922. Their cart is shown on the left side of the group.

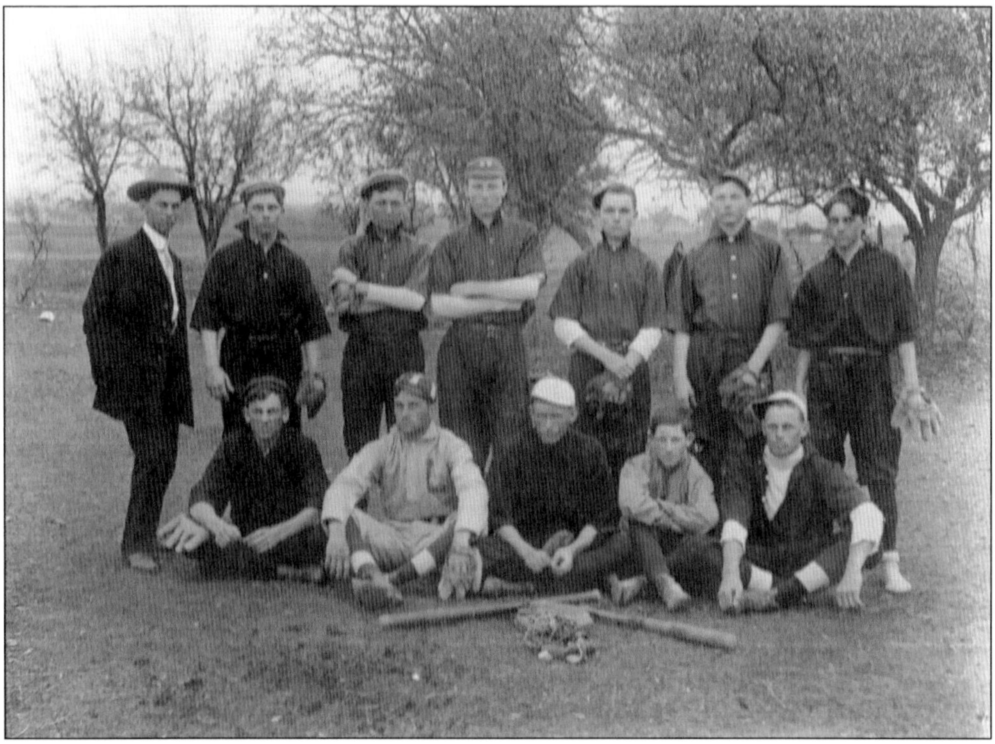

LOMETA BASEBALL TEAM. Note how styles of baseball uniforms differed from those of today.

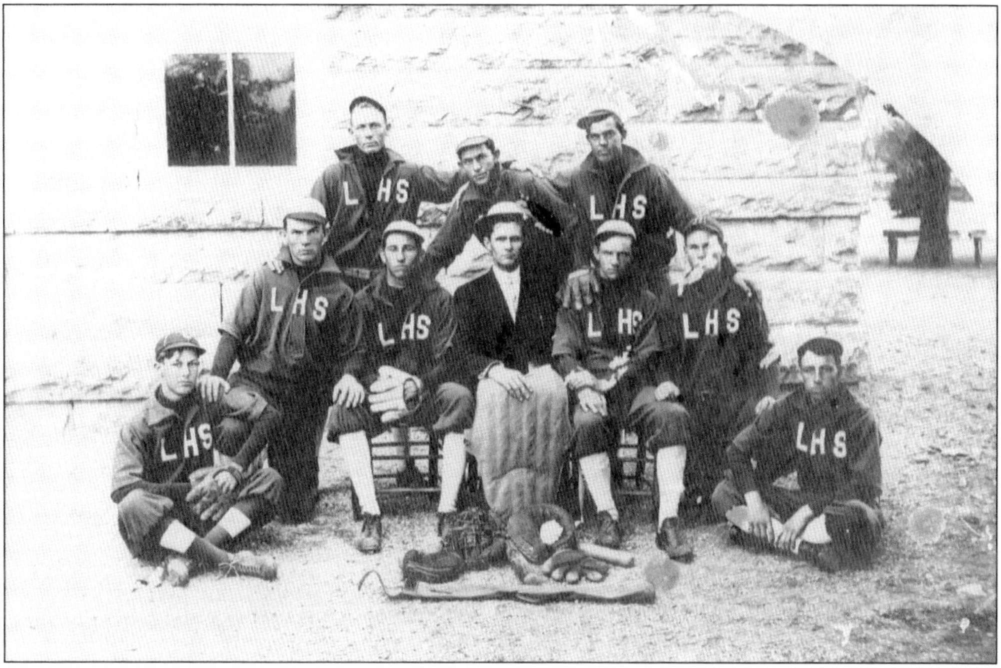

LAMPASAS HIGH SCHOOL BASEBALL TEAM, 1910S. Dudley Moore (1895–1961), a future teacher and coach for the Badgers, is seated at the right of the second row of this baseball team.

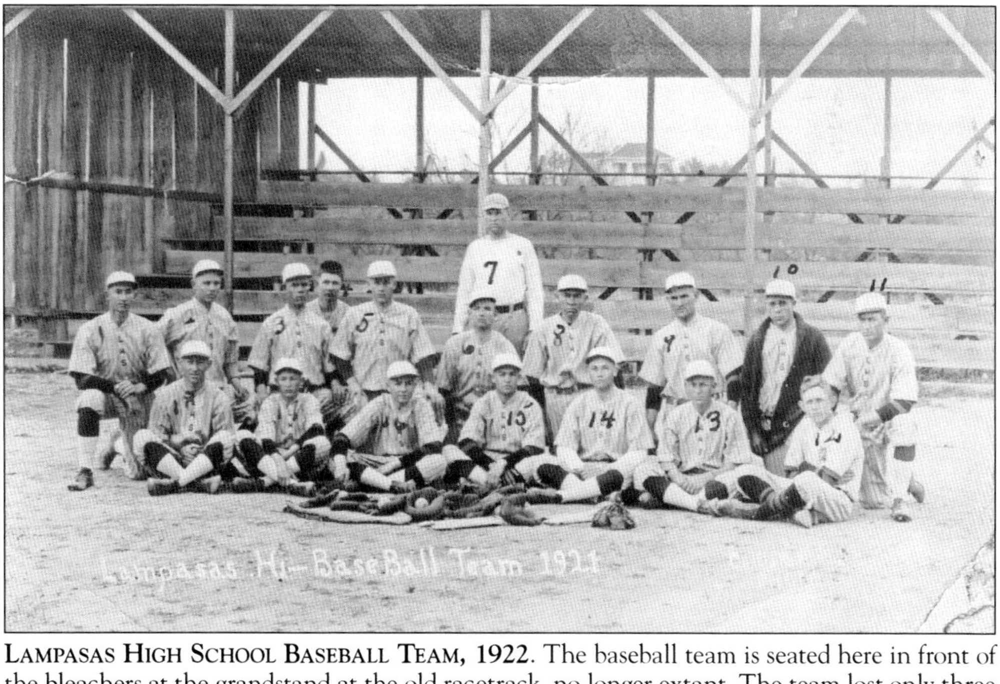

LAMPASAS HIGH SCHOOL BASEBALL TEAM, 1922. The baseball team is seated here in front of the bleachers at the grandstand at the old racetrack, no longer extant. The team lost only three games that season. Coach Dudley Moore is No. 7, standing at the back.

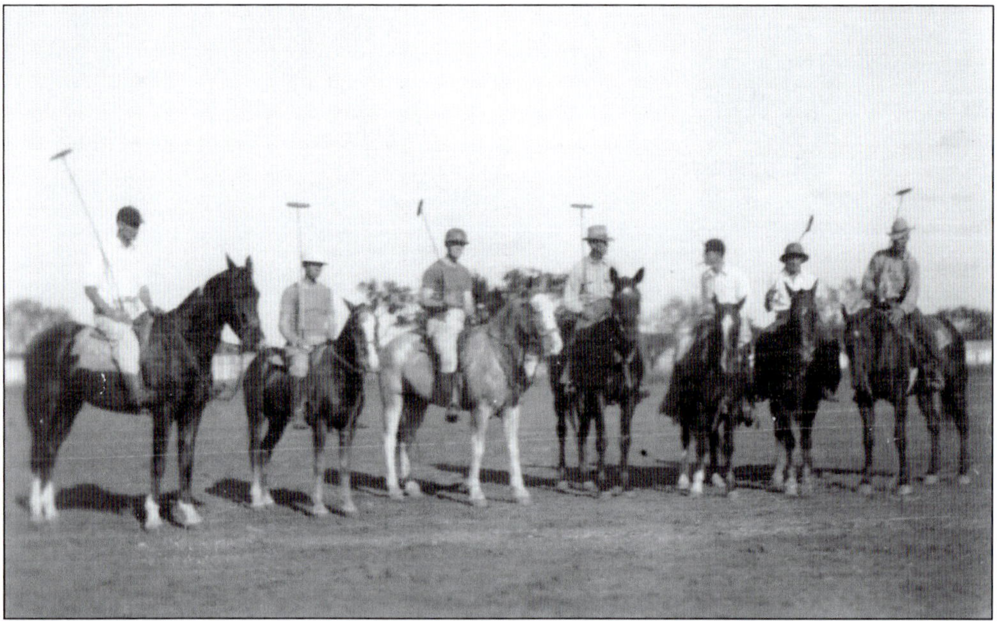

LAMPASAS POLO TEAM. Members of the Lampasas polo team, the Yellow Jackets, are lined up with their mallets up. An August 1933 newspaper article described a game between the University of Texas and the Yellow Jackets: "This was one of the fastest polo games ever played on the local field. Despite the fact that Lampasas lost, the contest was thoroughly enjoyed by the large crowd in attendance."

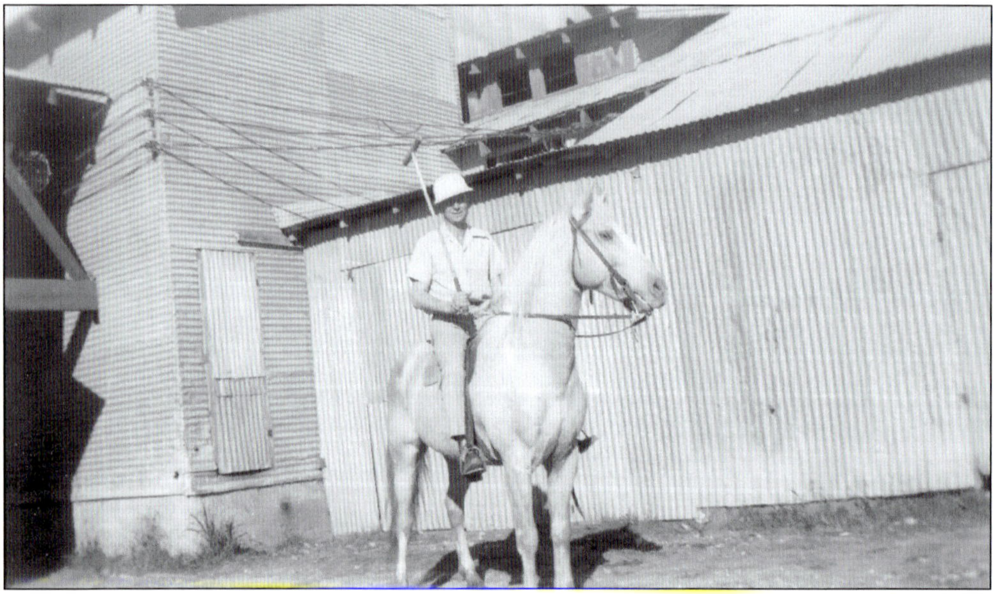

CHOC GILLEN ON POLO PONY, LATE 1930S. Charles "Choc" Gillen's father, William Cortis (W. C.) Gillen, bred and trained race horses and established the first polo team in Lampasas. His sons, including Choc, were on the polo team. Choc is shown here on one of the Gillen ponies. (Courtesy of the Gillen family.)

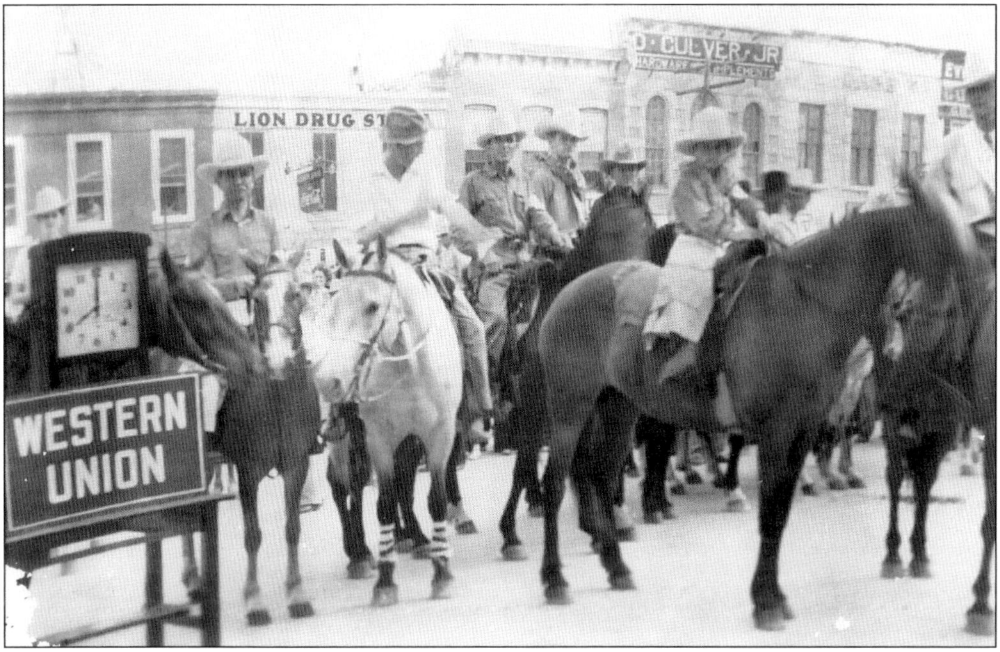

Riders in Lampasas Ready for the Marathon, 1936. The Lampasas-Dallas Marathon was held in 1936 in observance of the 100th anniversary of Texas Independence. Participants rode on horseback the distance between the Lampasas County Courthouse and the gates of the Centennial Exposition in Dallas. Bill Shirley Standard is the young rider shown astride a horse at the right.

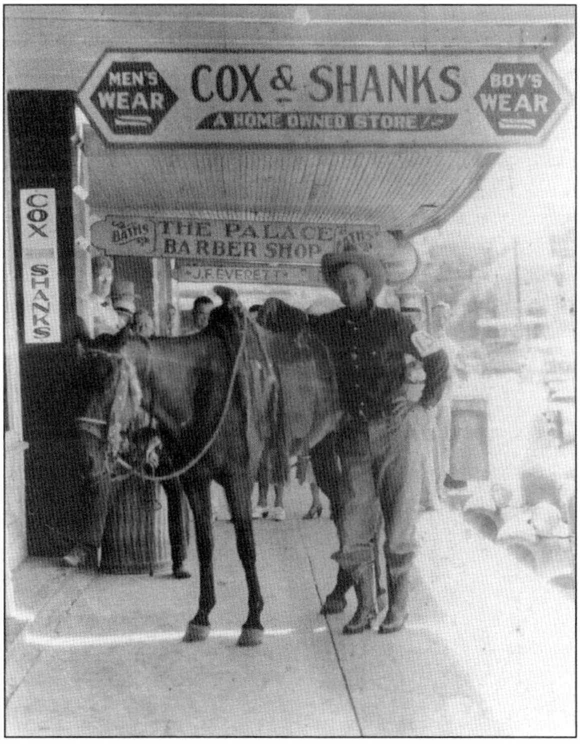

D. A. "Leck" Roberts with Hazel, after Winning the Dallas Marathon, 1936. Roberts won the Great Texas Centennial Horse Race in a contest of 100 horses and riders. The prize was $500 in cash and a Texas Centennial Saddle. Hazel, his horse, wears the saddle in this photograph, and Roberts shows off a pair of boots given to him by the store Cox and Shanks. (Courtesy of Linda Rogers.)

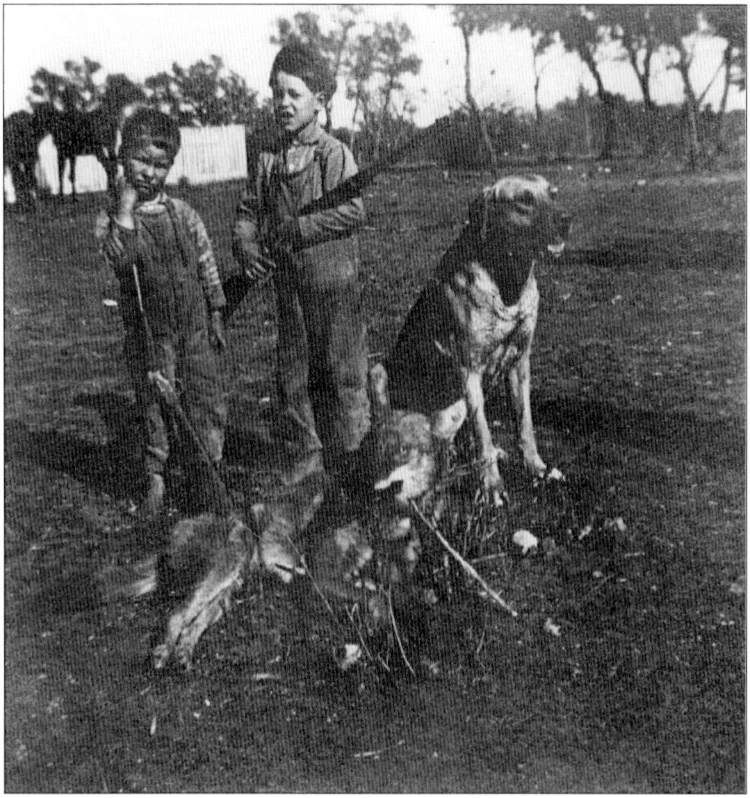

Otis Wright and Norman Wright, 1911. These two shot this wolf and were proud enough to have it recorded for posterity. (Courtesy of Suzane Killingsworth.)

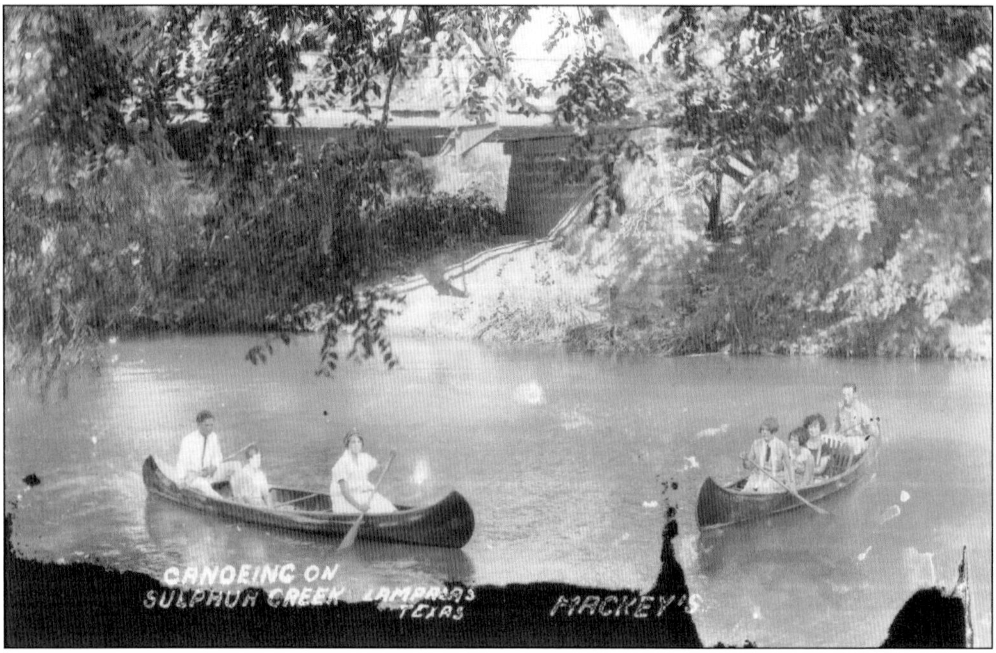

Canoeing on Sulphur Creek, Lampasas. Sulphur Creek offered calm waters for boating. The Chestnut Street Bridge can be seen in the background.

THREE LARGE CATFISH, SEPTEMBER 1955. From left to right, Randolph Scott, Jimmy Wright, Wayne Faught, and baby Lowell Wright admire the enormous catfish the men caught in the Colorado River in Lampasas. (Courtesy of Suzane Killingsworth.)

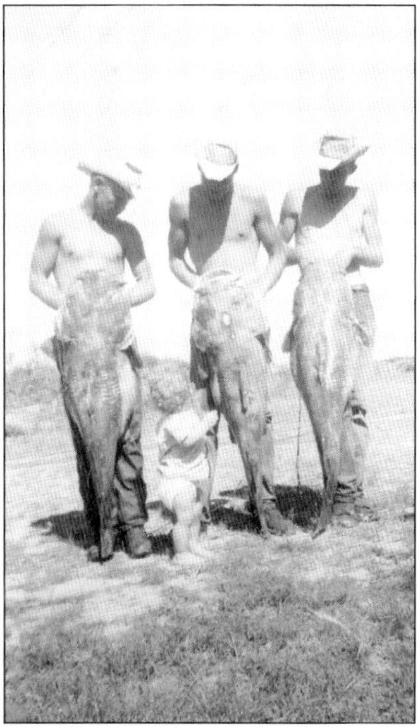

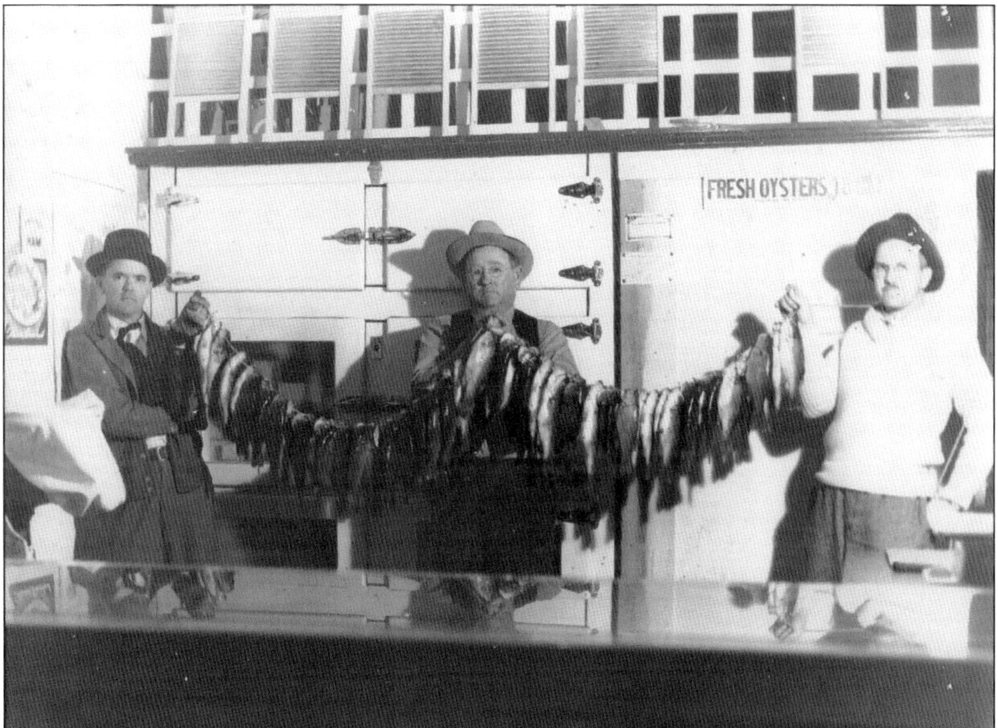

CATCH OF THE DAY. From left to right, Clyde Northington, Oscar Bolding, and James Abney hold up their impressive catch in the Ice House on Fourth Street in Lampasas. Notice the sign "Fresh Oysters Today." (Photograph by Lucile Standard.)

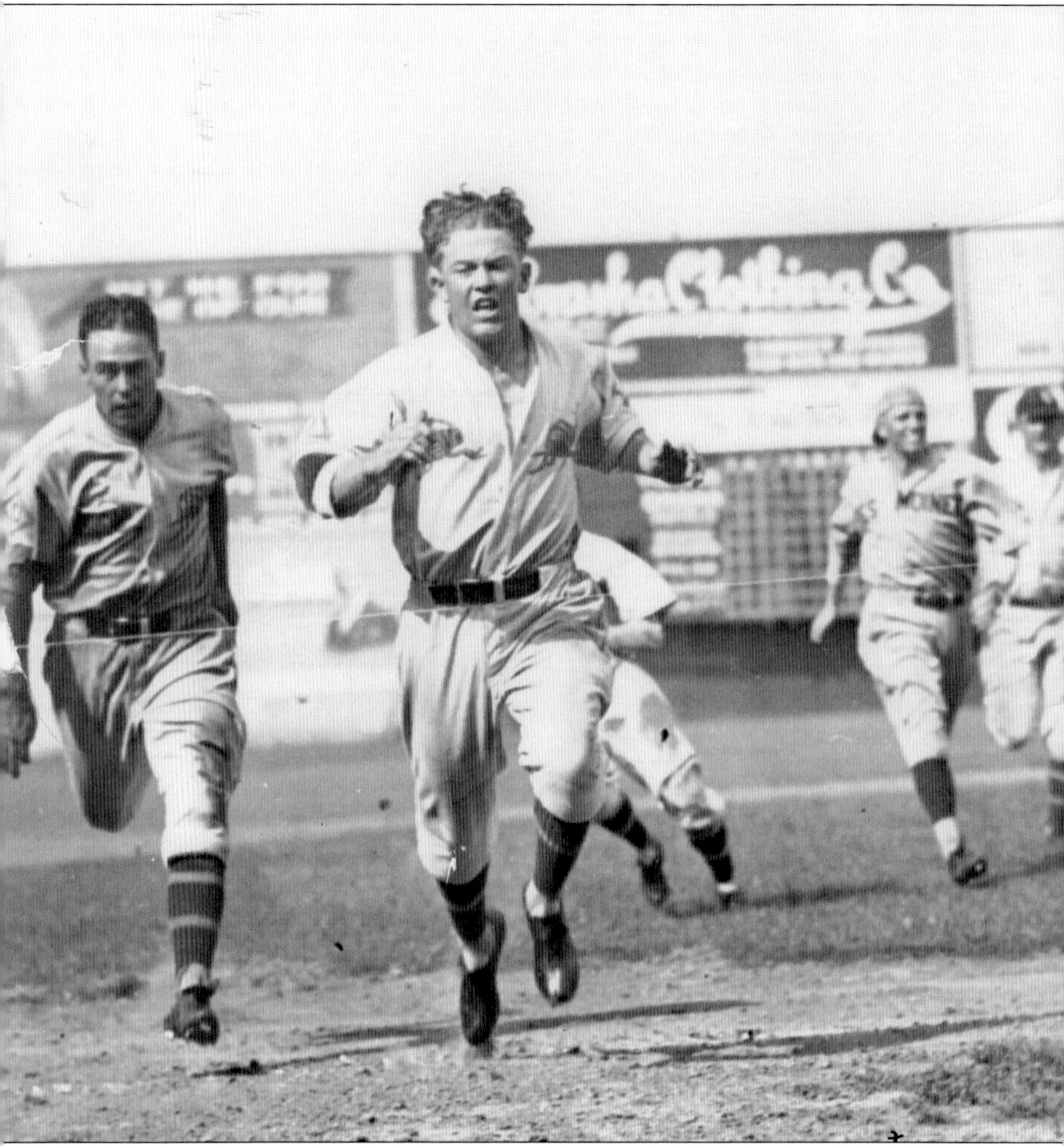

Fats Hetherly. C. W. "Fats" Hetherly (1907–1969) was drafted by the Detroit Tigers after playing in the minor leagues during the late 1920s and early 1930s. He joked, "I stuck in the majors just long enough to get a ham sandwich." After leaving professional baseball, he went on to manage a successful concrete business in Killeen, but settled in Lampasas with his wife and children. (Courtesy of Judy Hetherly.)

Eight

SPREADING THE WORD

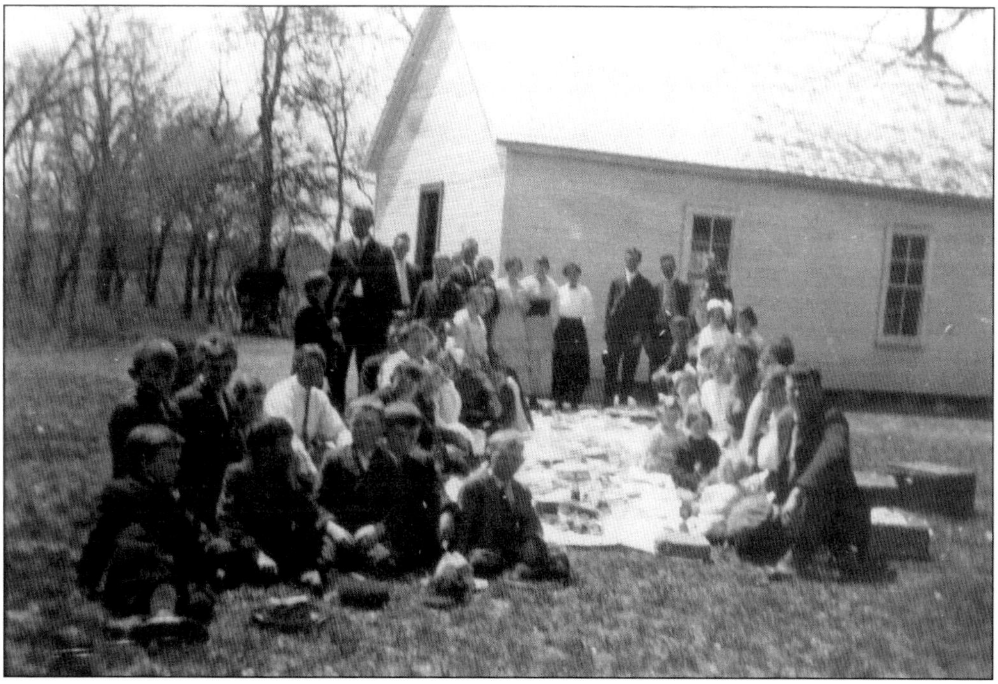

LUCY CREEK BAPTIST CHURCH. Sometimes after church, congregations would spread tablecloths on the ground and have lunch together. Here the members of the Lucy Creek Baptist Church are having "dinner on the ground," as the practice was called, about 1914. Until the church disbanded in 1927, its services were held in the Pecan Grove School.

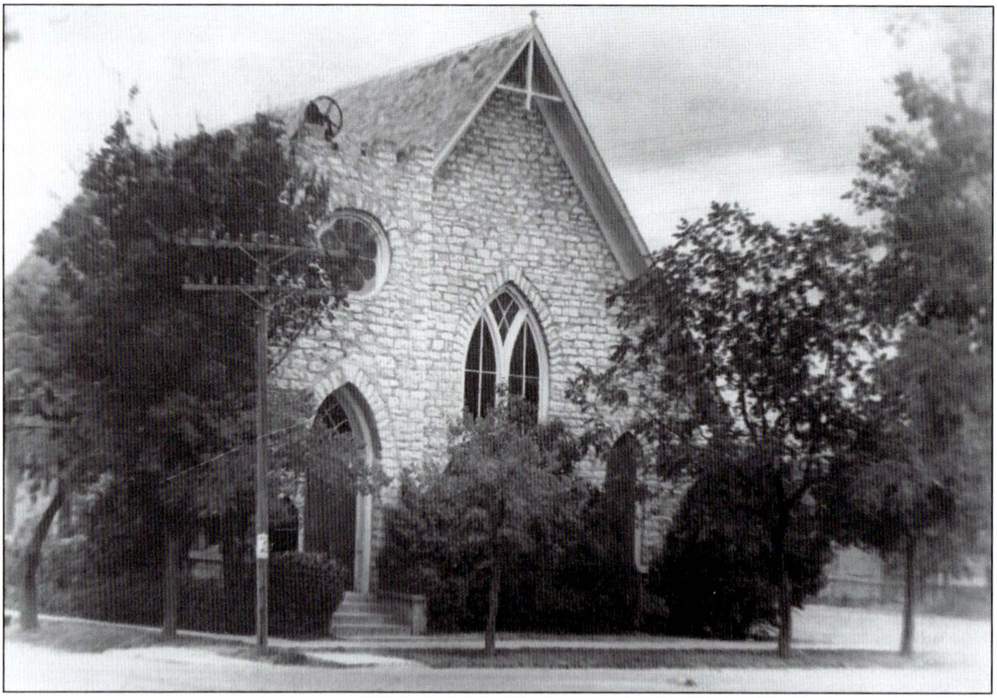

ST. MARY'S EPISCOPAL CHURCH. Built from 1884 to 1890 at 501 South Chestnut Street, St. Mary's Episcopal Church is the oldest church building in Lampasas. This photograph shows the original central window, which featured Gothic-style tracery and simple colored-glass panes. It was later replaced by the stained-glass memorial window seen today.

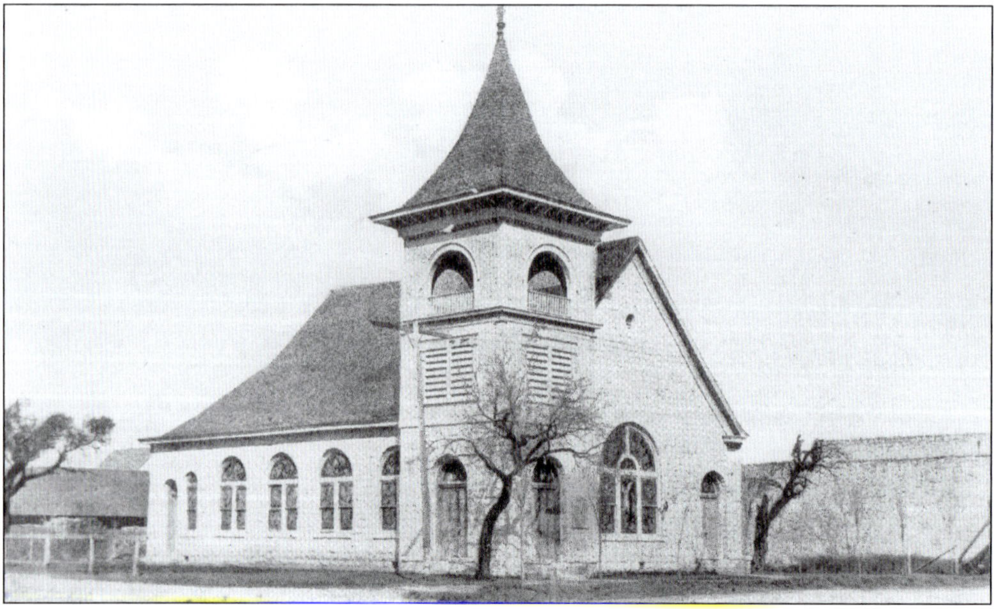

CENTRAL CHRISTIAN CHURCH. A funeral chapel since 2006, this building located at 201 East Third Street was constructed in 1905 by the Central Christian Church (Disciples of Christ). The Resurrection window, which dominates the front of the building, was donated by the church's Ladies Aid Society.

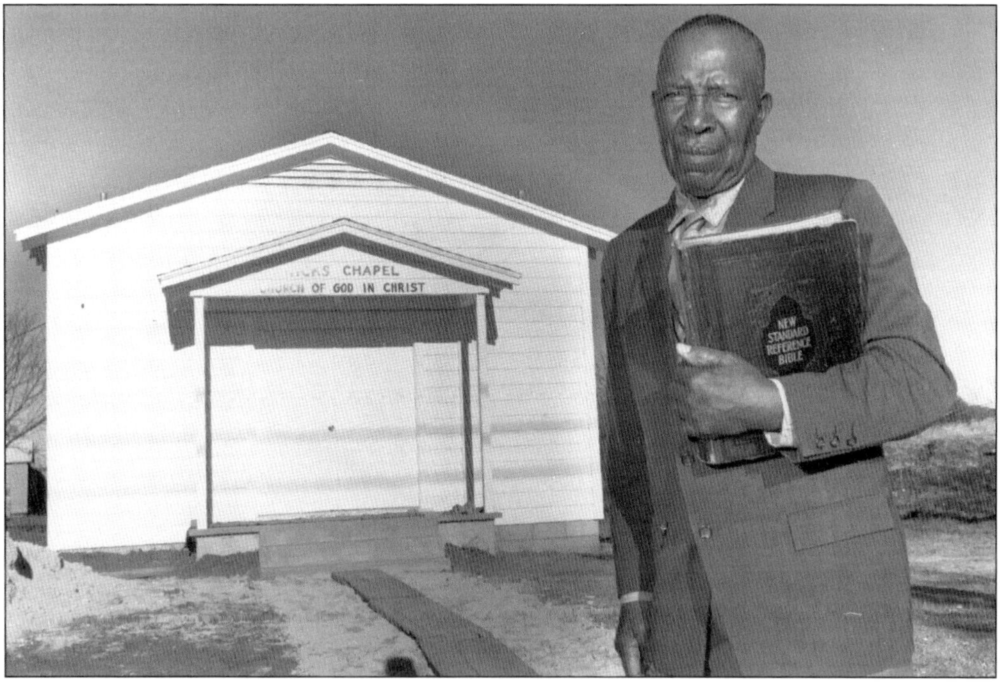

HICKS CHAPEL, CHURCH OF GOD IN CHRIST. The Reverend Thomas Hicks came to Lampasas in 1928 to establish a church. When he died in 1982, he had led his flock for 51 years, with his wife, Ruby, at his side all the while. The Hicks Chapel still stands on the banks of Sulphur Creek near the Key Avenue bridge. (Courtesy of the *Lampasas Dispatch Record*.)

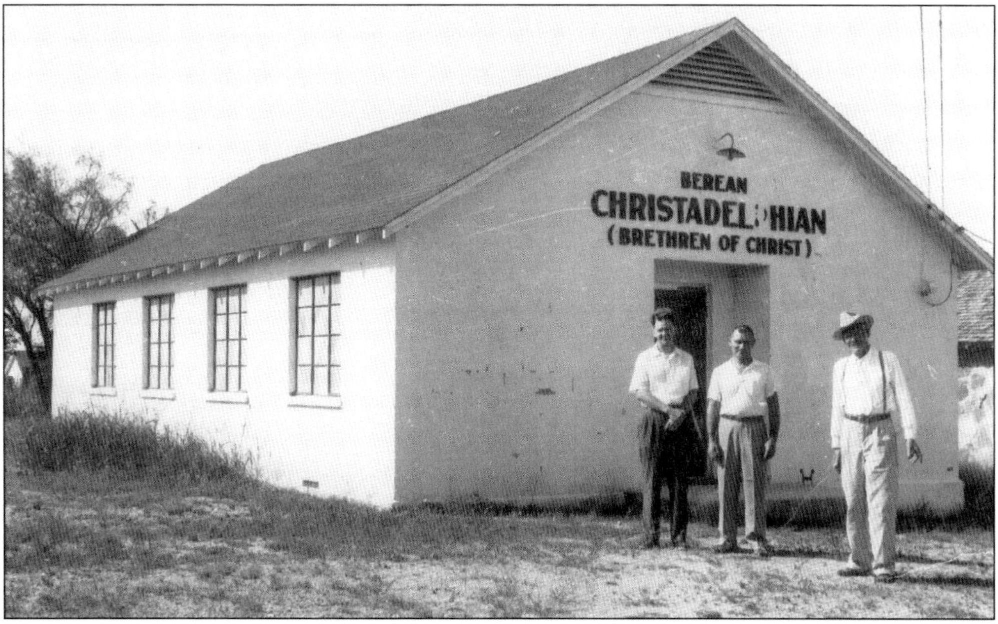

CHRISTADELPHIAN CHURCH, 1955. The denomination was active in Lampasas as early as 1885, when Christadelphians from more than 20 Texas counties held a 10-day Fraternal Gathering at Hanna Springs. Despite the auspicious beginning, the Lampasas congregation dwindled. However in 1936, the church began to flourish again. (Courtesy of Ruby Wolfe.)

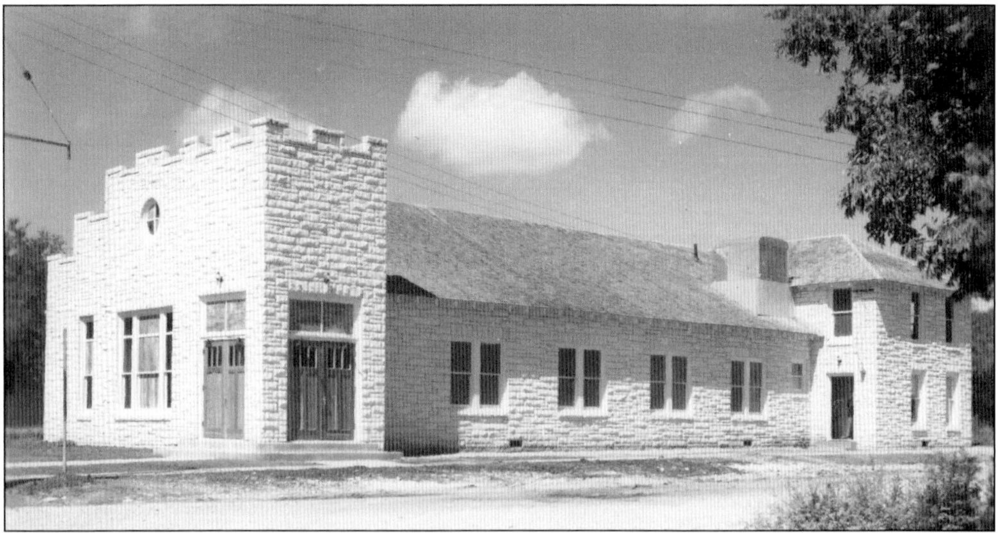

FIRST STREET CHURCH OF CHRIST, C. 1953. In 1931, First Street Church of Christ completed its first building at First and Walnut Streets. Rapid growth necessitated several additions, until the modest frame structure became a large stone-faced complex. On Christmas Eve 1978, much of the church was destroyed by fire. Rebuilding began immediately. The new church was dedicated on April 13, 1980. (Courtesy of the First Street Church of Christ.)

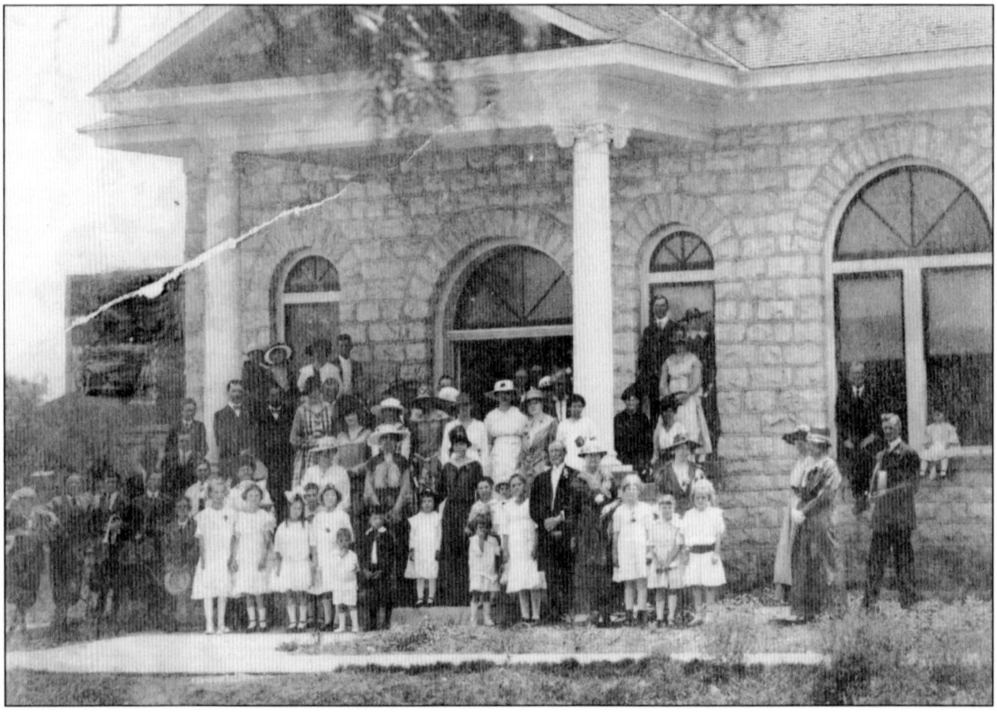

FIRST PRESBYTERIAN CHURCH. A proud congregation gathers in front of the First Presbyterian Church in Lampasas, which was built in 1916 at Chestnut and Third Streets. The original church was built in the early 1880s at Fifth and Walnut Streets, along the mule-drawn trolley route. The 1916 building filled the needs of the congregation until 1959, when the present church building was constructed on the same site.

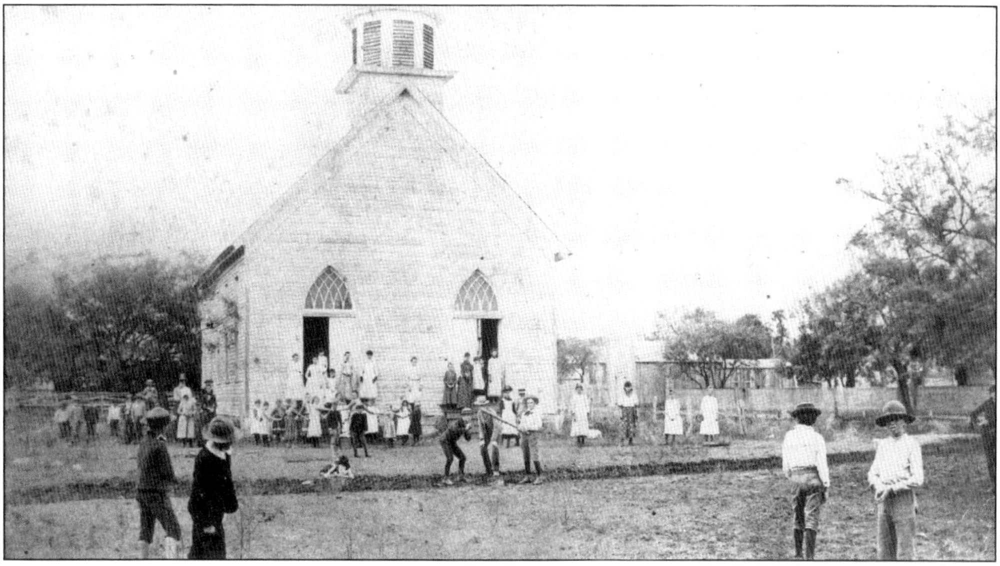

ESPYVILLE PRESBYTERIAN CHURCH, C. 1907. The original Presbyterian church at Espyville was built in 1894, and it also served as a school. These Presbyterians also had a church in Lampasas at Walnut and Second Streets called the Lampasas Espyville Congregation. In 1920, the Espyville church and all of its property became part of the First Presbyterian Church in Lampasas.

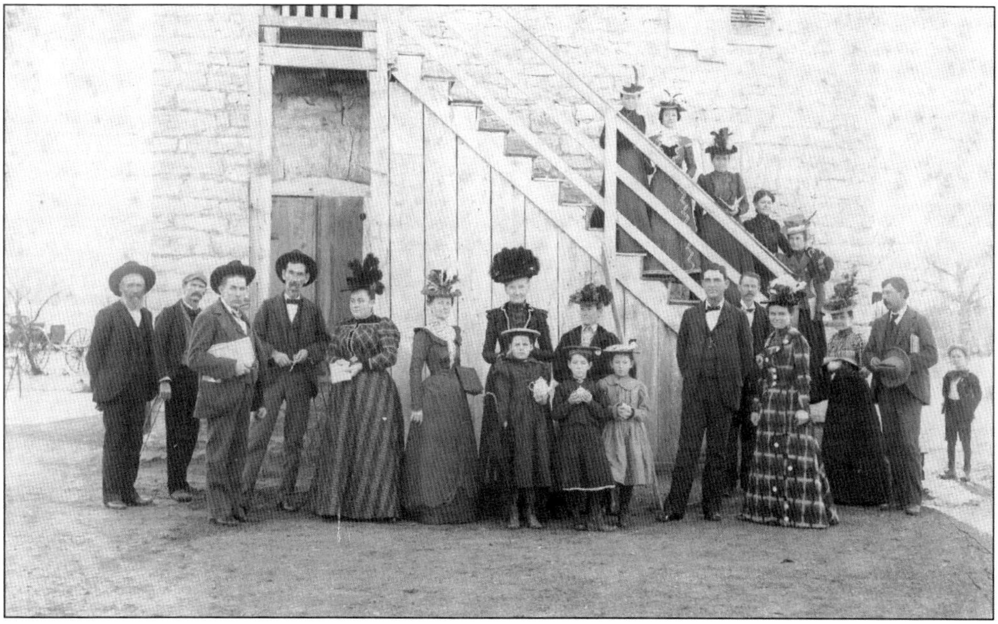

FIRST CHURCH OF CHRIST, SCIENTIST. Christian Scientists pose at the old Aten College building before they constructed their church at 204 South Broad Street about 1906. Two people have been identified to date, G. W. Clements, third from the left, and his wife, Annie Laurie Stokes Clements, fifth from the left. (Courtesy of Ann Richey Oliver.)

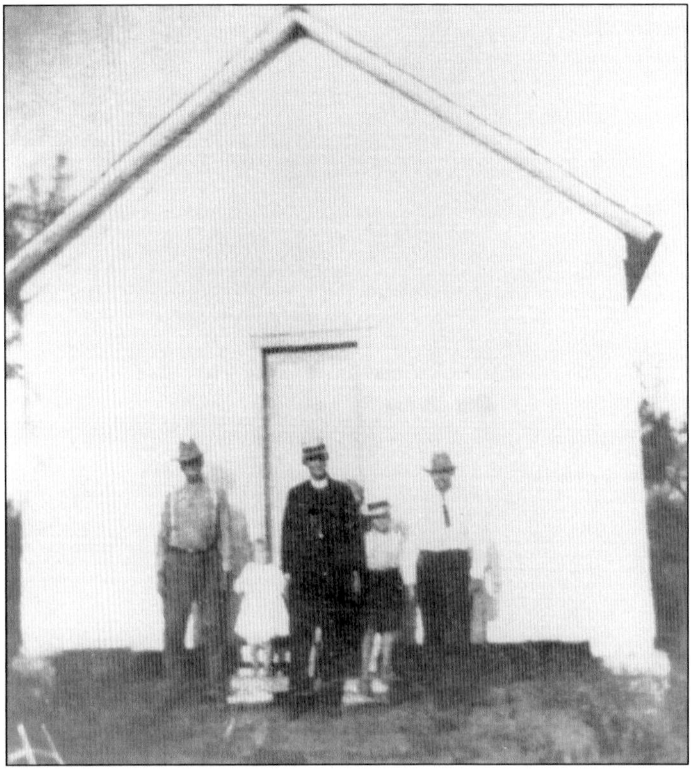

WITTENBURG CHAPEL. The first Roman Catholic church in Lampasas County was built on the ranch of William Mark Wittenburg, who came to Lampasas County in 1879 and settled near what would one day be Lometa. Pictured here in front of the chapel, from left to right, are William E. Wittenburg, Cecilia Wittenburg, Fr. P. A. Heckman, Earl Blake, and Joe Morgan. (Courtesy of Linda Klose.)

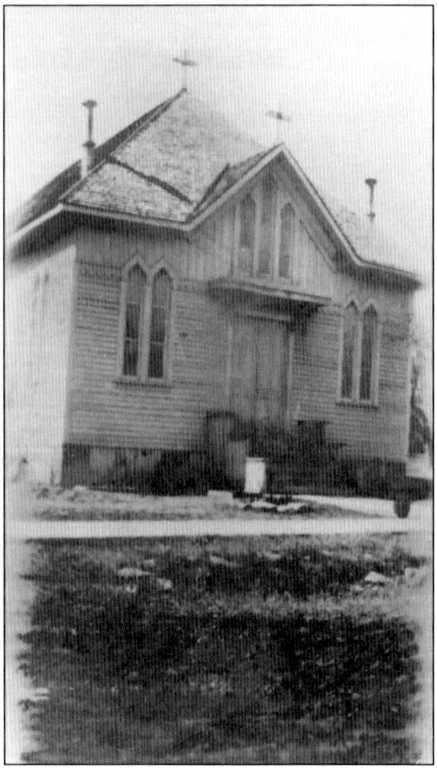

ST. MARY'S CATHOLIC CHURCH, 1885. The first St. Mary's building in the city of Lampasas was constructed in 1885 at Broad and Fifth Streets. However, the church did not get its first resident priest, Fr. Thomas A. Ryan, until 1927. It was during his tenure that the Church of the Good Shepherd was built in Lometa.

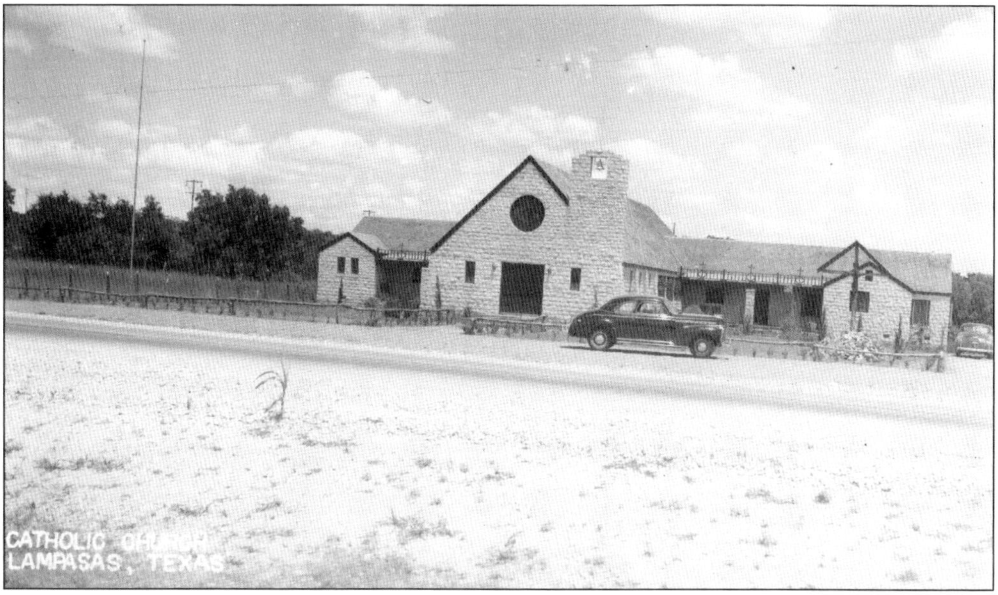

ST. MARY'S CATHOLIC CHURCH, 1941. Fr. William F. Roach, who served from 1939 to 1945, undertook a building program that included a church and rectory on North Key Avenue. For Spanish-speaking communicants, St. Christopher's was built on the banks of Sulphur Creek near the Fourth Street bridge. St. Mary's on Key Avenue was destroyed by fire in 1970. A new structure built on the site was dedicated in 1972. (Courtesy of Jane McMillin.)

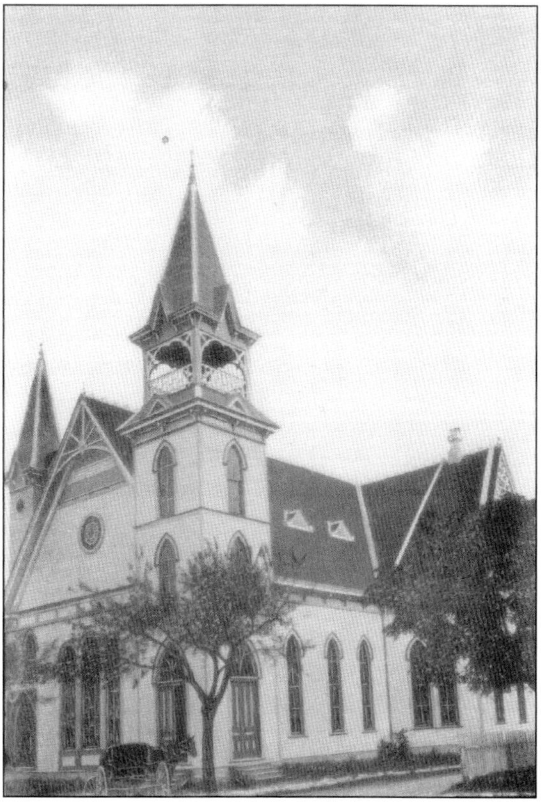

FIRST UNITED METHODIST CHURCH. In 1900, the congregation of the First United Methodist moved into this building, located at Grand Avenue (later Key Avenue) and Second Street. The new church accommodated the steadily growing membership until 1966, when it moved to its present location on U.S. Highway 190 East. (Courtesy of Merritt Romans.)

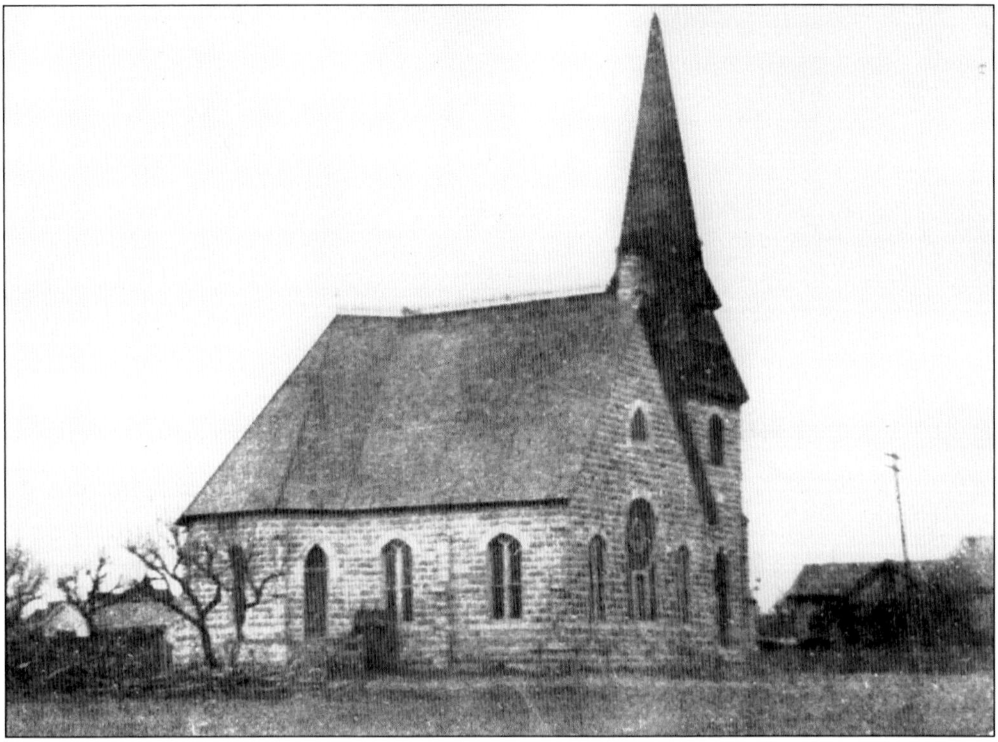

First Baptist Church of Lampasas. Destroyed by fire in 1937, this church building, located at Grand Avenue (later Key Avenue) and Third Street, had been the place of worship for the First Baptist Church since 1891. After the building was destroyed by fire, a brick and stone structure was built on the same site. Stone that had been salvaged from the original church was used around the foundation of the new sanctuary.

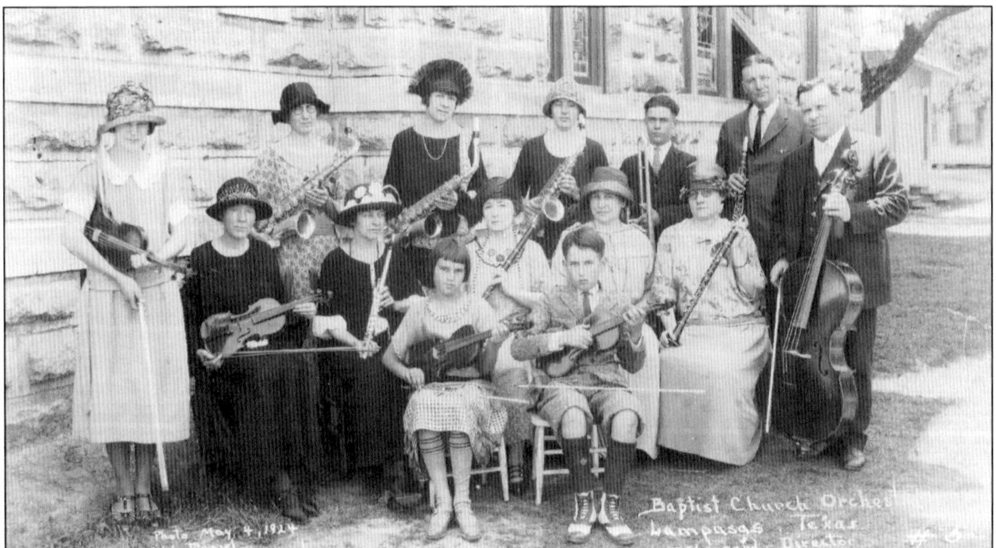

First Baptist Church Orchestra. Musicians pose for a picture outside the church building that burned in 1937. Three of the orchestra members have been identified: Dora Packer, seated first from left; H. H. Packer, standing first from right; and Ester Stokes, seated third from left.

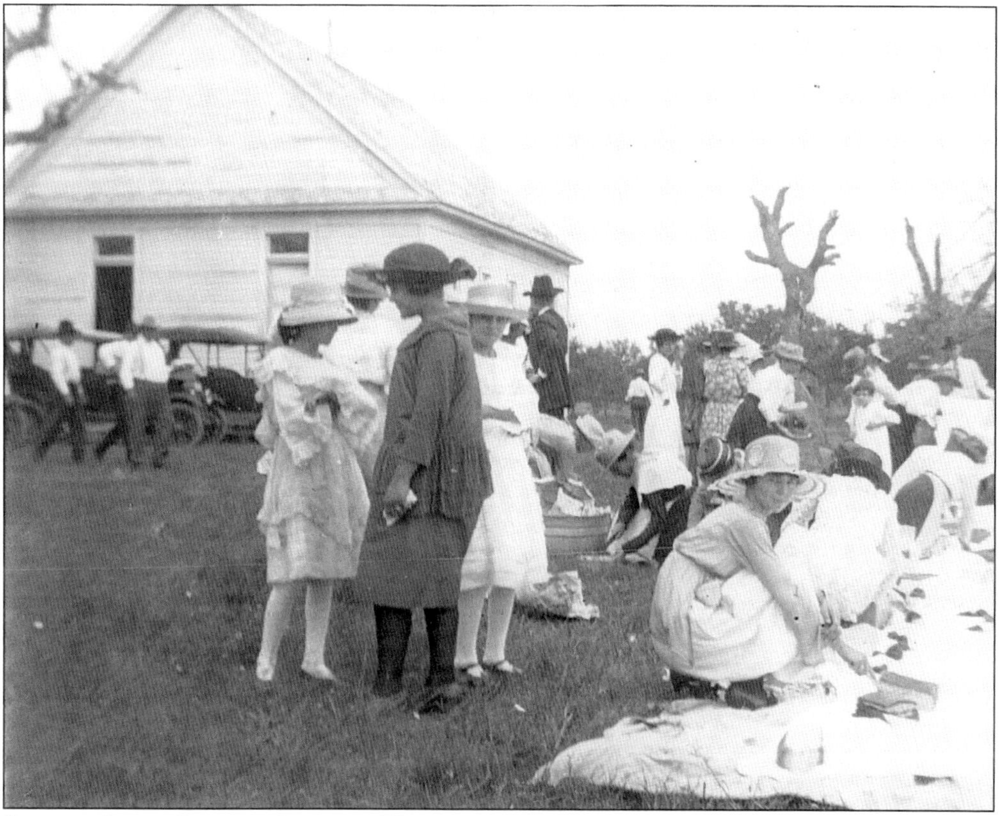

School Creek Baptist Church. The first and only church building of the School Creek Baptist Church was completed in 1891. The congregation, organized in 1879, is active and celebrated the dedication of a historical marker for the church in 2007. Pictured here is a 1920s "dinner on the ground." (Courtesy of Henry Langford.)

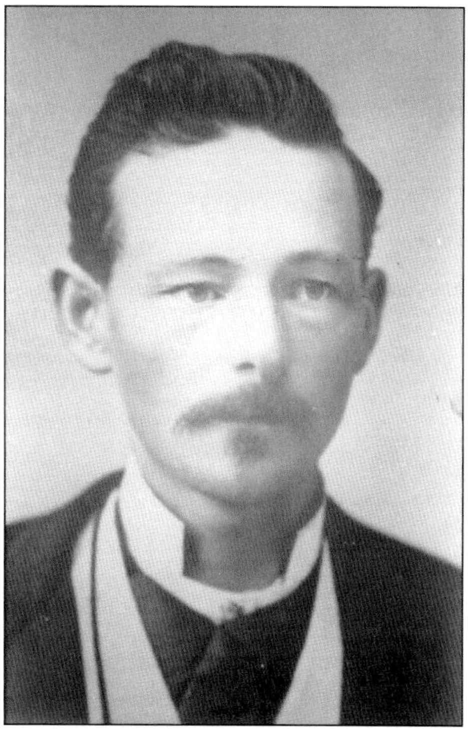

Leander Randon Millican (1853–1938). Once a deputy sheriff of Lampasas County, L. R. Millican was converted at the 1874 Methodist Camp Meeting at Bend. Ordained at the First Baptist Church in Lampasas, this "cowboy preacher" established churches throughout west Texas, beginning with the School Creek Baptist Church. (Courtesy of Phyllis Poehlmann.)

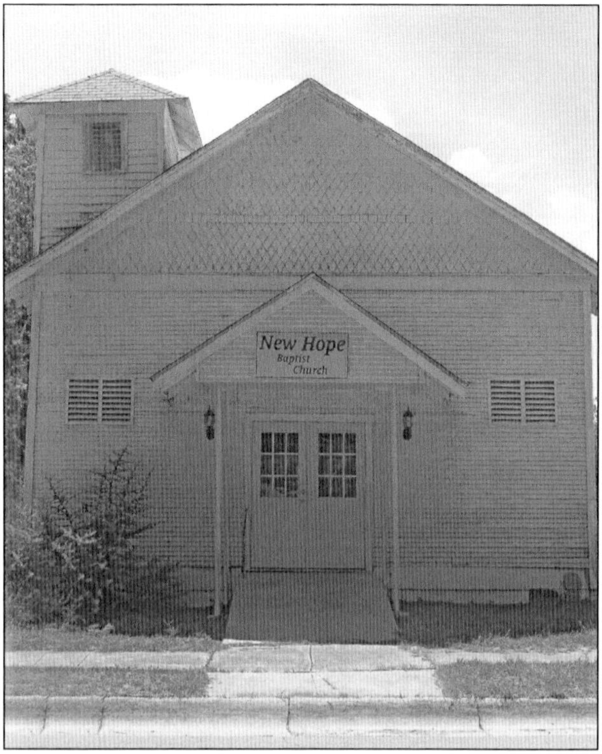

NEW HOPE BAPTIST CHURCH. The congregation marks April 10, 1869, as the date of its founding. The church building, located at 600 College Street, has been its home for many years. It was built after an earlier church at another location burned. Sulphur Creek, located just behind the church, was the site of many baptisms. New Hope Baptist is presently affiliated with the Willow Grove Association of Waco.

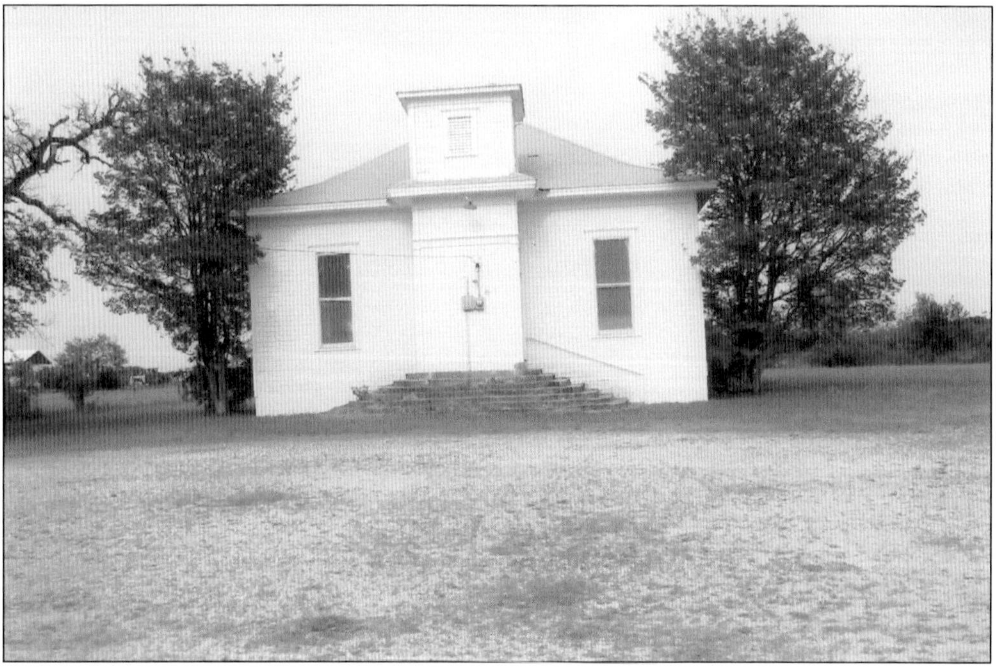

FIRST PRESBYTERIAN CHURCH OF ADAMSVILLE. Organized in 1880 as Pleasant Valley Cumberland Presbyterian Church, the congregation did not construct its church building until 1917. The structure is still used today by a small but active congregation designated as the First Presbyterian Church of Adamsville. (Courtesy of Wanda Lang.)

Nine

COWBOYS AND CROPS

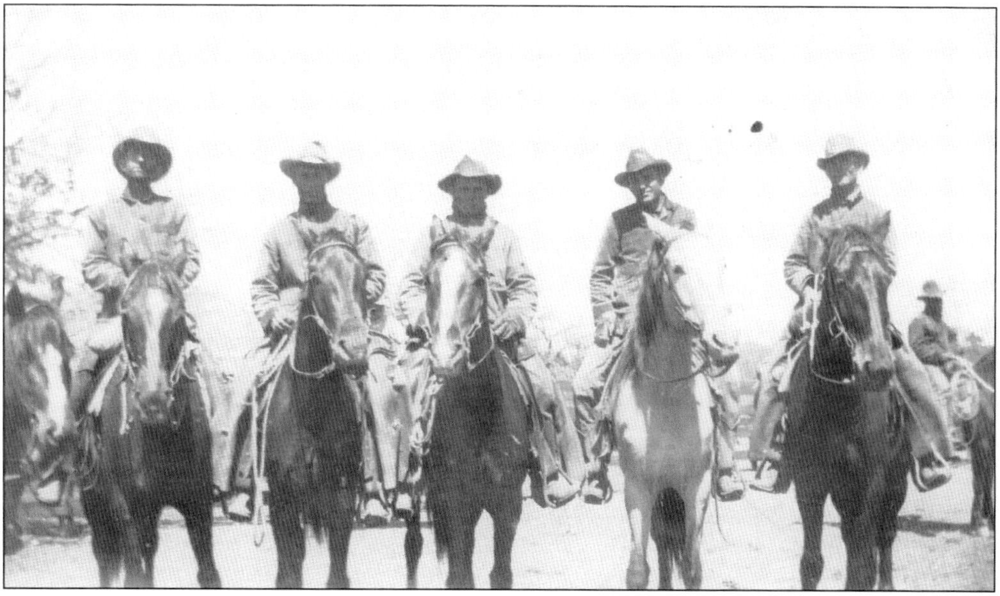

COWBOYS ON UPPER WHITE RANCH. Agriculture has always been a mainstay of the economy, but ranching has also been a way of life for generations in Lampasas County. Many local farming and ranching families have lived on the same land for a century or more. Pictured here are five horsemen, likely taking a break from gathering or working cattle on the Upper White Ranch (now the Oliver Ranch) on the Colorado River during the 1920s. From left to right are John Landers, two unidentified, Norrell Landers, and Albro Haynie. (Courtesy of Suzane Killingsworth.)

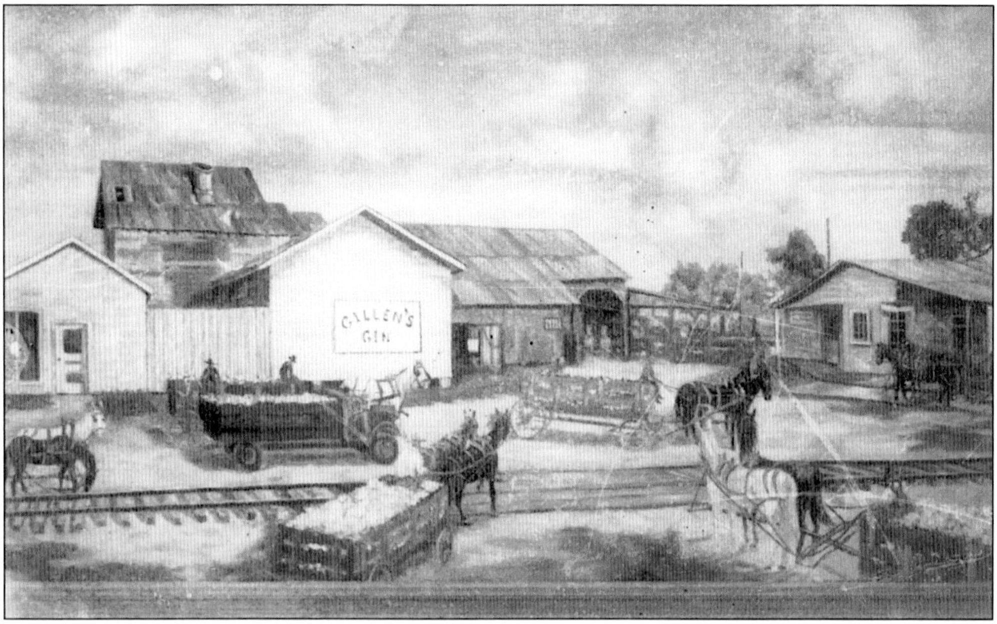

Gillen's Gin, Lampasas. W. C. Gillen's cotton gin was located off of East Fourth Street not far from Sulphur Creek. Early on, cotton and other crops were grown by families for their own use. With the arrival of the railroad in 1882, cotton became an important cash crop in Lampasas County. This drawing is in the collection of the Gillen family. (Courtesy of the Gillen family.)

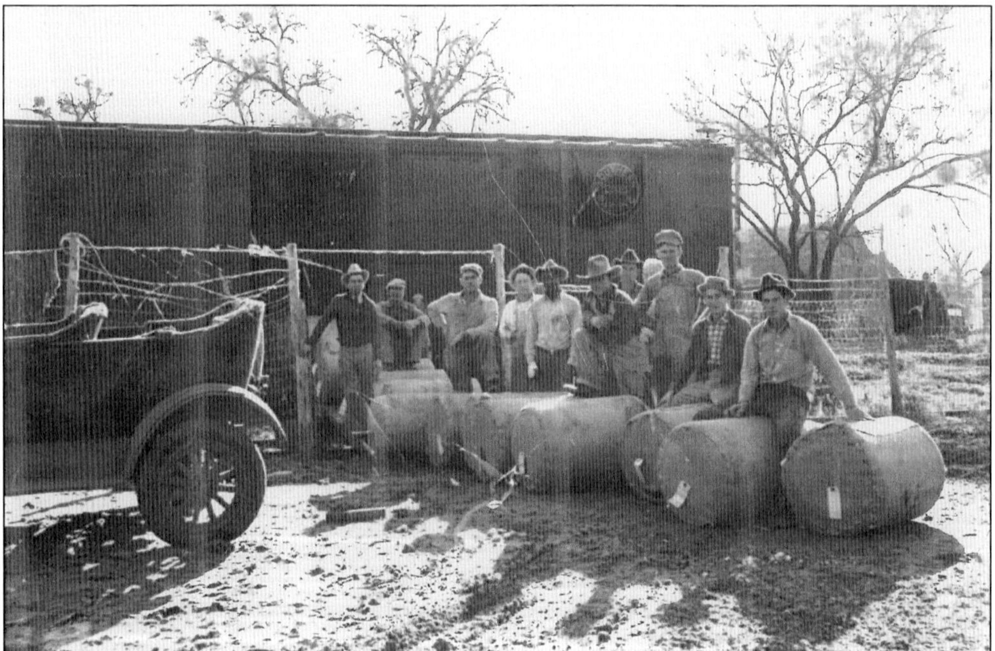

Cotton Bales. These cotton bales are ready to be loaded onto a Southern Pacific Railroad boxcar for transport. This cotton was baled at Gillen's Gin, near the railroad, in Lampasas. (Courtesy of the Gillen family.)

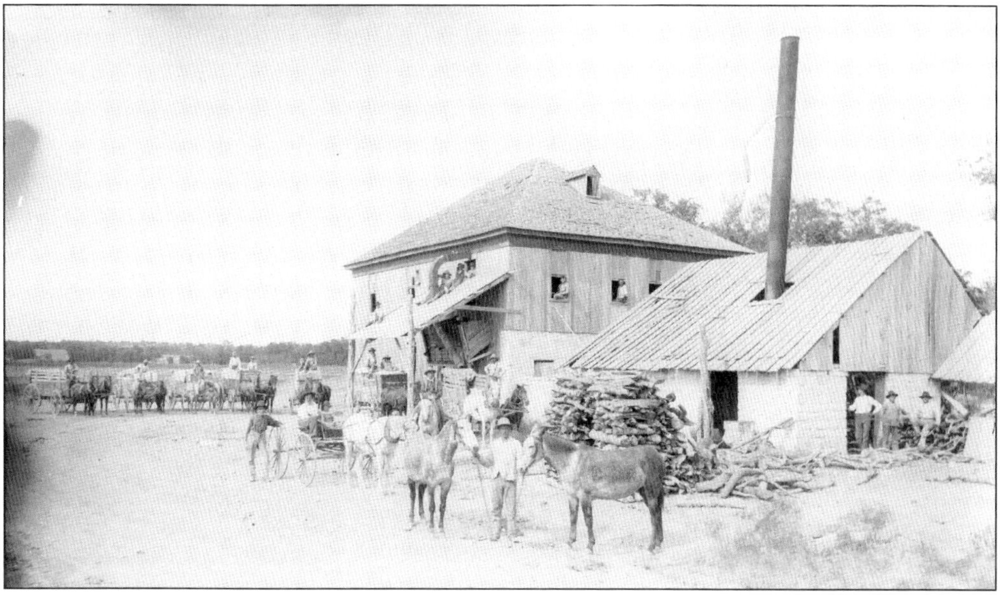

TOWNSEN'S MILL, NEAR ADAMSVILLE. In 1872, Perry and Jasper Townsen built Townsen's Mill on Mill Branch (now Mill Creek), which flows into the Lampasas River. Townsen's Mill was steam powered and cut lumber and ground wheat and corn.

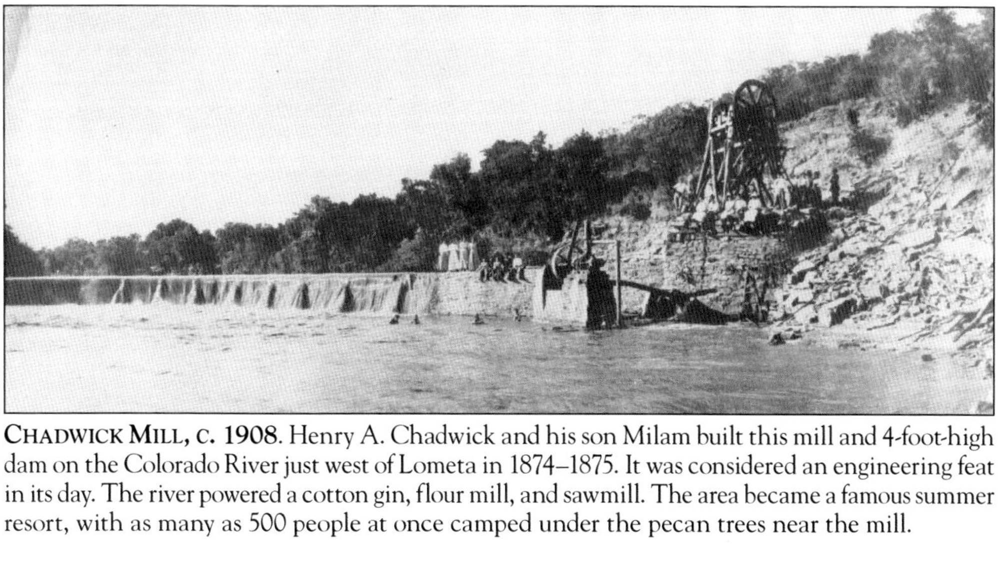

CHADWICK MILL, C. 1908. Henry A. Chadwick and his son Milam built this mill and 4-foot-high dam on the Colorado River just west of Lometa in 1874–1875. It was considered an engineering feat in its day. The river powered a cotton gin, flour mill, and sawmill. The area became a famous summer resort, with as many as 500 people at once camped under the pecan trees near the mill.

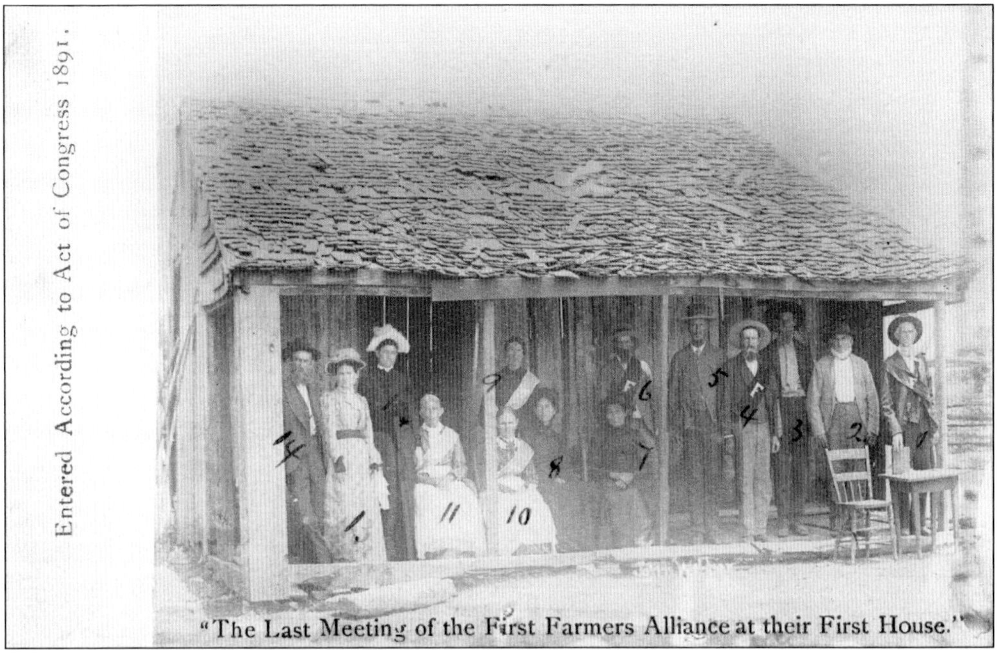

The Last Meeting of the First Farmers' Alliance at Their First House, 1891. This photograph shows the original members of the Pleasant Valley Alliance No. 1, formed in 1877 in response to falling prices for cotton and other agricultural products after the Civil War. They met in the rough lumber meeting house, shown here, on Donaldson Creek, about 7.5 miles southeast of Lometa. (Courtesy Loita Ramsey.)

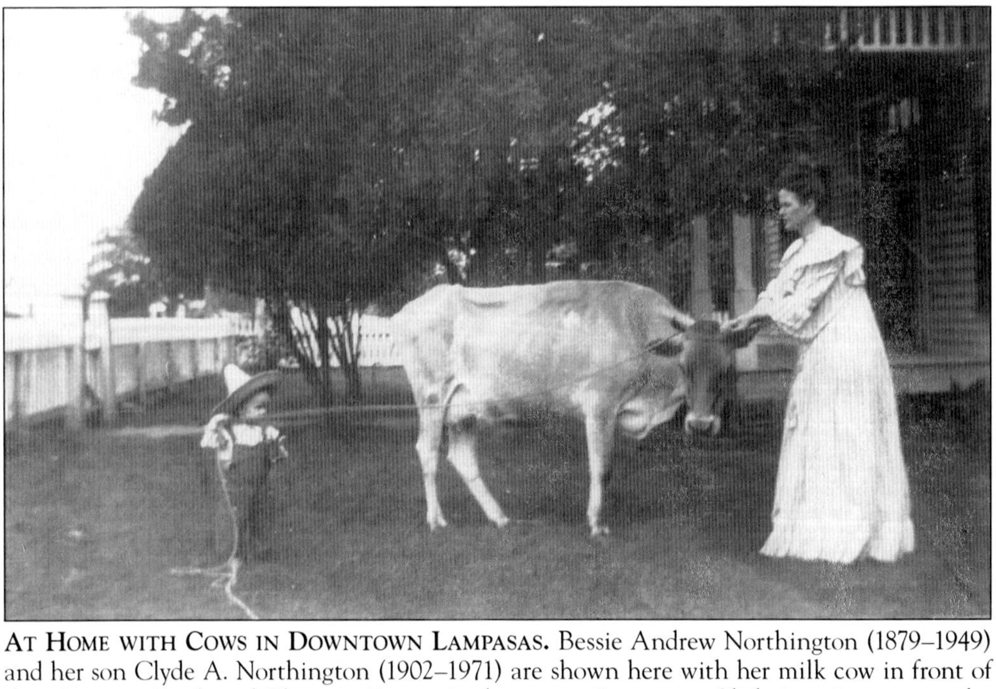

At Home with Cows in Downtown Lampasas. Bessie Andrew Northington (1879–1949) and her son Clyde A. Northington (1902–1971) are shown here with her milk cow in front of their home at Sixth and Chestnut Streets in downtown Lampasas. Clyde is trying to rope the cow. (Courtesy of Carol Northington Wright.)

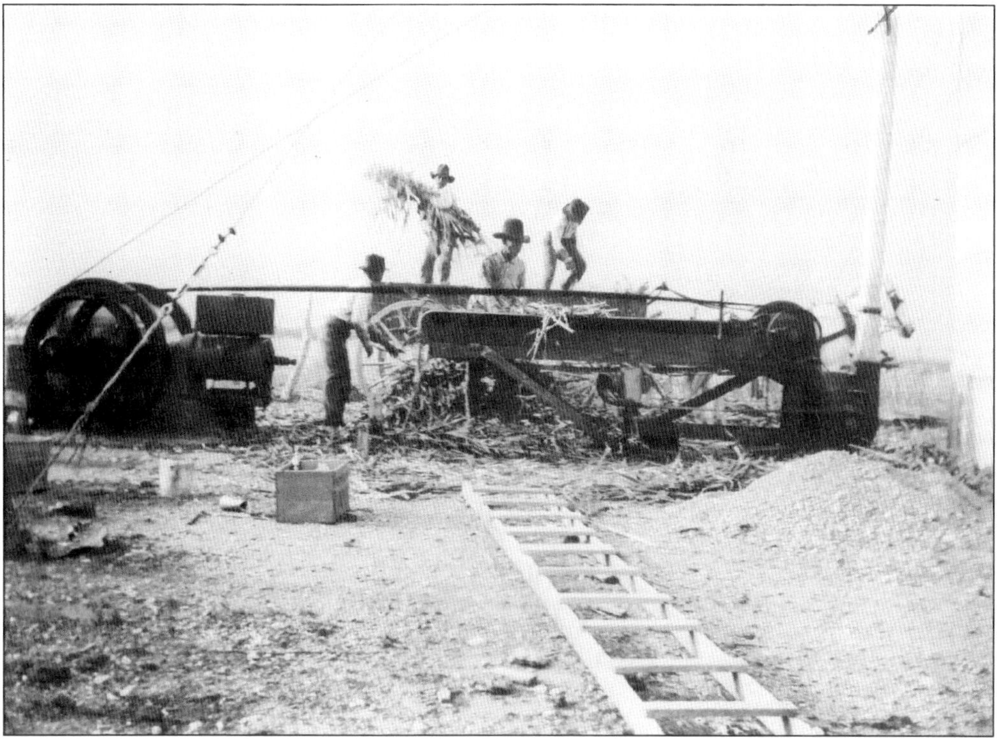

Filling the Silo. On the back of the postcard, Lee Landers wrote, "This is the chopper and blower that fills the silo. Papa is feeding the critter. The silo holds 240 tons. Only a small part of it shows in the picture. The feed is blown up the pipe under the X into the silo at the top." (Courtesy of Suzane Killingsworth.)

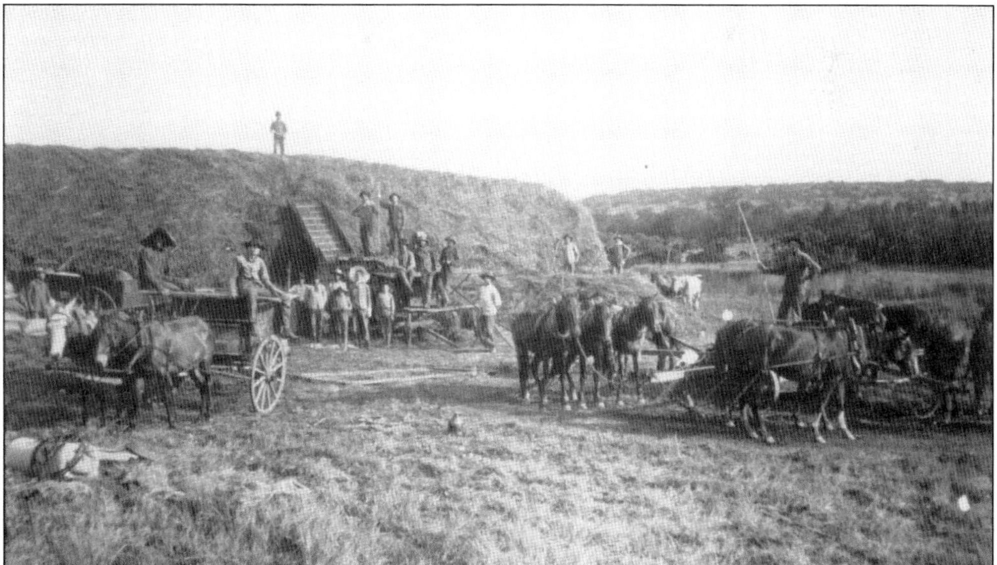

Horse-Powered Thresher, c. 1900. Horse power and mule power were employed to pull threshers on farms around the beginning of the 20th century. This horse-powered thresher was on the W. P. Irwin farm in Long Cove. (Courtesy of Ruth Gadbury.)

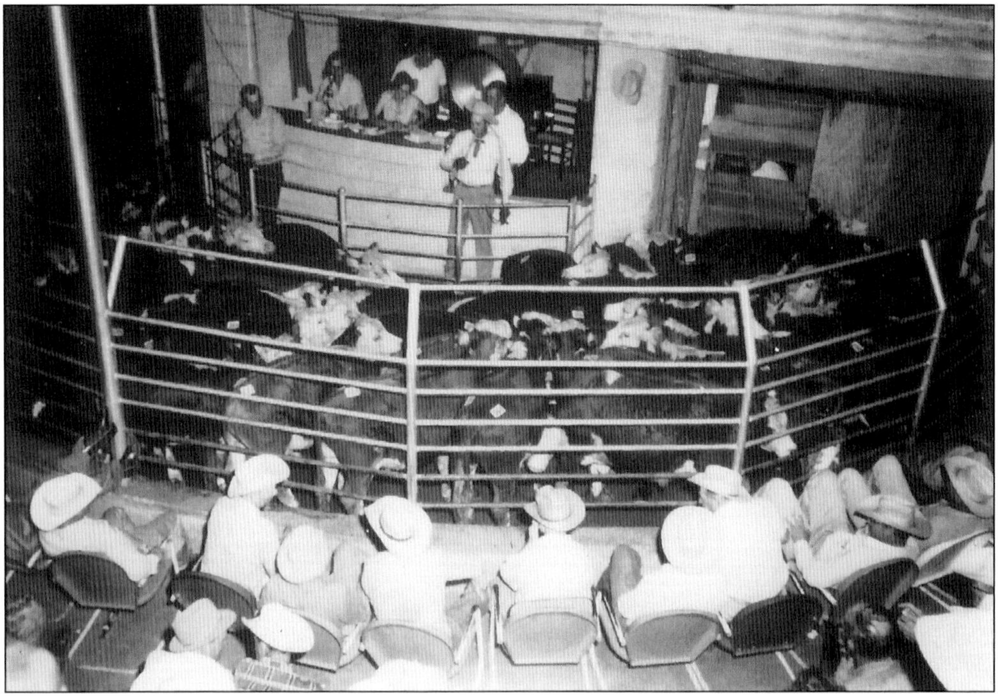

BIDDING AT AUCTION IN LOMETA. Every Friday in Lometa people brought their cattle to auction to be sold. Here Charlie Boyd starts the bidding at the Lometa Commission Company, which he operated from 1946 to 1961. The auction took place on land donated by the Lometa Lions Club. (Courtesy of Ruth Gadbury.)

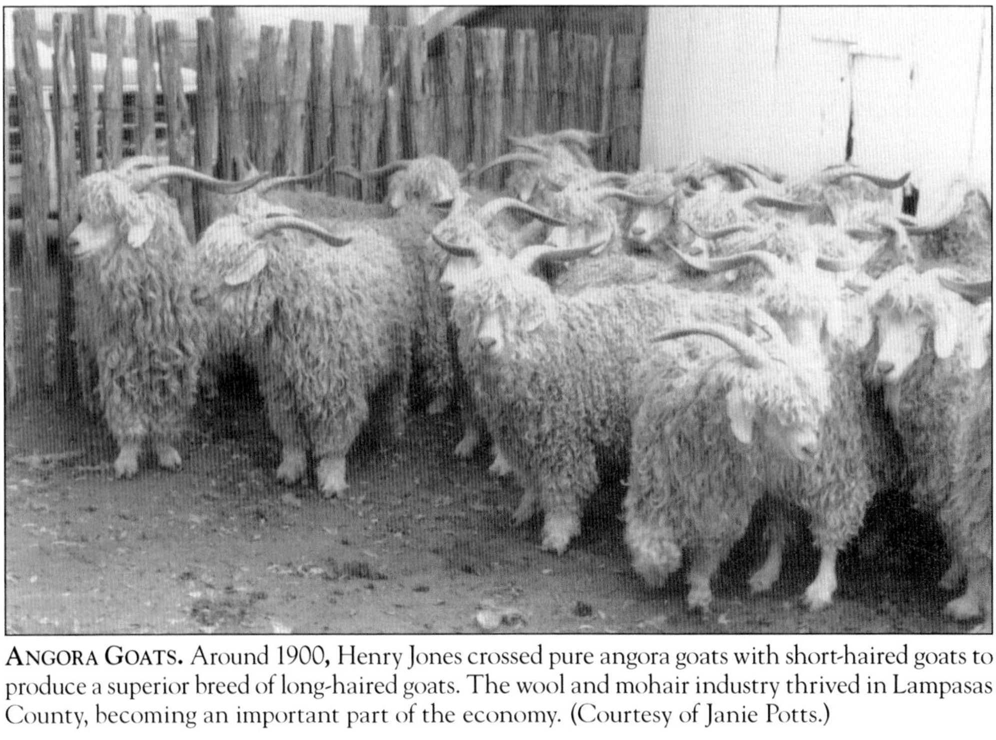

ANGORA GOATS. Around 1900, Henry Jones crossed pure angora goats with short-haired goats to produce a superior breed of long-haired goats. The wool and mohair industry thrived in Lampasas County, becoming an important part of the economy. (Courtesy of Janie Potts.)

HERDING SHEEP. Here Willard Potts's prize-winning border collies, Ben and Roxie, are shown herding sheep near Lometa. For taking top honors at the U.S. Supreme Competition in Des Moines, Iowa, in the mid-1950s, both were invited to exhibit their skills in Canada at the Calgary Stampede. (Courtesy of Janie Potts.)

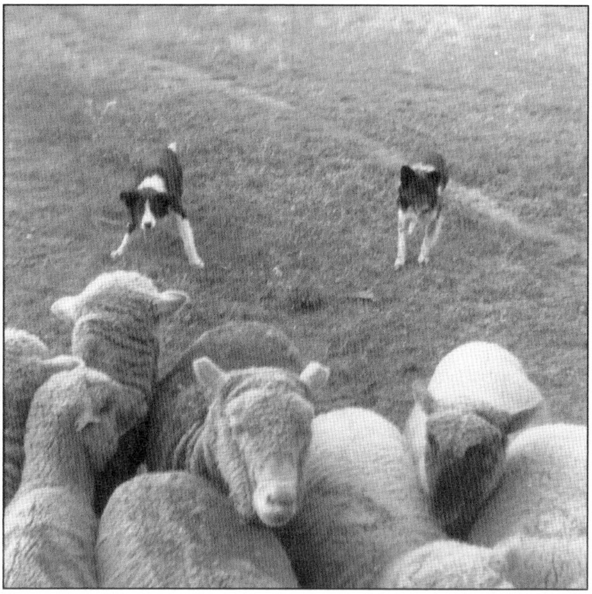

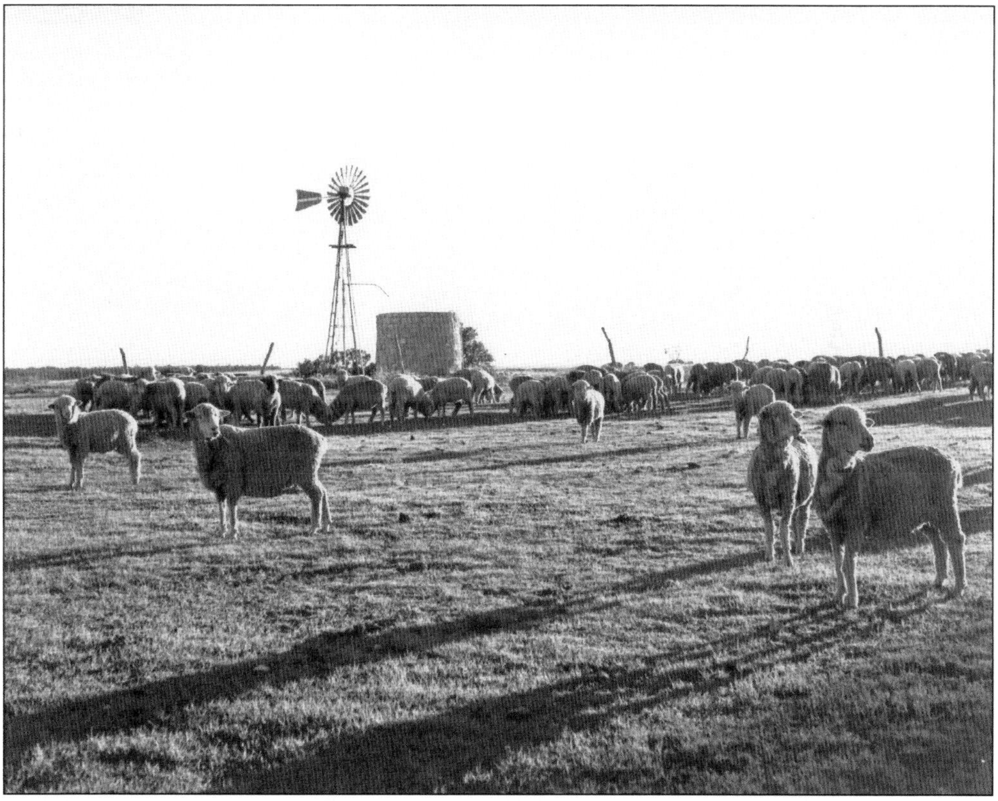

W. A. COWAN RANCH. Pictured here are Rambouillet sheep grazing on the W. A. Cowan ranch near Kempner. The Cowans have raised sheep and cattle in Lampasas County since at least 1889. The Rambouillet breed gained popularity in the United States for its fine wool production and adaptability to most climates. It was named for the estate of King Louis XVI, where it was developed from Spanish stock. (Photograph by Virgil Wooten.)

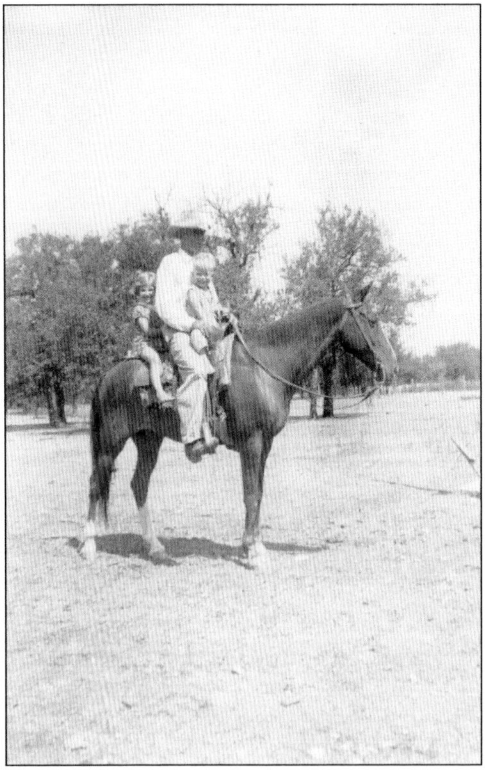

JESSE PICKETT WITH TRAVIS HERRING AND MARY KAY HERRING, C. 1938. Jesse Pickett was a legend in Lampasas County for his skill as a cowboy. He was also a respected horse, mule, and cattle trader. Son of a white man and a former African American slave, he lived on the Herring ranch, two miles north of Lometa. His nephew was the famous inventor of bull-dogging, Bill Pickett. (Courtesy of Travis Herring.)

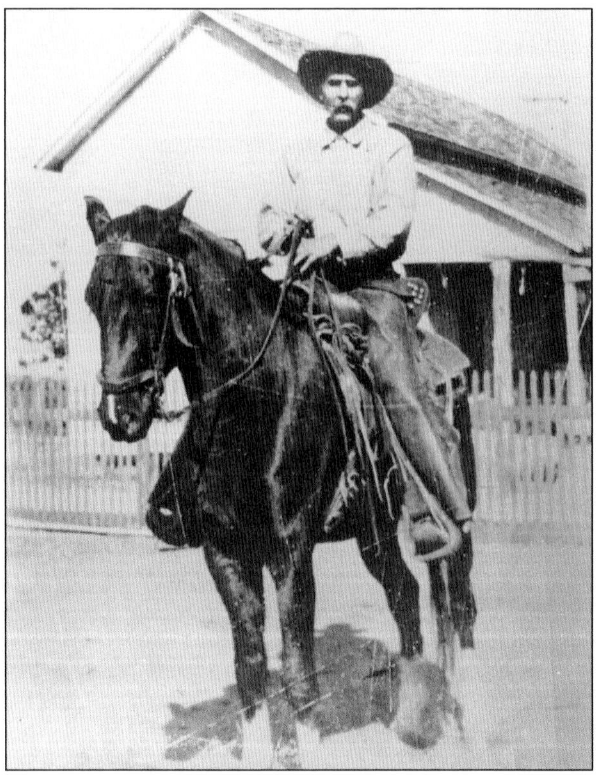

ON HORSEBACK. Robert "Bob" Springer is shown here on horseback in western Lampasas. Traditional clothing for a cowboy included chaps and boots with high tops, which protected his clothing from brush, cat claw, and cactus as he rode. The high heels of the boots prevented his feet from going through the stirrups if the horse fell. The bandana protected his neck from sun and his mouth from dust.

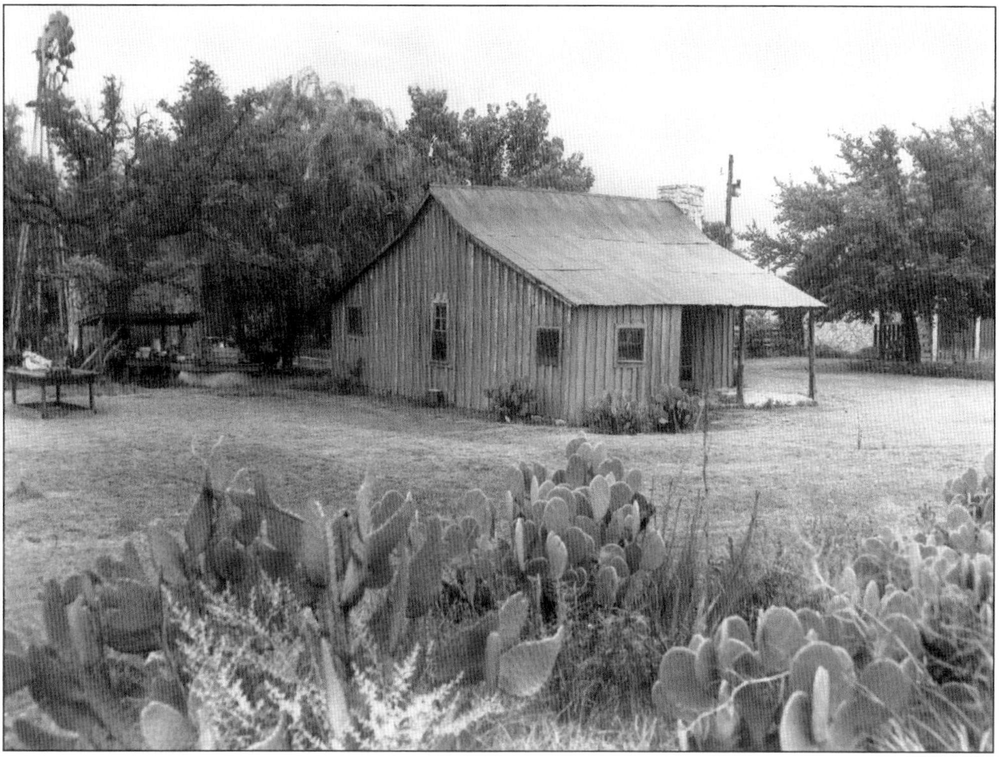

STANLEY WALKER PLACE. Celebrated journalist Stanley Walker (1898–1962) was born and reared in the Unity Community in northeast Lampasas County. After working on major dailies in Austin and Dallas, Walker went on to work for the old New York *Herald*, which later became the New York *Herald Tribune*. He returned to Lampasas County in 1946 and lived with his wife, Ruth, in the old house pictured here. (Photograph by Joe Swan.)

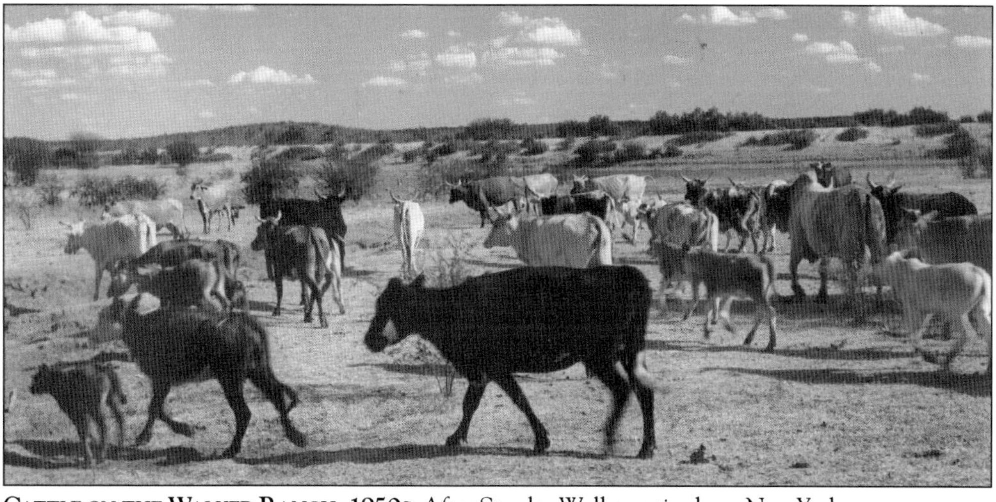

CATTLE ON THE WALKER RANCH, 1950S. After Stanley Walker retired as a New York newspaperman and returned to Lampasas County, he stocked his place with cattle, including those pictured here, pigs, chickens, and assorted other animals. He also continued to write for such prestigious publications as *National Geographic* and the *New Yorker.* Among the six books he wrote was his autobiographical *Home to Texas*.

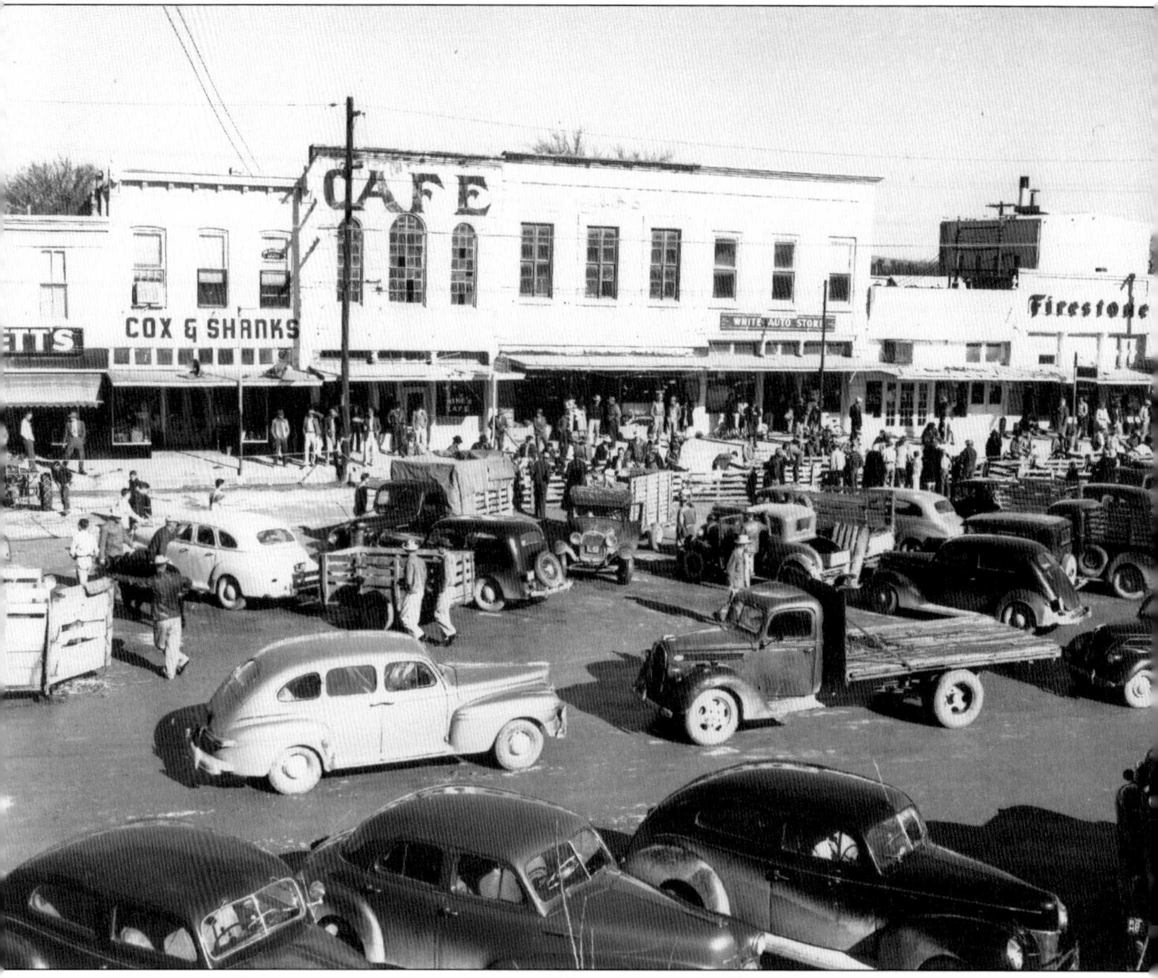

LIVESTOCK SHOW ON THE COURTHOUSE SQUARE, 1940S. Exhibitors hauled their prize cattle, sheep, and goats to town for this event. The wood-slatted trailers shown here were used for this purpose. This view of the north side of the square shows the range of businesses located downtown in the 1940s. Everything from menswear (Cox and Shanks) to auto parts (White Auto Store) could be procured. (Photograph by Virgil Wooten.)

BIBLIOGRAPHY

Adamsville Heritage Association. *Adamsville through Their Eyes: History and Reflections.* Killeen, TX: Spectrum, 2008.

Carpenter, Glynda Carson, comp. *History of Hancock Springs, Texas.* Lampasas, TX: Daughters of the Republic of Texas, 1992.

Elzner, Jonnie Ross. *Lamplights of Lampasas County, Texas.* Austin, TX: Firm Foundation, 1951.

———. *Re-lighting Lamplights of Lampasas County, Texas.* Burnet, TX: Hill Country, 1974.

Lampasas County Historical Commission, comp. *Lampasas County, Texas: Its History and Its People.* Marceline, MO: Walsworth, 1991.

Lampasas County Historical Commission, files housed at the Lampasas County Courthouse.

Lampasas County Museum Foundation, Inc., research files housed at the Keystone Square Museum, Lampasas.

Lampasas Dispatch Record

Martin, Ruthie, comp. *Lampasas Flood 1957.* Lampasas, TX: Preservation Lampasas, 2007.

Moses, Prima Baker. *Stories of Lampasas.* Reprint. Lampasas, TX: Pierian Club, 1986.

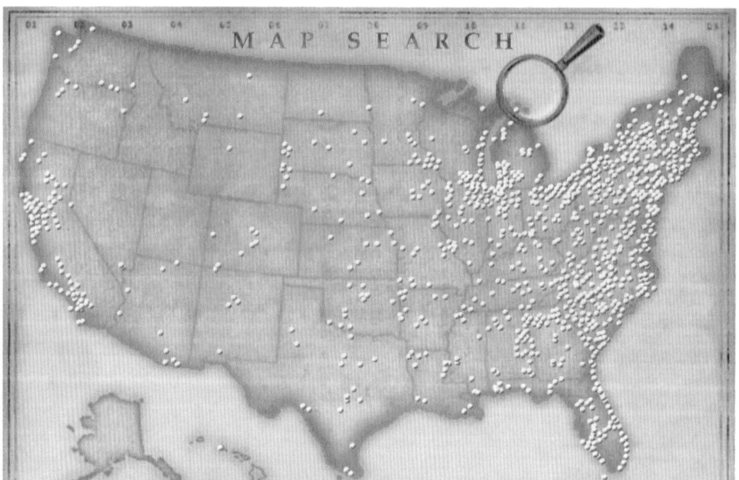
MAP SEARCH